NATO AND THE UNITED STATES, UPDATED EDITION

The Enduring Alliance

TWAYNE'S INTERNATIONAL HISTORY SERIES

Akira Iriye, editor
Harvard University

NATO AND THE UNITED STATES,
UPDATED EDITION

The Enduring Alliance

Lawrence S. Kaplan
Kent State University

TWAYNE PUBLISHERS • NEW YORK
MAXWELL MACMILLAN • TORONTO
MAXWELL MACMILLAN INTERNATIONAL • NEW YORK OXFORD SINGAPORE SYDNEY

Twayne Publishers
Macmillan Publishing Company
866 Third Avenue
New York, New York 10022

Maxwell Macmillan Canada, Inc.
1200 Eglinton Avenue East
Suite 200
Don Mills, Ontario M3C 3N1

Twayne's International History Series, No. 1

Library of Congress Cataloging-in-Publication Data

Kaplan, Lawrence S.
    NATO and the United States : the enduring alliance / Lawrence S. Kaplan —Updated ed.
        p. cm. — (Twayne's international history series ; 1)
    Includes bibliographical references and index.
    ISBN 0-8057-7926-4 — ISBN 0-8057-9221-X (pbk.)
    1. North Atlantic Treaty Organization. 2. United States—Military policy. I. Title. II. Series.
UA646.5.U5K37 1994
355'.031'091821—dc20
                                                                                    93-47497
                                                                                       CIP

The paper used in this publication meets the minimum requirements of American National Standard for Information Sciences—Permanence of Paper for Printed Library Materials, ANSI Z39.48-1984. ∞ ™

10 9 8 7 6 5 4 3 2 1 (alk. paper)
10 9 8 7 6 5 4 3 2 1 (pbk.: alk. paper)

Printed and bound in the United States of America.

In memory of
a friend and colleague
WARREN F. KUEHL
seeker of world order

CONTENTS

ILLUSTRATIONS

FOREWORD

Twayne's International History Series seeks to publish reliable and readable accounts of post–World War II international affairs. Today, nearly 50 years after the end of the war, the time seems opportune to undertake a critical assessment of world affairs in the second half of the twentieth century. What themes and trends have characterized international relations since 1945? How have they evolved and changed? What connections have developed between international and domestic affairs? How have states and peoples defined and pursued their objectives and what have they contributed to the world at large? How have conceptions of warfare and visions of peace changed?

These questions must be addressed if one is to arrive at an understanding of the contemporary world that is both international—with an awareness of the linkages among different parts of the world—and historical—with a keen sense of what the immediate past has brought to human civilization. Hence Twayne's International History Series. It is to be hoped that the volumes in this series will help the reader to explore important events and decisions since 1945 and to develop a global awareness and historical sensitivity with which to confront today's problems.

The first volumes in the series examine the United States' relations with other countries, groups of countries, or regions. The focus on the United States is justified in part because of the nation's predominant positions in postwar international relations, and also because far more extensive documentation is available on American foreign affairs than is the case with other countries. The series addresses not only those interested in international relations but also those studying America's and other countries' histories, who will find here useful guides and fresh insights into the recent past. Now more than ever it is imperative to understand the complex ties between national and international history.

Lawrence S. Kaplan's *NATO and the United States* was the first volume to be published in this series. It has been widely used as a textbook for students and as a reference guide for government officials. The author has now brought the story up to date by appending chapters covering developments since the mid-1980s. These developments, of course, have been momentous, signaling nothing less than a complete transformation of the international system as symbolized by the tearing down of the Berlin Wall and the disintegration of the Soviet Union. To narrate this story and to put it in proper perspective takes the skills of an imaginative historian. In this book the reader will find Professor Kaplan, a recognized authority on the history of the North Atlantic Treaty Organization, presenting not only a concise summary and balanced assessment of recent changes in U.S.-NATO relations but also a thoughtful inquiry into their future possibilities. The revised volume is thus a highly welcome addition to the series.

Akira Iriye

PREFACE

This book owes a considerable debt to the Lyman L. Lemnitzer Center for NATO Studies at Kent State University. The center provided an environment of learning that nourished my understanding of NATO's history. Colloquia, symposia, and conferences, as well as visiting scholars and officials, offered information and insights that compensated in good measure for the paucity of unclassified records. Additionally, I have drawn from my own contributions to publications resulting from the Lemnitzer Center conferences, notably, NATO after Thirty Years (1981), The Warsaw Pact: Political Purpose and Military Means (1982), NATO and the Mediterranean (1985), and East-West Rivalry in the Third World: Security Issues and Regional Perspectives (1986). I am grateful for the support of my colleagues at the Lemnitzer Center: Robert W. Clawson, S. Victor Papacosma, Mark R. Rubin, and Ruth Young.

The aid of the U.S. Information Agency and the NATO Information Directorate in promoting my travels in Europe deserves recognition. James Kelman of the USIA and Fernand Welter, director of NATO's fellowship program, have been particularly supportive. S. I. P. van Campen, former director of the Office of NATO's Secretary-General, and Alice C. Cole, formerly of the Historian's Office in the office of the U.S. secretary of defense, have read the manuscript and have offered valuable criticism. Steven L. Rearden has added useful comments on the last two chapters of this edition. I have profited from all of it, even if I did not always follow their advice. Phyllis G. Weinstein of Cuyahoga Community College gave me useful commentary on portions of the manuscript, thereby sparing this book certain infelicities. Those that remain are present on my own initiative. Janis Hietala, editor at the National Defense University Press, and Robert S. Jordan, of the University of New Orleans, were helpful in making available the photographs of NATO events. Marjorie Evans typed the manuscript with her usual skill and her unusual tolerance of my handwriting. Ellen Denning efficiently processed this updated edition.

Lawrence S. Kaplan

INTRODUCTION

It has been six years since I completed *NATO and the United States*. When the book appeared in 1988 there were few indications that within three years the Baltic states would regain their independence, that Germany would be reunited, and that the Soviet Union would be disbanded. If there seemed to be a sense of satisfaction in 1987 in NATO circles, it was the result of the success of the alliance in moving toward a détente with Mikhail Gorbachev that the summit meeting in Reykjavik, Iceland, in 1986 had promoted and the Intermediate-Range Nuclear Force (INF) negotiations of the following year accelerated. There were glimmers of recognition that change in NATO itself was on the horizon, either in the form of increasing European leadership through the Conference on Security and Cooperation in Europe (CSCE) and the Western European Union (WEU) or in the form of a new relationship with the "out-of-area" world, necessitated by variations on the Iraq-Iran war and the Soviet invasion of Afghanistan. But for the moment the putative power of the Soviet-dominated Warsaw Pact dictated the continuation of a transatlantic alliance centered on a credible military foundation built a generation before.

Given the vital roles of the Soviet Union and Communist ideology in the functioning of NATO, the disappearance of both challenges left member nations asking what further purpose the alliance could have. It seemed that the predictions of such articulate pundits as Ronald Steel about the imminent demise of NATO would be realized in the 1990s. Military budgets, long a source of tension among the allies, suddenly became needlessly bloated. Indeed, the intricate military apparatus that had been so carefully constructed since 1951 appears to be obsolete. If a military organization should be required for the future security of Europe, the rapidly growing European Community presumably should be strong enough and confident enough to defend Western Europe without American involvement.

The consequences of these changes could make the subtitle of this book, "The Enduring Alliance," an anachronism today, and the publication of an updated edition unnecessary. A NATO dissolved, or a NATO without a future purpose, scarcely deserves a new edition. Perhaps, then, this might be the time for historians to take over from journalists, military analysts, and political scientists the exploitation of anticipated openings of NATO's archival resources and attempt a definitive study of the alliance's rise and fall, much as historians have done with the Quadruple Alliance of the early nineteenth century and the Triple Alliance of the early twentieth century.

Writing in December 1993, I believe that an obituary would be premature. Unlike the Southeast Asia and Central treaty organizations, which collapsed in the late 1970s, unheeded and unlamented, NATO today occupies the front pages of all major newspapers. The crisis in Bosnia has thrust the organization onto center stage even as it has exposed many of its weaknesses. But even if the NATO allies fail to arrive at a consensus on this important "out-of-area" issue, there is no other organization in place that could offer even a hope for security and stability in Europe. Neither the United Nations, the CSCE, the WEU, nor the Franco-German brigade possesses the infrastructure for military action that NATO has positioned in Germany and the Mediterranean. It is significant that none of the allies, divided as they are over the American role, is seeking the removal of American troops from Europe let alone that of itself from the alliance. Instead, members of the former Eastern bloc are clamoring to join NATO. While it is reasonable to question the future of the "enduring alliance," its successful contest with its Soviet antagonist merits the adjective "enduring" for NATO's past—and for its present as well.

Lawrence S. Kaplan
December 1993

chapter 1

ORIGINS OF THE AMERICAN REVOLUTION OF 1949

The idea of treating the birth of the Atlantic alliance as if it were a latter-day American Revolution was the subject of a brief essay by a prominent American diplomatic historian a generation ago.[1] Few scholars, journalists, or politicians have adopted his image, although implicitly many of the retrospective examinations of NATO have taken for granted or commented only in passing on the radical transformation in American foreign policy marked by the signing of the Treaty of Washington in 1949.

NATO represented as sharp a break with isolationism as any diplomat could imagine. Abstention from European political and military entanglements had been the hallmark of American diplomatic history. It was formulated in Washington's farewell address in 1706, confirmed in Jefferson's inaugural address in 1801, and codified in the Monroe Doctrine of 1823. And yet in 1949—149 years after the termination of the Franco-American alliance of 1778—the United States entered into an entangling relationship not only with its former British and French adversaries but also with seven other European nations, along with Canada and Iceland. The reasons for this major break have resonance a generation later.

Less dramatic, because it was less complete, was the change that NATO has implied and subsequently promoted on the European side. NATO may be identified as Europe's recognition that the chaotic national rivalries that had produced two catastrophic twentieth-century wars by 1945 had to be mitigated. Some form of European unification was necessary to dampen old antagonisms, provide a way to defuse internecine conflict, and establish machinery to foster the growth of a United States of Europe.

NATO has accomplished both more and less than these objectives required. As it developed, the alliance served to erode elements of military and political sovereignty as well as to create an atmosphere of security against potential aggression from the East. It has not yet led to a European community as the undisputed heir to the old nation-state system in the manner that the United States of America has superseded the sovereign states of the prefederal period. Indeed, NATO, with its American base, has raised a still insoluble question concerning the compatibility of an Atlantic community and a European community. While neither has been fully achieved, a community of interests in Western Europe has developed that has made future warfare within the area difficult, if not impossible, to envision. NATO has been the umbrella beneath which vital changes could occur in the politico-military and economic relations of France, Germany, and the United Kingdom—nations that had been the focal points of conflict for over 300 years. Europe has acted in concert in new unimagined ways since 1949.

1945—YEAR ZERO

The end products are not yet in sight and—given divisive nationalist strains—they may never be. Europe's need for change in 1945, however, was more vital than America's. The balance of power system, the shifting arrangements of national alliances, and the competition among the nation-states had existed since modern Europe had grown out of the Renaissance. Essentially the France of Francis I, the England of Henry VIII, and the Austria of Charles V in the early sixteenth century comprised the same Europe that suffered the disasters of the twentieth century. Nothing much really had changed. While Adam Smith and free trade appeared to have challenged and overcome the narrow mercantilism built on the accumulation of precious metals, the glorification of the nation-state as the supreme loyalty of the citizen remained in place. Colonies continued to be valued for their exploitable wealth, even if the wealth was no longer expended on mercenary soldiers. The French Revolution intensified nationalism rather than modified it. The balance of power was still to be maintained by carefully arranged alliances. For Great Britain it would exist in the absence of a single European entity that could deny Britain access to the Continent; for France it would be the prevention of Austria and later Prussia and Germany from winning superiority or even equality; for Germany it would be the frustration of enemies in the West or East—France and Russia—coming together to deny it a place in the sun.

But even as the Congress of Vienna in 1815 presumably offered a century of coexistence, of relative peace among the competing powers in Europe, there were fissures visible that were to grow deeper and more dangerous in the twentieth century. Some of them were class-based, as the proletariat growing out of the industrial revolution threatened the established order in 1848; others were a continuation of the national rivalries in the world beyond Europe. European powers competed as vigorously in Asia and Africa as they had in the Americas in the seventeenth century. But by the twentieth century technology had shrunk the size of the world; nationalist passions ran more fiercely than they had in the past; new destructive weapons of war on land and on sea made conflict more dangerous than before. And when war came in 1914 there were no mechanisms available to prevent a minor explosion in the Balkans from escalating into a major European war, as one country after another was swept into the maelstrom. This calamity could have occurred in 1854 or 1878 in the Crimea or in the Balkans, or in Africa at the turn of the century. It did not. British maritime and industrial superiority may have been the balancing force that kept the peace. But that superiority departed with that nation's empire in the twentieth century.

Conceivably, as one looks back on that fateful year 1914, a strong British action on 25 July might have inhibited Germany. The acute French critic Raymond Aron observed that when the British made it unmistakably clear 25 years later that the British empire would not remain neutral if France had to face the Reich again, Neville Chamberlain was as good as his word. But Chamberlain's energy was "touchingly ineffectual." Perhaps the results would have been different before Munich. Perhaps not. What the coming of World War II revealed was not just that the Great War had settled nothing but that by the time of the Munich Agreement Hitler's Germany had already upset the balance of power in Europe. As Aron went on to say, Chamberlain's "word was not doubted in Berlin, but the times had changed. In 1939 the equivalent of the British warning of 1914 could only have come from Washington." And while Franklin D. Roosevelt predicted catastrophe he could not or would not replace British power with American power.[2]

In the Year Zero, 1945, Europe was a wasteland. It is estimated that the war cost the lives of at least 35 million and possibly 60 million people. Germany, the instigator of the war, lost over 4 million combatants and civilians, while the Soviet Union's figures were over four times that number. Leading the grisly list of civilian deaths was most of Europe's Jewish population, some 6 million victims of the Nazi terror. Additionally, hundreds of thousands of Europeans whose countries were overrun by the Germans perished in the war. The resultant population uprooting left 50 million displaced persons to be resettled after the war. Material damage was commensurate with the human destruction; burning cities, disruption of communications, and razing of production facilities were the inevitable consequences of this total war.[3]

The years following the war witnessed no revival or rebirth of spirit but rather a continuing, even deepening, despair over the future of Europe. In Germany such cities as Cologne and Dresden lay in ruins, while Berlin, Frankfurt, Hamburg, and Munich were severely damaged. Into this wasteland came 10 million ethnic Germans expelled from Soviet-occupied and -controlled Eastern Europe. Starvation was worsened by a fuel shortage that led not only to people freezing to death but also to the closing of the surviving

German factories. By February 1947 German production had declined to 29 percent of what it was in 1936.

But life was not much better for the nominal victors of the war. Britain's means for paying for food and such raw materials as shipping, foreign investments, and manufactured exports had been a casualty of war. Only exports remained a possibility, but to capitalize on this potential American loans and austerity programs were vital. Despite all its efforts, including a bread-rationing policy that had not even been instituted during the war, Britain had not been able to do more than reach its prewar production level. When the great cold wave of 1946–47 struck, British transportation came to a standstill. Since industries could not get fuel, gas and electricity were in short supply and factories were closed. Britain was in a state of crisis. Even if this doomsday note is exaggerated, as Alan Milward has claimed, the perceptions are as significant as the reality.[4] Western Europe appeared to be on the brink of collapse, and it was this sense of imminent peril that dominated the thinking of Europeans and Americans alike in 1947.

TOWARD A UNITED EUROPE

It was in this setting that two movements, closely intertwined but different in composition and implications for the future, took place. One was the rise of the concept of European union in a variety of forms to replace the worn-out remnants of the nation-states that survived the war. The other was the necessity to rely on the new imperial power of the West, the United States, both to counter the imperial power of Soviet communism in the East and to assist in the rebuilding of devastated Europe. According to the leading historian of European integration, Walter Lipgens, there was little choice about roles for the new superpowers: the "two former peripheral powers, Russia and America, driven to reshape the world by their opposing political ideologies . . . divided [Europe] de facto between themselves into spheres of influence."[5]

In any event, the three-century domination of the world by Western European nation-states had come to an end. Amid the horrors of the 1940s there was at least the possibility of change for the survivors—toward a Communist world, toward an American world, or even, it was hoped, toward a new and united Europe.

The notion of a unified Europe itself was not new. Indeed, philosophers and scholars had talked about it over the centuries, as either a recovery of the largely mythical concept of medieval Christian Europe, or, before that a reconstruction of Charlemagne's Europe, or an idea for the future in the ideas of Grotius and other seventeenth-century savants.

Although the Peace of Westphalia of 1648 ratified the division of Europe into warring competing national entities divided by dynasty, religion, and language, the fragmented Europe inspired attempts at least to mitigate the chaos inherent in national statecraft. Grotius in his *De Jure Belli et Pacis* had earlier, in 1625, looked to some sort of body, with its assemblies, where the litigations would be judged by those not involved, so as to force the parties to reconcile themselves in reasonable conditions. Later in the century France's Duc de Sully conceived of a "grand design" in a united Europe, while William Penn in the same period envisaged an assembly of the united Europe making decisions on a three-fourths vote of a weighted majority. Inevitably, the philosophies of the eighteenth-century Age of Reason spawned even more elaborate schemes.

The French Revolution, with its appeal to mass nationalism, made a mockery of these aristocratic schemes. But so did the presence of charismatic dictators. A Europe of Louis XIV in the seventeenth century or of Napoleon Bonaparte in the nineteenth and Adolf Hitler in the twentieth indeed would have put forth a European unity, but one built on domination, or national and racial inequalities, not on a free association of nations.

It was appropriate, if ironic, that only at the beginning of the twentieth century did there arise a concerted movement with pragmatic methods and reasonable objectives—and it coincided with the most destructive of European wars. The establishment of an International Court at two conferences, in 1898 and 1907, was tangible admission of the need for a law among nations. The Great War a few years later inspired the next impressive step, a League of Nations, that, while recognizing national sovereignties, would erode them with plans to solve international problems through law, negotiation, and conciliation rather than through warfare. It was the failure of the league, as World War II threatened, to raise among Europeans a closer and deeper vision of a new Europe that revived the concept of a federated Europe. This would go beyond a League of Nations or a United Nations organization and would look with fear and dismay on the kind of unity communism would bring.

In the broadest sense, the leaders of the revived interest in European unification, the "European Movement" as it was called in 1949, consisted of those who wanted a federated Europe with relatively limited powers as well as those who wanted an integrated European union. The former was represented largely by the British; the latter was influenced both by the national groups activated in the resistance movements of World War II and by the prewar planning of a remarkable European organizer, Count Richard Coudenhove-Kalergi, nominally of Switzerland.

Coudenhove-Kalergi, an Austrian nobleman of Japanese, Greek, and Flemish ancestry, was the propagandizer for a United States of Europe for almost 50 years, from 1923 until his death in 1972. Having judged the League of Nations inadequate, he presented in his book *Pan Europe* ideas that were to signify "self-help through the consolidation of Europe into an ad hoc politico-economic federation."[6] A lonely voice until the war, he was then able to rally a variety of individuals and groups around his cause. His

European Parliamentary Union became the focal point of the activities of Hendrik Brugmans's Europeesche Acte of the Netherlands, R. W. G. Mackay's Federal Union Movement of the United Kingdom, and Edouard Herriot's Conseil français pour l'Europe unie. Perhaps even more important was his ability in the immediate postwar period to win the attention of national leaders, including, it seemed, such figures as Winston Churchill, Ernest Bevin, Duncan Sandys, and Georges Bidault.

Coudenhove-Kalergi's efforts were enhanced in part because he found not one but two enemies to combat: the old self-destructive nationalisms of the past and the newer rising threat of communism that would extinguish liberty along with nationalism. The Communist Europe that the Soviet Union threatened to impose through its increasingly aggressive parties in every country would have made a mockery of the federal democratic system promoted by Coudenhove-Kalergi and his colleagues. And yet the Communist alternative was inevitably a possible and even understandable solution to the chaos of Europe.

Communism's leading exponent, the Soviet Union, had been the only victor on the Continent in the war with Hitler. Like Britain, it had been grievously damaged by the conflict; much of European Russia had been occupied and devastated by the war. At its height the Germans were at the gates of Leningrad, Moscow, and Stalingrad. Unlike Great Britain, however, the Soviet Union had the resources to absorb its losses and the dynamic ideology to celebrate its survival as proof of the inevitability of communism.

The evidence, particularly in retrospect, does not reveal the Soviet Union to have been a superpower equal in any sense to that of America in 1945. But its sense of direction and its strength relative to the weakness of the rest of Europe made it a formidable competitor to a restored capitalism and certainly to groups seeking a democratic federation of Europe. Soviet confidence was bolstered by the genuine patriotic roles that Communist parties in such countries as Italy and France played in the fight against fascism. Memories of the Comintern controlling the destinies of Communist parties in the service of the Soviet Union had dimmed. So had the Soviet Union's unholy alliance with Nazi Germany in 1939, which had been rationalized as the Communist response to potential betrayal at the hands of the West. In 1945 the Communist fighting forces had been the best organized and the most resolute among Western resistance movements, and they could reasonably claim a share in the new order to follow the war. Communism seemed to offer a rational answer to the disorder and disarray of capitalism and democracy in postwar Europe.

The model the Soviet Union showed to the West, however, was that of a new oppressor, as the Soviets remained in Germany and in Eastern Europe after the war. This act demonstrated that totalitarianism was an integral part of the Soviet system and, at the same time, served to guarantee a friendly government on the borders of the Soviet Union. As the malaise of Europe continued and even worsened, possibilities of a Communist Europe appeared to be on the near horizon.

It was not because the principles of communism were more attractive or because Soviet armies were poised to take over the capitals of Western Europe. Life under Joseph Stalin was life under a dictatorship, an exchange of Soviet for German domination. And although the Soviets did not rule with quite the same barbarism as the Nazis, their totalitarian control of society was more absolute. The utopian goals of Communist ideology were unlikely to be realized, and this was widely recognized in the West. If France or Britain embraced communism it would not be because of the lure of its promises; the history of the past generation in the Soviet Union undermined communism's slogans. Nor would it be because of a Soviet invasion; that was not expected. It would not be necessary. If the Europeans turned to the Soviet Union and its system it would be out of despair for the future.

This was the context in 1946 and 1947 in which European leaders turned to the United States for aid. To secure this aid they turned also to the idea of European unity. Their primary interest, however, was not the pursuit of any particular form of unification. Indeed, it may be claimed that they had no interest in unification itself. They were concerned with the survival of their nations, threatened as they were with social as well as economic bankruptcy and exposed to Communist blandishments and threats. Only the United States had the resources and the power to save the West.

But European leaders were well aware of American history and the power of isolationism in that history. By raising the impression that the Old World, or at least the democratic part of it, had changed its outlook drastically, the United States could be persuaded to change its own long-held convictions about foreign relations. European union could be the instrument to impress America with the worthiness of Europe's claim to support. To place European importunities in this context implies a cynicism about Europeans that is only partly justified. Certainly Ernest Bevin in Britain, Georges Bidault in France, Alcide de Gasperi in Italy, and Paul-Henri Spaak in Belgium were genuinely persuaded that the old system could and should not be reestablished. Unity of some kind was necessary. But they also recognized that guile was necessary to woo a nation whose tradition precluded the kind of entangling military and political alliances Europeans felt they needed in the postwar world.

THE LEGACY OF ISOLATIONISM

European cautions were well grounded. From a perspective of almost 45 years of an intimate, continuing European-American alliance it is difficult to imagine the first century and a half of American foreign policy. The American attitude toward Europe may be summed up in one word: isolationism. While the term is still used from time to time, often as "neo-isolationism,"

it is essentially an opprobious shorthand insult that politicians hurl at opponents. It not only lacks resonance today; it is an anachronism. But scarcely
55 years ago, on the eve of World War II, the nation and its leaders were all
isolationists, from President Roosevelt down to the British-baiting Irish
Catholic politician and the midwestern Republican farmer. World War I, or
the Great War, had seemingly taught once again the wisdom of abstention
from "the toils of European ambition, rivalship, interest, humor, or caprice,"
to use the language of Washington's farewell address.

The term needs definition, which Washington assumed rather than
offered. To cite the most famous dictim of that address, "the great rule of
conduct for us in regard to foreign nations is, in extending our commercial
relations to have with them as little *political* connection as possible." The
emphasis of "political" underscores the character of isolationism. It did not
refer to commercial connection and certainly not to cultural relations. It did
mean political and military alliance, or entanglements.

A considerable literature has accumulated in the past generation concerning Americans' use of alliance to include both commercial and political connections, and concerning the objectives of the foreign policies of the
founding fathers. Felix Gilbert, writing 30 years ago, identified the United
States with a "new spirit of international relations," breaking away from the
power politics of the day, in which war as well as unnatural restrictions on
international trade would be abandoned. America was introducing a new
concept of international relations befitting a new world confronting the old.[7]

While Gilbert intimated a certain naïveté in America's idealism, James
Hutson, writing a generation later, rejected both the naïveté and the idealism when he claimed that the founding fathers had no intention of establishing a new international economic order but rather intended to exploit the
European balance of power for American objectives.[8] Whichever interpretation is correct, both accepted isolationism as the American mode—the former to elevate the world by serving as a distant model of correct posture, the
latter to abjure entangling alliances to play off more effectively one European
power against another.

The idea of an innocent America—projected naively or guilefully—turning away from European corruption was part of a self-image that rose to
prominence during the American Revolution and ran openly or subter-
raneanly through the next 200 years. The Declaration of Independence
seemed to celebrate the differences. On one side of the Atlantic were the
imperialistic kingdoms of Europe competing with one another for the wealth
of the New World and at the same time exploiting the colonies for the
greater benefit of the Old World. Through its revolution America repudiated
this way of international life and asked for a better form of relations in its
place. Since Europe would not heed America's advice, it was vital for the
new nation to have as little to do with the European system as possible. The
price of connection was victimization and destruction. So Jefferson had

believed in 1801 as he distanced himself from both France and England. Had it been possible, he also would have removed America from the international commercial system that kept the United States in thrall to the British credit structure.

The American experience of the nineteenth century seemed to dramatize periodically the wisdom of the founding fathers. The War of 1812 became the second war of independence, with the United States developing a continental economy that further removed the nation from European affairs. The Monroe Doctrine of 1823 represented a temptation to ally with England, as the country had once allied with France, to protect the hemisphere from Spanish, French, or Russian intervention. President James Monroe was tempted also to involve America in the popular Greek revolution against the Ottoman Turks. In both instances the strong stand of Secretary of State John Quincy Adams against European entanglement won the day and set the course for the next century. The argument that Britain would only exploit an American connection in an alliance against France or that association with even the most idealistic Greeks would still be a dangerous attachment to an Old World cause found resonance in American reactions to the liberal revolutions of 1848, to the Franco-Prussian War of 1871, and to the Boer insurrections in South Africa at the end of the century. These crises either were of no concern to the United States or seemed to be siren calls to disaster.

Apparent proof of the wisdom of political abstention in world affairs was offered by Woodrow Wilson's intervention in the Great War of 1914. The United States, by then a great power itself, entered the war in 1917 on behalf of such causes as democracy, peace, and a new world order that had no intrinsic relationship to the welfare of the United States. Such was the sense of America at large in 1919, when the country rejected the League of Nations and turned its back on Wilson's Democratic party in the presidential election of 1920. What it rejected was not simply Wilson's leadership in pushing America into a needless war but also the European powers that once again proved their perfidy. Although the United States was not an "ally" in a formal sense, it associated itself with British and French imperialism. Those nations had fought the war, according to American opinion, to expand their empires: witness the fate of German territories in Africa. Britain made sure that the German navy, which had been a rival of the British before the war, had no function in the new German republic; France used its victory to keep troops in the Rhineland, to revise the borders with Germany in the classic pattern of European power politics. The League of Nations that purported to end the balance of power was perceived as another instrument of British and French suzerainty over Europe.

The result was a reaffirmation of isolationism and a deepening of the political rejection of Europe. The United States in the interbella period refused to join the League of Nations, observed the rise of fascism in Italy and Nazism in Germany with distaste but also with resignation, and refused to commit American power on behalf of the British and French when they made their deal with Hitler at Munich in 1938. Rather than recognize that the national interest may have had a stake in the outcome of Benito Mussolini's invasion of Ethiopia, or Hitler's occupation of the Rhineland, or the Spanish Civil War, America had erected new barriers in the 1920s and 1930s to penalize Europe for its betrayal in 1919. These barriers ranged from restrictions on movement of trade through tariffs to restrictive immigration laws to neutrality acts in the 1930s that were specifically based on the premise that the situation in Europe was the same as it had been in 1914 or 1915. Economic aid and governmental loans, let alone military arms and supplies, could ensnare the United States just as they had 20 years before. And the competing menace of Soviet communism, which rivalled if not surpassed Nazism in its hostility to American values, was another proof of the wisdom of abstaining from the entanglements of the Old World. A pox on all their houses was a prevailing sentiment in the 1930s.

It was the apparent intensity of American passions on this subject that helps to account for the hesitancy and deviousness of President Roosevelt's attempts to nudge the nation out of its isolationism. By the end of the decade he had come around to recognizing that America's security rested on the survival of the European democracies against the Axis powers of Germany, Italy, and Japan. The world was too small and America's presence potentially too large to isolate the United States from the European conflict. Given the strong memories of World War I, it was remarkable that the nation not only modified its neutrality laws to serve as a silent nonbelligerent partner of Britain in 1940 but as the major cobelligerent with the Soviet Union in 1941. Still, it is questionable if the United States would have entered a European war through an act of Congress, as in 1917, had Japan not attacked a U.S. naval base, for the United States had no isolationist tradition with respect to the Pacific and East Asian worlds.

When World War II ended with America and Russia as the two dominant forces in Europe, it was hardly surprising that voices of isolationism would be heard once again. If isolationists could no longer berate Europe as a threat to America, given the pitiable condition of both Britain and France, they could claim that American concerns should be confined once again to the Western Hemisphere. The pell-mell demobilization of troops and the deregulation of the economy, along with the rise of a new disillusionment based on the putative power of communism in Europe, could have given rise to a mood similar to that of the 1920s.

These fears were understandable, particularly among Europeans who realized that their nations' futures depended on America's actions. But times had changed. The widespread acceptance of the United Nations, the successor to the league, may have indicated some substitution of a vague internationalism for the older isolationism; but if the United Nations would be seen as a surrogate for American foreign policy, new disasters lurked in the future. U.S.

membership in the United Nations may also be seen as a pledge of participation in extrahemispheric affairs. When the U.S.–Soviet partnership originally projected in the United Nations broke down early in the administration of Harry S. Truman, concerns about the expansion of communism as well as the recovery of Western Europe replaced neoisolationist reaction over the breakdown of the new peaceful world envisaged under the United Nations.

A new foreign policy elite had come to maturity during World War II, supportive of American leadership in the outside world. This "Eastern Establishment" had an uncertain start as long ago as Theodore Roosevelt's generation. Its Ivy League, Wall Street internationalism fitfully manifested itself in Wilson's administration[9] and became dominant in the third administration of Franklin Roosevelt. Anglophilia and a Republican bias, personified in Secretary of War Henry L. Stimson, characterized this new and influential group of policymakers. 1947 was not 1919 or even 1939. An American revolution was in the making, if its progress could be carefully managed on both sides of the Atlantic. Even as the threat of entanglement was made, the founding fathers of the Atlantic alliance were not fully convinced that the great rule of Washington that had left America without an entangling alliance for almost a century and a half was now irrelevant.

chapter 2

THE BRUSSELS CONNECTION AND THE TREATY
OF WASHINGTON, 1947–1949

If any year can be designated as a turning point in postwar American thinking about international obligations it would be 1947. The severe winter of 1946–47 underscored not only the woeful lack of food, heating fuel, jobs, and any kind of hope in Europe but also the temptations communism offered as a solution to the failure of democratic capitalism. It was a year in which the drift in foreign policy, or at least an apparent aimlessness in the direction of the Truman administration, was replaced by the underlying concept of containment, produced by an acceptance of George F. Kennan's thoughts about living with the Russians.

Up until the end of 1946 the Truman administration seemed to veer from sharp challenges to Soviet behavior in Berlin and Hungary to a willingness to accept quid pro quo arrangements, such as those Secretary of State James F. Byrnes had sought in foreign ministers' meetings with the Soviet Union. American pressure for representative government in Bulgaria and Romania at the London meeting of October 1945 produced some token changes in the Moscow meeting in December of that year. But nothing more. Byrnes and Truman lost faith in Joseph Stalin as a conventional political figure and lost their tempers with what appeared to be Soviet betrayal of their Yalta agreements of February 1945. Yet while Truman or Byrnes might rail at the Soviets, cut off lend-lease abruptly, and refuse loans, they devised no long-term policy toward the USSR. Indeed, Truman had failed to respond to Churchill's Iron Curtain speech in Missouri in 1946 and seemed, as late as September 1946, to accept Secretary of Commerce Henry Wallace's vocal opposition to a "get tough" position with the Soviet Union. Byrnes later

Secretary of State Dean Acheson signing the North Atlantic Treaty in Washington, D.C., on 4 April 1949. President Harry S. Truman and Vice President Alben Barkley stand behind him. *Courtesy National Defense University Press*

blamed Wallace's Madison Square Garden speech for undercutting his policy of firmness toward the Soviet Union.[1]

In retrospect it appears that the United States was groping for an active coherent foreign policy that had not been necessary in the isolationist years. The United Nations, which was supposed to keep the great powers together, had failed from the outset to perform this function; it could not serve as a surrogate foreign policymaker for the United States. What the Truman administration could not see or understand was that its "Open Door" urgings on a suspicious Soviet Union, its demand for free elections in an American tradition, would be interpreted as undermining Soviet security in postwar Europe. It took time before the American negotiators recognized that the Soviet regime under Communist ideology was different in kind from that of other nations. Conventional diplomacy would not work. And as the Soviets strengthened their hold on the western borders, communism in Western Europe appeared prepared to take over more than just the Soviet Union's immediate neighbors.

TOWARD CONTAINMENT

It was at this point that George F. Kennan's long telegram of 1946 from Moscow had begun to sink into the consciousness of policymakers in Washington. Kennan, along with Charles Bohlen, was among the few specialists in Soviet affairs emerging from the Foreign Service in the 1930s. Unlike most of his peers, he found no answer in the United Nations to the problems in store for American foreign relations. Even less did he consider a return to America's prewar isolationism. The world was too small after World War II; a vacuum existed in Europe and elsewhere that the United States was obliged to fill. The alternative would be the rise of Soviet influence sparked by a worldwide Communist movement. The merger of traditional Russian imperialism with a dynamic new ideology made even the war-weakened Soviet Union a formidable obstacle to the international development of the open capitalist-democratic societies that the United States had envisioned for the world after the allied victory in 1945.

In this new outlook there was little room for conventional diplomacy. The Soviets would respond only to counterpressure, to firmness of posture not to words. Confident that history was on their side, they would retreat in the face of power and wait for another opening at another time. Kennan's ideas were not published until the summer of 1947 in the influential journal *Foreign Affairs*, but they became the linchpin of what Walter Lippmann publicized as the "Cold War" and what would be loosely called the policy of "containment."[2]

Kennan's call for a new direction in American foreign policy was heard in 1947, although in terms too simplistic for him to accept. The Truman Doctrine and NATO were reasonable translations of containment, but they seemed too dependent on military strength and too neglectful of moral leadership to appeal to Kennan's sensibilities. In brief, the instruments employed by the Truman administration to cope with Soviet expansionism appeared too crude.

Perhaps it was the abruptness of American action that created uneasiness in Kennan as he looked at one consequence of his recommendations. The president used the civil war in Greece, where Communists threatened to overturn the Western-oriented monarchy, as an occasion to enunciate the Truman Doctrine. In a message to Congress on 12 March 1947 Truman asked for emergency aid to Greece and Turkey. But he did more than ask for funds. He announced that "it must be the policy of the United States to support free peoples who are resisting attempted subjugation by armed minorities and outside pressures."[3] Here the gauntlet was thrown down, with the challenge extending to any part of the world threatened by Soviet aggression. Primarily it covered Western Europe where Communist parties were strong and where Soviet influence would be buttressed by subversive allies in the affected countries.

Still, the Truman announcement was insufficient of itself, although it paved the way for massive American involvement in Greece. Military aid needed an economic infrastructure to support it. The president had pointed out in the Truman Doctrine that "the seeds of totalitarian regimes are nurtured in misery and want."[4] So while the containment policy began with military assistance, it was quickly buttressed by a plan of economic aid that was conceived in the State Department and was propagated by such able spokesmen as under secretaries of state William L. Clayton and Dean Acheson. This plan, the Marshall Plan, was embodied elliptically but emphatically in Secretary of State George C. Marshall's commencement address at Harvard University on 5 June 1947, less than three months after President Truman unveiled his doctrine to the world.

Considerable debate has been held over the question of whether the two conceptions were different in kind, as pundit Walter Lippmann and Kennan preferred, or were complementary as the administration firmly believed. State Department official Joseph M. Jones, in an enthusiastic book linking the two, paraphrased Wordsworth in exulting that "It was a great time to be alive, one of those rare times in history when shackles fall away from the mind, the spirit, and the will, allowing them to soar free and high for a while and to discover new standards of what is responsible, of what is promising, and of what is possible."[5] From February to June 1947 (*Fifteen Weeks*) Jones found not only the origins of aid programs to Greece and Turkey and the Marshall Plan but also NATO, the military assistance program, and Point 4 of Truman's second inaugural address. The Fifteen Weeks then equalled if not overshadowed the celebrated Hundred Days of Napoleon or Franklin D. Roosevelt in heralding radical changes in the lives of nations. Military and economic aid seemed inextricably connected.

The unilateral nature of the Truman Doctrine was an important distinction between that proclamation and the Marshall Plan. Aid to Greece was an emergency relief, with Americans wholly as benefactors and embattled Greeks as desperate beneficiaries. The Truman Doctrine was America's alone, and its success or failure rested on the willingness of the United States to carry out its promises, as it drew from apparently bottomless resources.

The Marshall Plan, on the other hand, involved a proposal to Europeans whose desperation had not yet reached the breaking point. If they showed themselves worthy of rehabilitation, they must take actions on their own to complement American support. As Marshall put it, "such assistance, I am convinced, must not be on a piece-meal basis as various crises develop. Any assistance that this Government may render in the future should provide a cure rather than a mere palliative." And before such steps can be taken, "there must be some agreement among the countries of Europe as to the requirements of the situation and the part those countries themselves will take in order to give proper effect to whatever action might be undertaken by this Government. . . . The initiative, I think must come from Europe."[6]

This speech not only recognized the dangers to Europe but also emphasized that, since the Communist threat did not proceed from military action alone, it could not be countered by military means alone. The Marshall Plan acknowledged that communism would more likely take root where hunger and hopelessness prevailed and stressed that economic revival must stem from the energies and will of the people themselves. Accordingly, the program should rest on joint participation rather than rely on a unilateral system devised by the United States or a bilateral arrangement made between the United States and a particular country. In order to be effective, it would have to be "agreed to by a number, if not all, European nations."[7]

The keys to the success of the Marshall Plan were individual initiative and mutual aid, and the results anticipated were the breakdown of the economic barriers that had hindered Europe's trade in the past. More distant, but still in sight, was an erosion of the principles of national sovereignty that had brought such disaster to Europe in the past. A new, stronger Europe, assisted by the United States, would then be able to face the Soviet Union from a position of confidence. A democratic society embracing a free economy in a united Europe would no longer be bothered by the blandishments of communism.

THE BRUSSELS PACT OF 1948

Despite bouts of euphoria over a new direction for American foreign policy, there was depression in European and American chanceries at the very time the Marshall Plan seemed moving into orbit. There was a widespread fear of irrelevancy. What use would there be to massive efforts at economic recovery unless strong measures were taken to stabilize the political lives of the affected countries? Economic aid would not help an economy threatened with political chaos. Such was the perception of foreign ministers Ernest Bevin of the United Kingdom and Georges Bidault of France as they witnessed the continuing and expanding political power of domestic Communist parties in the West and the increasingly threatening gestures of the Soviet Union in the East. The Soviets had already turned down a nervous invitation by the British and French to participate in the recovery program and had intimidated such neighbors as Poland to do likewise. Bevin and Bidault doubted that the Soviet Union would stand idly by while American assistance restored the societies of Western Europe to the point where capitalism would be proven superior to communism. Not even scientific knowledge of the history of Marxism, with its expectations of ultimate triumph, would be sufficient to deter the Soviet Union from stirring civil war in France or Italy, or from intervening militarily where resistance seemed least likely. Or so the foreign ministers feared.

Germany was the focus of most of the concerns as 1947 drew to a close. Even before the Truman Doctrine had been articulated the West had stopped reparations shipments from the American zone to the Soviets, and in December 1946 the British and Americans had combined their zones into "Bizonia." How much of Soviet militancy stemmed from fears of the West's stoking German revanchism is still not measurable in the 1990s. That the Soviets interpreted all American moves, from demands for democratic elections in Poland or Hungary to proposals for restoration of the European economies, including the German, as signs of hostility is unquestionable. One result was the stimulation of Western anxieties about potential Soviet aggression, which the Marshall Plan could not allay. The complete failure of the London Conference of Foreign Ministers in December 1947, primarily concerning the settlement of divided Germany, signalled a moment of decision for Bevin and Bidault.

Their reactions assumed two forms: one overt, the other covert. The first was to take steps for self-defense by establishing an alliance that would pool the military strengths of the West. The Treaty of Dunkirk earlier in the year between France and Britain had already made arrangements, on paper at least, for the two to act in concert against any future German menace. Now the enemy, or the hostile force at any event, was right at hand; a larger scale alliance of Western Europe involving even sacrifice of traditional sovereignty was needed to cope with the Soviet threat. On 22 January 1948 Bevin delivered a remarkable speech to the House of Commons in which he announced that in concert with the French, Dutch, Belgians, and Luxemburgers the British would propose a political community that eventually would be open to other Europeans in time.[8] This was a dramatic departure from Britain's traditional sense of separation from the Continent, a recognition that the West's peril required a new departure: namely, a union of European states.

The end product of this January initiative was the signing less than two months later of the Brussels Pact on 17 March 1948, linking Britain, France, and the Benelux countries to a 50-year treaty. The heart of the arrangement was a promise of mutual support in the event of armed attack (Article 4). A Consultative Council would be created for continuing discussion (Article 7). But even more noteworthy was the attempt to translate Bevin's call of January into a promise of European unity by emphasizing, in Article 1, the promotion of European economic recovery that would result from the alliance's activities: "the High Contracting Parties will so organize and coordinate their economic activities as to produce the best possible results, by the elimination of conflict in their economic policies, the coordination of production and the development of commercial exchanges."

If this language seemed to fit into the American objectives for the Marshall Plan, it was no coincidence. The American role, unstated in Bevin's speech and in the text of the treaty, was vital to the success of the venture, and even to the survival of a Western Union. Ideally, it was felt, the United States should be a partner in the Western Union created by the Brussels treaty. Bevin and Bidault recognized this in their conversations about European defense, which incidentally began in earnest in Paris, where they met in June to respond to Secretary Marshall's overtures. In its initial form, the pact was to have been an Anglo-French condominium, with Belgium and the Netherlands playing smaller roles. Under pressure from the Benelux countries, the British and French agreed to a more equal distribution of authority. The allies agreed that there could be no economic recovery without the political confidence that military security could offer and that there could be neither political confidence nor military security without guarantees of American involvement in the defense of Western Europe. More than military aid was needed. In short, the covert objective of the British and French leaders was nothing less than American membership in the Western Union.

If the idea of European-American union was not in the American vision in 1947, European union certainly was. In January John Foster Dulles, the Republican shadow secretary of state, made a major address at the Waldorf Astoria in New York pressing for European federation. His theme was taken up and expanded on by influential journalists Walter Lippmann and Dorothy Thompson and ultimately embodied in the resolution of Senators J. William Fulbright and Elbert Thomas on 21 March 1947 that expressed Congress's support for the "creation of a United States of Europe within the framework of the United Nations."[9] There were other even more radical ideas in the air. Led by journalist Clarence Streit, the Atlantic Union Committee, as it came to be called in 1949, worked toward full American membership in a European federal union. This was too extreme for most Americans in 1947 or 1948 and more than Bevin or Bidault wanted. The American mood, one that was even shared by isolationists, was well expressed in historian Carl Van Doren's popular *Great Rehearsal*, a recasting of the writing of the U.S. Constitution with broad hints that the American model was the path that the rest of the world, particularly Europe, should follow for the sake of security and prosperity.[10]

Neither the French nor British government was genuinely interested in a United States of Europe, and even less in the United States joining such a new entity. They wanted American involvement in the defense of Europe and the military assistance to achieve it, and they hoped to use the American sentiment on behalf of European unity to break down American inhibitions against entangling alliances.

American official reaction was far more cautious than that of senators, opposition politicians, and other notables outside the executive branch.

Bevin's speech to Parliament of 22 January 1948 won enthusiastic applause in Congress and in the press. It accorded with the views of middle-echelon State Department officials who understood the direction Bevin and Bidault were moving in and recognized its necessity even as they shied away from immediate political commitments. Theodore C. Achilles, director for Western European Affairs, recalled a confession about the future of Europe to his superior, John D. Hickerson, director of the Office of European Affairs, at a New Year's party: "I don't care whether entangling alliances have been considered worse than original sin since George Washington's time. We've got to negotiate a military alliance with Western Europe in peacetime and we've got to do it quickly."[11]

The Europeans could not have known just how committed some officials were, reluctantly or not. Hickerson felt that there was no alternative to full commitment. The question was how to realize the commitment without bringing the wrath of isolationists down on the policymakers' heads and without letting the Europeans relax their efforts toward sacrifices and unification. When Bevin made his speech to the House of Commons in January he had Marshall's "wholehearted sympathy in this undertaking,"[12] but nothing more specific than that. By the time the Brussels Pact was signed two months later, American willingness to make commitments was greater but still insufficient from Europe's point of view. Both Hickerson and Kennan had reservations about a Western union on the model of the Dunkirk treaty—the former because it was too negative, the latter because it rested too much on a military connection. Hickerson saw as a model the Treaty of Rio de Janeiro of 1947, in which the United States associated itself with the defense of the Americas. Objections made by the chief diplomats—Marshall and his deputy secretary of state, Robert A. Lovett, who wanted evidence of European activity toward self-defense before making public American obligations—prevailed, however, although they did not conceal from the British foreign secretary a fundamental American accord with Europe. Bevin was ready to wait for American involvement in a "second stage" of a Western union.[13]

Events of the winter of 1948 pushed the United States into close collaboration. Three crises, or anticipated crises, galvanized the West. The first and most dramatic was the coup d'état in Prague in February that ended the valiant attempts of Czech democracy under President Eduard Benes to survive in the face of Soviet pressures. A new Communist government under Klement Gottwald took power on 25 February; Foreign Minister Jan Masaryk, another famous name associated with America, fell or was pushed to his death on 10 March in Prague. The coup summoned images of ruthless Soviet aggression, squeezing victims by external pressure and internal subversion. As John Hickerson put it, the coup "scared the living bejesus out of everybody."[14] The fate of Czechoslovakia was a warning that Europe could not withstand Communist intimidation without an American guarantee. So wrote James Reston in the *New York Times* on 27 February 1948.

Reston's eye, and that of the State Department, was most immediately on Italy, the next potential victim. Elections scheduled for April of 1948 could be the occasion for the powerful Communist bloc, the largest and best-organized party in Italy, to repeat the experience of Czechoslovakia. Even if there was no Soviet military presence in that beleaguered country, the need for action to save Italian democracy seemed overwhelming. The National Security Council (NSC) and the Policy Planning Staff of the State Department were summoned to come up with solutions and responded with a series of proposals. They ranged from scenarios involving U.S. military intervention—and this from George Kennan—to urging a strong letter-writing campaign by Italian-Americans on behalf of anti-Communist parties in the forthcoming election. Not incidentally, the NSC report recommended that the administration "press for immediate inclusion of Italy in negotiations for Western Union and the announcement thereof to the British and French."[15]

On the very day that the NSC report on Italy was submitted, and one day after formal talks opened in Brussels, a new danger arose in the north. Norway expressed its fears that the Soviets were on the point of demanding a treaty that would reduce that country to a position similar to that of Czechoslovakia. There were echoes of Hitler and his nonaggression pacts as well in these demands and in the fears they evoked. In many ways this was the least of the three threats, and yet it was the one that precipitated the Pentagon talks later that month. The British responded with a proposal that the United States and Canada join to talk about a regional Atlantic approach to mutual assistance. Its scope would embrace all countries threatened by a Soviet thrust to the Atlantic, most notably Norway itself. Hickerson's response to the Norwegian problem had been similar to Bevin's: namely, that the United States not only participate in and support such arrangements as the Europeans may make but also explore the possibility of participating in a North Atlantic–Mediterranean regional defense arrangement.[16] Italy as well as Norway was on his mind.

THE VANDENBERG RESOLUTION

In retrospect, it appears that Soviet behavior rather than European plotting pushed America out of its isolationism and into a European alliance in 1948. The aggressiveness of the Soviets and the involvement of the Americans were both to deepen in the course of the year, and the symbiotic relationship between the two nations' actions is striking. They were in many ways brothers in paranoia. From a Soviet perspective the long-expected American hostilities had begun in earnest. American refusal to accept friendly regimes along Soviet borders in 1946 had been joined with intervention on behalf of reactionary forces in Greece in 1947. These activities were preludes to the reform of German currency that created, at least in

West Germany, a bizonal economic community. Since one of the aims of the Marshall Plan was the restoration of Germany, this was a signal that an anti-Soviet Germany was being prepared as part of the assault on the Communist world. In this light the Czech coup, the warnings to Norway, the frantic efforts to manipulate the elections in Italy, and even the Berlin blockade later in the spring may have been defensive moves to stave off Western aggression as much as they were targets of opportunity for an expanding Communist world.

The records in Moscow are still unavailable, but they are open in Washington, London, and Paris. And while the contents may offer reasons for Soviet suspicions, they were provocative acts only by inadvertence, insensitivity, or by loose construction. The reconstruction of a capitalist Europe was itself an offense even without a capitalist plot to undergird it. But the primary lesson to be read from the archives of Western chanceries is that the common fear of Communist subversion broke down traditions of isolation and independence on both sides of the Atlantic.

The question then was just how far the United States was ready to go in articulating its "full support" as promised in the president's special address to the Congress on 17 March 1948.[17] The answer must be: a considerable way. The European Cooperation Administration (ECA) bill, which had been in process throughout the winter, passed into law in April. Congress had been won over to the seriousness of Europe's plight and equally to the seriousness of Europe's willingness to bury its divisive past. Secret meetings in the Pentagon were held with British and Canadian representatives from 22 March to 1 April. Because of suspicions about Communist influence in France, there was no French delegate. These secret conversations set the stage for the calling of a conference that would include all the Western Union countries, Canada and the United States, with other European countries as well, to create a "collective defense agreement for the North Atlantic area."[18]

Impressive as these steps were, they did not satisfy the leaders of the Western Union. For the British and French, in particular, a "military ERP" (designed along the lines of the European Recovery Program) was a major objective, and it was not obtainable in 1948. Even more important was the rejection in the Pentagon talks of American membership in the new Western Union. It seemed that the lures that Bevin and Bidault had cast out to catch the American superpower had failed, despite the warm sentiments that flowed across the Atlantic.

Once the panic induced by the Communist coup in Prague of February and March had subsided, obstacles to America fully abandoning its isolationist past inevitably appeared. The most obvious block was that the tradition itself stood in the way of a military alliance with any European nation, let alone a group of five nations. Would public opinion permit it? Polls indicated that it would, that the public had been conditioned by the crises of postwar international life, by the frustrations of the United Nations, and perhaps too by the administration's successful manipulation of the Red menace. Still, the policymakers could not be certain. Passage of the ECA turned out to be more difficult than they had expected, and economic aid was less sensitive an issue than military aid.

The visceral suspicion that Europe would take advantage of American innocence and wealth lay behind the administration's hesitations. And nowhere was the uneasiness greater than in the military establishment. The Joint Chiefs of Staff (JCS) recognized the need for both alliance and aid without wishing to proceed on either front. Military assistance, they feared, would deplete their own stocks, which were already badly damaged by a tight military budget in 1948. Nor were they happy with implications of NSC recommendations for new commitments. In other words, the Truman Doctrine seemed to them to involve commitments that would overextend America's already strained military resources. With all the talk of collaboration with Europe, there was little faith in the ability of Western powers individually or collectively to stop a determined Soviet advance on Western Europe. In this the JCS shared the views of the Europeans themselves.

In retrospect, how significant were these caveats? They may have been enough to slow but not stop change. The machinery was already in place, expressed in three major NSC documents. The first, NSC-7, a general report on "The Position of the United States with Respect to Soviet-directed World Communism," recommended on 30 March a counteroffensive against the enemy that would "strengthen the will to resist of anti-communist forces throughout the world."[19] Although the JCS squirmed over the possibility that machine tools might be provided to European arms industries or that technical information subject to capture by invasion forces might be included under an endorsement to the Western Union's defense, their caveats delayed but did not stanch a military aid program that went into effect in 1949.

Two weeks later NSC-9, on 13 April, came forth with even broader offers to Europe.[20] Under the title of "The Position of the United States with Respect to Support for Western Union and Other Related Free Countries," the administration presented its considered response to the Western Union's importunities. This time it was the Senate, led by Arthur Vandenberg, that was discomfited, and the Senate's voice could not be ignored. Three major modifications of NSC-9 had to be made, the last on 28 June, before modifications could be sent to countries of the North Atlantic, including Italy, Ireland, Norway, Sweden, Denmark, Canada, and Portugal, as well as the Western Union members. Vandenberg and his colleagues were still suspicious about the Old World taking advantage of the New, about its expectation of having America do what was properly Europe's work; they were also concerned that the Senate and the Republican leadership receive some of the credit for the seminal changes being made in American foreign policy.

Vandenberg was reputed to exclaim, "Why should a Democratic President get all the kudos in an election year? Wouldn't the chances of Senate 'consent' to ratification of such a treaty be greatly increased by Senatorial advice to the President to negotiate it?"[21]

The result was an apparent setback for adherents to a European-American alliance. The Vandenberg Resolution, reported by the Foreign Relations Committee to the Senate on 19 May and adopted as Senate Resolution 239 on 11 June, placed a number of conditions on American involvement with Europe.[22] The most visible of them was the requirement of compatibility of all efforts, European and American, with the U.N. Charter: five of the six paragraphs of the amendments refer specifically to the charter. The key third paragraph tied "association by the United States, by constitutional process, with regional and other collective arrangements as are based on continuous and effective self-help and mutual aid." This struck many Europeans as a unilateral declaration and an insufficient response to the Western Union's hopes and to the projections of the Pentagon conversations.

For some senators on the right, such as George Malone of Nevada, the amendment was unacceptable simply on the grounds of Europe's traditional duplicity; no amount of juggling with words would change their minds. Milder but nonetheless serious reservations were expressed by critics on the left, such as Fulbright, who wished to see America firmly attached to the principle of European integration. In place of "individual and collective defense" in the second paragraph he wanted to insert the phrase "for mutual defense and political unity." Both Malone and Fulbright were effectively ignored. The Senate passed the resolution by a margin of 64 to 4.

WASHINGTON EXPLORATORY TALKS

The passage of the Vandenberg Resolution cleared away the last obstacles to negotiations for an Atlantic alliance. NSC-14, adopted on 1 July, lived up to its title, as it presented "The Position of the United States with Respect to Providing Military Assistance to Nations of the Non-Soviet World."[23] In brief, when the exploratory conversations about an Atlantic agreement finally began on 1 July in Washington, they opened largely on terms desired by the framers of the Brussels Pact. Only the Western Union powers, along with Canada, were present. Although the NSC document insisted on exploring with Italy, Iceland, Norway, and Denmark, and even Portugal and Sweden, possibilities of security agreements, this was something to be done in the future. In the meantime, it was the Western Union that was the exclusive European conversational partner of Washington.

The resulting negotiations that began with the exploratory talks in the summer of 1948 were long and drawn out. Some of the responsibility for delay clearly belonged to the United States. Despite new tensions in June over the Soviet completion of the Berlin blockade, there was no sense of haste. The airlift was working. The greater block to U.S. action was recognition that an election would be held in November and that a Republican president would have to assume and accept the consequences of the labors of diplomats. This was not altogether a formidable problem. Senator Vandenberg presumably would continue as chairman of the Foreign Relations Committee unless he was catapulted into the presidency. And John Foster Dulles, appointed to the Senate in July 1948, would be secretary of state in the Republican presidency of Thomas E. Dewey. Given the rifts in the Democratic party, there were few expectations that Harry Truman would win the election. If he was nominated at all it would be largely because the Democrats could not locate a suitable replacement. Even in the unlikely event of a Truman victory, it seemed reasonable to postpone definitive decisions until the new administration was in place.

Delay also developed from confusion shared by Europeans and Americans alike. The most consequential devolved on the dimensions of the relationship. On a superficial level this could be translated into geographical terms. Many of the talks centered on the scope of the association. If it had to be wider than the Brussels Pact, which the British and French wished to keep as the bargaining unit in dealing with the United States, then which countries should be included? Norway had different concerns from Belgium and the Netherlands. Iceland and Portugal were hardly part of Europe at all, even if they fitted into an Atlantic scheme. And Italy and Denmark were even further removed from European consideration, if only because of their distance from the Atlantic. The nub of this problem seemed to be the resistance of the Western Union initiators to share American largesse with outlying nations. Eelco van Kleffens of the Netherlands had an answer that would satisfy Europeans when pressed to accept other nations: the alliance would resemble "a peach, the Brussels Pact would be the hard kernel in the center and a North Atlantic Pact the somewhat less hard mass around it."[24]

But the putative selfishness of Europeans and the lingering suspicion of American masked irresolution about the kind of community the new alliance would create. Was it a European community to which the United States would lend its strength and its association? This was the hope of European federationists, who had met triumphantly in May in the Hague to anticipate the coming of the United States of Europe. It was also the hope of American friends of European unification, such as Fulbright and Dulles. The Vandenberg Resolution seemed to point in this direction when it mentioned U.S. encouragement of "progressive development of regional and other collective arrangements for individual or collective self-defense." The removal of political and economic barriers that had divided the Europeans in the past would facilitate use of American aid in providing effective defense. With the United States on the sidelines as provider, the Senate resolution could accelerate the European impulse for unity. Such is one construction that can be made of the U.S. position in the summer of 1948.

This scenario would be an inaccurate reading of events, however. No matter how fervent the wishes of the European federationists may have been, neither the United States of Europe nor open-ended American aid was on the agenda of the State Department or of the Western Union policymakers. The use of "Atlantic" rather than "European" alliance was a key to intentions. An Atlantic community meant an American presence inside Europe, a prerequisite both for a steady supply of American aid and, more important, for the sense of security so sorely lacking in the past. If the signals were not clear it was in part because of fear of American isolationism reasserting itself. Would Vandenberg have gone along with a clear-cut understanding that negotiations with Europeans were for an American political and military alliance outside the charter of the United Nations?

With a blurring of the questions Americans could be taken step by step into a new entangling arrangement, a situation that most of the policymakers, Kennan excluded, felt was necessary in 1948. But one of the costs to be paid was an alliance in which European integration would be compromised by the massive presence of America inside the new community. Conceivably, the Europeans could develop freely within a larger Atlantic framework to create a federated entity—and the history of the next generation reflects some slight progress in this direction. But was this entity's growth stunted because American membership invited continuing European dependence on American bounty on the one hand and American vetoes of European initiatives on the other? No definitive answer can be given, but one can note some caveats at the time. Kennan had a "dumbbell" concept he would have preferred: a European unit separate in identity and membership but connected to a United States–Canada grouping through participation in mutual security planning. When the Atlantic treaty was finally signed it received Kennan's reluctant blessing, along with Dulles's, who mused at the time that "the Economic Recovery Act and the Atlantic Pact were the two things which prevented a unity in Europe which in the long run may be more valuable than either of them."[25]

These voices, along with those of a few dedicated Europeans, went unattended in 1948. The negotiators in Washington knew that the attendance of Americans, under Major General Lyman L. Lemnitzer, at the Western Union military talks in London in June were on a "nonmembership basis"; but they also knew that the Washington exploratory talks were intended to change that status. The question was simply how to manage the change successfully.

As noted above, most of the exchange in Washington during the summer and early fall of 1948 seemed to center on details of who would be in the alliance and how much assistance would be given to its members. These problems, vexing as they were, never threatened to break up the meetings. They were soluble. Sometimes solutions came from looking the other way. American military leaders, particularly the JCS, knew quite well that the elaborate framework of the Western Union's Military Committee was a charade. It was intended to follow the ERP precedent in demonstrating to the Americans the many advances in self-help and mutual aid it would make: concerting short-term military plans in the event of Soviet military action in Europe, drawing up a coordinated supply plan, and arranging for the United States to screen estimates of military needs for the Western Union as a whole. All these requirements were presented to Europe when General Lemnitzer spoke with military leaders in London. None of them was met in the course of the year, and yet the United States accepted the professions of unified activity because of the exigencies of the time. It was obvious, however, that the joint plans were vehicles for Europe to gratify national needs, particularly France's. America's compensation for acquiescing in the European pretenses was in denying the Brussels Pact powers, the core nations, the exclusive role of Europe's bargaining agent. It was American pressure that brought in the maritime nations with Atlantic Ocean bases and arranged for bilateral terms for any military assistance given.

Still, the accusation of shortsighted and selfish considerations is not wholly justifiable. Granted that arms and supplies were high on most nations' lists, granted also that they attempted to keep the primacy of the Western Union intact as the chief American partner, the Brussels Pact leaders had reasons to worry about an excessively "Atlantic" approach to the new alliance. The Americans seemed too intent, on Iceland, Portugal, and Norway for their strategic reasons. Such an emphasis would deflect attention from the most vital of all concerns in 1948: the means of entangling the United States in the defense of Europe. The American response was to agree with the objective but to work out ways to make the solution appear to be compatible both with the Constitution and with tradition.

THE NORTH ATLANTIC TREATY—4 APRIL 1949

Nine more months had to pass before a treaty could be signed. The Europeans were surprised and dismayed by continuing delays, most of them caused by American tactics. Pending settlement of the foregoing article, the Brussels Pact nations through their Consultative Council had formally given their approval to the alliance on 26 October. Canada had followed suit in December. The United States, by contrast, had slowed the pace in the summer and seemed to dawdle in the fall.

The initial reason for delay, as noted, had been expectation of a change of administrations. The startling upset in the presidential election of 1948 should have permitted quick American action because there was no new president to be educated to the nuances of the Atlantic alliance. Other explanations are needed and are available.

Among them was the relative quiescence in Soviet pressure in the winter of 1948–49. The defeat of the Communist party in Italy had removed the immediacy of the menace that Western European communism held for Americans. In Eastern Europe the Tito rebellion had succeeded in detaching Yugoslavia from the Soviet grip, spoiling the image of a Communist uniformity in the Communist world. And in Germany the successful airlift induced the Soviets to send a cautious signal that they were prepared to negotiate terms for ending the Berlin blockade. Conceivably, the muted Soviet response to the negotiations for NATO may have been part of its elaborate plans to present the USSR as the peace party against an aggressive, militaristic NATO. Major demonstrations by peace movements that had been orchestrated by the Soviets broke out in the spring of 1949 in New York and Paris. And since judgments about Soviet intentions have to be speculative, it is conceivable that the information from the Communist mole in the British Embassy in Washington, Donald Maclean, may have convinced the Soviets that they had nothing to fear from the new Western alliance. Maclean was involved in all NATO negotiations and presumably communicated his knowledge to Moscow.

To complicate matters further, the behavior of the Western Union was in itself sufficient to raise eyebrows in Washington. The JCS, still suspicious of European designs on their military stocks, were equally doubtful about the defense plans the Western Union's Military Committee was supposed to prepare as a condition for military assistance. By the beginning of 1949 the most the committee offered was an interim solution whereby the United States would receive by mid-1949 an outline for the defense of Europe to the Rhine rather than of an overall integrated plan. The best the European chiefs of staff could do was to present a summary of forces available for mobilization if the necessary equipment could be obtained. It was obvious that much more time was spent by British and French generals Lord Montgomery and Jean de Lattre de Tassigny in jockeying for authority than in integrating their nation's defense efforts. The solution was to have both generals designated as members of a commanders-in-chief committee.

But the most significant reason for delay was internal, not external. Truman may have won the election, but there was a new team in foreign affairs in both the executive and legislative branches. The Marshall-Lovett leadership was replaced by Dean Acheson in January 1949, and while Acheson had been a valued member of Marshall's staff in 1947, he had been in private life for a year and a half and thus unaware of the nuances of the negotiations that had consumed so much time in 1948. Although he was generally supportive of the Western Union—as he was to be of NATO—his personality was different from Lovett's. European diplomats encountered a mind as sharp as Lovett's but one more skeptical and more sardonic. Additionally, the loss of a Republican majority in the Senate assured another significant change: the replacement of Arthur Vandenberg with Tom Connally of Texas as chairman of the Foreign Relations Committee. Vandenberg remained an important figure as the minority leader on that committee and, as such, was the subject of Connally's considerable jealousy. Acheson was in almost equal measure contemptuous of both men's pretensions.

The result of all these tensions led to mutual suspicions between the United States and the Western Union that worsened as the new Acheson State Department reviewed the relationship. On the one side was smoldering resentment against the conditions the United States required for military assistance, and on the other was a belief that the Europeans were deceiving the Americans. Their programs for integration—military, economic, and political—all seemed elaborate ruses to trap the United States.

The negotiations for NATO almost collapsed when, without warning, Acheson informed the European ambassadors on 8 February that the Senate had objected to the wording of Article 5; the constitutional barriers against American military commitments were not sufficiently respected.[26] This blow came after months of negotiating over wording that had seemingly settled the question. It came also at a time when the JCS had unveiled a defense plan for Europe that would not range beyond the Rhine. In the event of war, Acting Chief of Staff Dwight D. Eisenhower did hope for "a substantial bridgehead" to be held in Western Europe, and if that were not possible, at least "a return at the earliest possible moment, to Western Europe, in order to prevent the communication of that area with long term disastrous effects on U.S. national interests."[27] His words were little comfort to Europeans. Small wonder that Premier Henri Queille could respond, "The next time the U.S. would probably be liberating a corpse and civilization would be dead."[28]

Blame for this crisis fell in part on Lovett's failure to communicate the language of the draft treaty of 24 December to the Foreign Relations Committee. The trouble was over "military and other action," and Acheson did not help matters much by calling the phrase an "unnecessary embellishment."[29] The brouhaha ended with a new compromise agreement, whereby the pledge of "such action as it *deems* necessary" would replace "as may be necessary." Europeans still worried over the ambiguous "deems" but were ultimately satisfied when "forthwith" was inserted into the clause.

Everything else then fell into place. Vandenberg was appeased by the liberal references to the United Nations in the final text. Canada and France had their own special causes to plead, and both succeeded in imposing their claims. Canada was a passionate advocate of Article 2 of the treaty, which would make it more than a military alliance; it spoke to an economic and social objective of the West. France was even more vehement about the inclusion of Algeria despite its North African identity in the alliance as part of metropolitan France. France's stubbornness on behalf of the southern balance to northern dominance explains its support of Italy's membership as well, although the Italian cause was as much American as it was French. Lastly, a 20-year duration (Article 13), rather than the 50 years of the Brussels Pact, was acceptable to Europeans, and the curse of permanent alliance was alleviated by a provision for treaty review after 10 years (Article 12).

The final disturbance developed over the time and place of the signing ceremonies. The Canadians suggested Bermuda for its Atlantic imagery, while Europeans recommended the Azores, also an Atlantic entity but closer to their capitals. Although the United States initially suggested Ottawa, Acheson finally decided on Washington, partly because he could not get away easily at that time and partly for the beneficial effect a treaty signed on American soil would have on public opinion. The British were upset over the scant courtesy shown by Americans and, along with their allies, were even more annoyed that invitations were issued to the non–Western Union nations to participate in the ceremonies as equals.

There were even some problems at the ceremony itself, in the auditorium of the State Department on Constitution Avenue on 4 April. Senator Connally complained about foreign states failing to provide appropriate recognition to senators.[30] The musical selections of the Marine Corps band also lacked some sensitivity. As Dean Acheson observed, Gershwin's "I've Got Plenty of Nothin'" and "It Ain't Necessarily So" fitted more comfortably in *Porgy and Bess*.[31] But with all the false notes and arrières-pensées, Achilles and Hickerson, the most important of the American creators of the treaty, felt that it was time to head for the bar in the basement of the old Hotel Willard. "After fifteen months of effort, worry, and tension," Achilles observed, "the Treaty was a fact. We could relax, grin at each other, and really enjoy a couple of bourbons."[32]

Secretary of State Dean Acheson addressing the North Atlantic Council in Lisbon, 2 February 1952. Minister for the presidency of Portugal, Costa Leite (Lumbales), and L. B. Pearson of Canada, president of the council, are seated behind speaker's stand. *Courtesy AP/World Wide photos*

chapter 3

FROM TREATY TO ORGANIZATION: THE IMPACT
OF THE KOREAN WAR, 1949–1952

Despite the jubilation shared by all the signers of the North Atlantic Treaty at the ceremonies in Washington on 4 April 1949, ratification by a slightly less jubilant Senate did not follow immediately. Not until 21 July did the United States approve the treaty. Canada was the first to ratify it, 3 May; and Italy was the last, on 24 August. But given the care with which the treaty was fashioned to soothe American sensibilities, the passage was more difficult than had been anticipated in the spring.

Some of the difficulty derived from the natural aftereffects of euphoria. It seemed that President Truman barely had enough pens to satisfy the foreign ministers and ambassadors who participated in that historic ceremony. The most serious problem on 4 April was the seating order of the dignitaries present. Or so it appeared on that day. Still, the very fact that the country was consciously turning its back on the nation's longest tradition in its 175-year history—nonentanglement with the countries of the Old World—inevitably led to some nervous moments in the succeeding weeks and months.

THE RATIFYING PROCESS

The allies did not help the national hangover by submitting a request for military and financial aid from the United States only one day after the treaty was signed.[1] It was an untimely signal. The seekers were the Brussels Pact powers, and while their request represented actions prepared well in advance of the signing with close American collaboration through the State Department's special European Coordinating Committee, it still came as a shock to Washington. The submission pointed up the special claims of the Western Union, with the problems they raised for the other members of the alliance, as well as priorities all the allies could share. Acting as a bloc within the alliance the Brussels Pact powers sought to serve as spokesman for Europe, but its list of military requests suggests that NATO was to be an alliance of the United States and the Western Union exclusively.

The immediate consequence was delay of any military assistance program. As expected, George Kennan led the opposition from within, claiming that an excessive emphasis on the military character of the program would make NATO's initiatives toward the Soviet Union too inflexible. Yet he recognized that military aid was a prerequisite to the kinds of changes the alliance was asking of its European members. "Our whole position in argument," he observed, "must rest largely on the predominance of our contribution and on what we are being asked to do for the others. If we have nothing to give, we can hardly expect the others to accede to our views."[2]

The Senate had fewer reservations about its objections. Arthur Vandenberg may have been demoted to minority leader in the Foreign Relations Committee, but his longstanding discomfort with military implementation of the alliance carried considerable weight with all his colleagues. Dean Acheson, reporting a telephone conversation with Vandenberg, noted that the senator "felt that the introduction of the Military Assistance Bill prior to ratification would present the Treaty in the wrong light in the country."[3] Tom Connally was less concerned with the implications of military aid than Vandenberg but was more concerned with the divisive impact of the issue in Senate debate on the treaty. The result was an agreement reached at a meeting of the Foreign Relations Committee on 21 April to postpone the administration's submission of a military aid bill until the treaty had been ratified.[4]

This compromise did not settle all the administration's problems with the treaty. Its managers first had to cope with public hearings of the Foreign Relations Committee in which the administration spokesmen defended the treaty against more than 150 inquisitors—from the public as well as from Congress—in late April and early May.[5] The inquisitors forced the witnesses to repeat in excruciating detail many of the arguments that had been made over the past year. The parade of critics from the outside seemed endless, ranging from ideologues of the extreme left to the extreme right and including representatives of the American Communist party, most of the mainline churches, veterans groups, labor unions, and business associations. While the range of their comments tended to divert attention from military assistance, it stretched the ingenuity of the administration to come up with credible responses.

The most persistent issue for hostile witnesses was isolationism and the damage to tradition that a military alliance would effect. More specifically, the criticism centered on the automatic declaration of war presumably required if one of the allies should be attacked. Critics from the left were concerned that the new alliance would undermine the United Nations, which was for them the true guarantor of collective security. Some of these complaints were unanswerable.

Isolationists frequently defied labels of right and left. Professor Curtis P. Nettels of Cornell, a distinguished historian of early America, could speak for both ends of the spectrum when he expressed his alarm over the abandonment of the oldest most valuable American heritage: nonentanglement with Europe. George Washington, he implied, would have recognized that the Atlantic treaty was no temporary alliance; it was a 20-year obligation that entangled the United States with Europe in a way that violated the prescriptions of his farewell address. Nettels did stop short of saying that Washington was turning over in his grave in reaction to the impending deviation from his "great rule of conduct": namely, to limit America's political connection with Europe as much as possible.[6] Secretary of State Acheson's response to such criticism was as hyperbolic as Professor Nettels's attack. He implied that technology had changed the world since Washington's farewell address and the Monroe Doctrine, to the degree that the Atlantic Ocean had been shrunk to the size of the Caribbean. In this light Europe was simply the eastern shore of a common body of water, no farther removed from America's concern than Venezuela on the southern coast of the Caribbean had been a century and a quarter earlier.[7] The model, then, that the administration sought was not the Brussels Pact but the Treaty of Rio de Janeiro of 1947, which multilaterized the Monroe Doctrine. Europe's problems were America's in 1949.

It was more difficult for the administration to dismiss the "alliance" factor from consideration, particularly when one of its leading members, Secretary of Defense Louis Johnson, had claimed before his assumption of office that the Brussels Pact was just the kind of military alliance that characterized balance-of-power politics in the Old World.[8] Granted that he was addressing the Daughters of the American Revolution at the time, it was an unfortunate and unnecessary burden for an administration sensitive to this issue and doing what it could to show that NATO was to be different from traditional alliances. The administration's task was made all the more difficult by Europe's premature pressing for military assistance immediately after the signing of the treaty. Had it been granted it would have proved to critics that the Atlantic alliance was just a device to open the American coffers to European raids or to build up a military force that would entangle the United States in European wars.

Consequently, military aid was carefully played down in the hearings. In its place was the American connection defending the common Western heritage against the Communist threat. Almost alone this factor could inhibit war. General Omar Bradley, chairman of the Joint Chiefs of Staff, emphasized that if the aggressors in 1914 and 1939 had known in advance of America's engagement from the beginning, World Wars I and II would not have taken place.[9] As for the problem then of an invasion of one or another European country automatically bringing the United States into war, the language of Article 5, specifically mentioning constitutional processes, was supposed to take care of this objection.

Still other troubles attended the question of the treaty's compatibility with the U.N. Charter. Many former isolationists, including Senator Vandenberg, had been converted to internationalism on the strength of the United Nations providing collective security for all. The treaty seemed to be a violation of the U.N. Charter by its emphasis on collective defense outside the scope of the United Nations and by its implicit recognition that the United Nations—where the Soviet Union occupied a seat of power—was unable to provide the security expected in 1945. Even worse, the failure of U.N. machinery meant that the old balance-of-power system of military alliances was necessary to replace it. Such was the twofold problem as the pact's managers saw it in 1949. They had to respond not simply to older isolationists wary of Europe's designs on America; they had to turn aside the newer internationalists who had been convinced that collective security within the United Nations was the appropriate direction for the United States to follow.

Two approaches were taken in anticipation of these objections. The most visible was the liberal sprinkling of the names of the United Nations and the charter in as many articles of the treaty as that document could bear. A hasty reading of the treaty could leave the impression that the pact was actually a codicil of the charter itself, and this was precisely what was intended. Articles 1, 5, 7, and 12 specifically mention the charter, and the preamble opens with an affirmation of the members' "faith in the purposes and principles of the Charter of the United Nations." Article 1 makes a point of the alliance's commitment to settle international disputes by peaceful means and "to refrain in their international relations from the threat or use of force in any manner inconsistent with the purposes of the United Nations." Article 7 solemnly claims that "the threat does not affect the responsibility of the Security Council for the maintenance of international peace and security."

That a semantic game was being played out did not elude opponents of the alliance at the Senate hearings. There was an inherent conflict between treaty and charter that could not be avoided. To announce publicly that NATO would be essentially a regional arrangement like the Rio Pact would have required the acceptance of Article 53, wherein regional associations were obligated to report regularly to the Security Council on which the Soviet Union would sit in judgment of their activities. The only rubric then open to NATO was Article 51 of the charter, with its emphasis on the right of individual or collective defense. Unlike Articles 53 and 54, it required no Security Council authorization; rather, it involved an issue inviolable to any nation-state, the right of self-defense. But the U.S. ambassador to the United Nations twisted on the witness chair as he provided a loose construction that would permit self-defense to include planning collectively in advance of any attack to deter hostility on the part of an aggressor. "In my mind," he said, "Article 51 does not grant a power. It merely prohibits anything contained in the Charter cutting across existing power."[10]

Whatever the contortions required, the arguments succeeded. The Senate passed the treaty on 21 July by the commanding margin of 82 to 13. A rearguard action was fought on the Senate floor under the leadership of Robert A. Taft. The most powerful single legislator of his day, his authority on foreign relations proved limited, as did his appeal to tradition. Taft would have extended the Monroe Doctrine to cover all the Atlantic allies, if only the act could be done unilaterally without entangling the nation unnecessarily and dangerously in the affairs of the Old World. His failure seemed to suggest that a national consensus had been reached, beginning with the promises of the Truman Doctrine and culminating in the commitments of the North Atlantic Treaty. It is possible that the administration had exaggerated the dangers of isolationism and internationalism and that the semantic devices used to win approval of the treaty had been unnecessary.

Perhaps so. But given the vehemence of critics and the potency of tradition, the administration's caution was understandable. Moreover, the storm over military assistance that threatened to erupt immediately after the signing of the treaty did indeed burst forth after the treaty was ratified. It required more strenuous efforts on the part of the administration, including rewriting of the bill itself, to push a billion-dollar aid bill through Congress. In fact, had the administration not publicly announced on 23 September that the Soviet Union successfully tested an atomic bomb, the Mutual Defense Assistance Act, signed on 6 October, might not have materialized at all. If this had happened, the failure of the United States to give life to Article 3 of the treaty might have done it mortal damage. Granted that Article 5, with its entangling obligation, was at the heart of the European-American alliance, military aid was a vital pledge of commitment for most of the allies, and for France the keystone of the pact. When it did pass, Senator Tom Connally, chairman of the Foreign Relations Committee, claimed that it was the most difficult foreign policy bill since the Lend-Lease Act of 1941.[11]

THE FIRST YEAR

The Brussels Pact powers provided a model for the building of a NATO structure in the summer and fall of 1949. Once the treaty had been ratified by its members a working group was constituted to establish institutions made possible under Article 9 of the treaty. Like the Constitution of the United States the treaty permitted a loose construction in that article by establishing a council "to consider matters concerning the implementation of the Treaty." Under its aegis there would be "set up such subsidiary bodies as may be necessary; in particular it shall establish immediately a defense committee which shall recommend measures for the implementation of Articles 3 and 5." Thus the treaty identified only the superior authority of the council, along with a defense committee, among the many that may be established in the future. That so many administrative actions were taken at the first meeting of the council in Washington in September was primarily because the Western Union's infrastructure could be either appropriated directly or used as a model for NATO. In the September meetings, and again in November 1949 and January 1950, also in Washington, the working group absorbed the Western Union's Military Supply Board into NATO's Military Production and Supply Board, while the Brussels Pact's Finance and Economic Committee became almost without change, aside from its membership, NATO's Defense Financial and Economic Committee. Until the NATO groups were completely organized the older Western Union committees would add NATO operations to their regular activities.

Aside from the support units, the most significant result of the first months of NATO was the work of the Military Committee. Unlike the NATO Council and the Defense Committee, composed of foreign and defense ministers of each nation respectively, the Military Committee was made up of chiefs of staff who could devote much more time to NATO problems than their civilian chiefs, who would meet infrequently and who were preoccupied for the most part with other concerns. The Military Committee, and particularly the three-nation Standing Group, its executive arm, was to be the major institution planning NATO defense, and here too the Western Union would play a major role.

The Western Union continued to occupy a key planning role. Among the five regional planning groups covering all the Atlantic world, the Western European Regional Planning Group was the most important. It consisted wholly of the five nations of the Brussels Pact. The other four groups were North Atlantic Ocean, Canada–United States, Northern Europe, and Southern Europe–Western Mediterranean. The United States was either a full or consulting member of all groups.

But the most important element in planning was the Standing Group of the Military Committee, composed of the chiefs of staff of the three major powers of NATO—the United States, Britain, and France. Given its weight, membership was a touchy issue. The British would have liked to continue the special Anglo-American relationship of World War II and to make it a combined chiefs of staff. The French, suspicious of Anglo-Saxon domination, insisted on parity and received it, in part because the Americans did not wish to bind themselves to any Anglo-American condominium.[12] While the Western Union then was not part of the directorates as such, its voice was heard through the two European members.

A case may be made, as Secretary of State Acheson did, that NATO planning in 1949 was only "a pre-integration organization, aimed to produce general plans for uncoordinated and separate action in the hope that in the event of trouble a plan and the forces to meet it would exist and would be adopted by a sort of spontaneous combustion."[13] Acheson wrote these words almost a generation later, influenced by the events of the Korean War of 1950–53. But a comparison with the lower state of planning in 1948 would suggest that Europe and America had achieved a degree of integration that would not have been possible outside the new alliance.

The high point of planning in the first year of the alliance was reached on the approval of the strategic concept, wherein each ally would assume obligations it was best equipped to perform for the common cause. Duplication was to be avoided as integration was to be encouraged. The United States would have the chief responsibility for strategic bombing and with the United Kingdom would share naval responsibilities on the open seas. Continental countries would carry the primary burden of tactical air warfare and provide the larger share of ground troops.[14] When the United States accepted the strategic concept on 27 January 1950, the balance of the military assistance appropriations was released for distribution among the allies. Enormous progress had been made, at least at the planning tables.

But there was always an air of unreality about the frenzied activities of 1949 and early 1950. It devolved on implementation of plans—for production of weapons, for provision of troops, for integration of forces, for standardization of weapons. It occasionally surfaced when the strategic concept was matched with the strategic plan. The American JCS, long skeptical of Western Union activities and concerned about draining American stocks to fill gaps in European forces, had formulated a short-term plan for the defense of Europe that would provide essentially for evacuation of American troops and the establishment of a credible line of defense at the Pyrenees at best. More likely, an outpost in the United Kingdom would be more realistic, given the budget limits in the Truman administration's military allocations in fiscal year 1950.[15]

Europeans were unwilling to accept this short-term plan. If disseminated it would destroy the alliance, as memories of past occupation and liberation would destroy morale. The plan of the Western Union, no matter how unrealistic, was a defense of Europe at least at the Rhine, preferably at the Oder. To appease the sensibilities of NATO allies the United States accepted the Medium-Term Defense Plan (MTDP), ultimately approved at the May 1950 meeting of the North Atlantic Council, to be completed in phases by 1954, that assumed 90 ready and reserve divisions and a tactical air force of approximately 8,000 planes.[16] These projections were based solely on hope, particularly that American aid would be increased and that European industry, already energized by Marshall Plan support, would generate the economic momentum to undergird the promises of this ambitious program.

A close look at the work of NATO in 1949 would find that every other activity functioned on the principle that the future would bring what the present so obviously lacked. Acheson's term "spontaneous combustion" was not far from the mark. The various committees designed to carry out the mandate of the strategic plan seemed to be spinning their wheels with great energy but with little effect. Indeed, the committees, which should themselves be models of integration as they sought integration within the alliance, were the very opposite. The Defense Financial and Economic Committee had its headquarters in Rome, while the Military Production and Supply Board was centered in London and the Standing Group of the Military Committee worked out of the Pentagon in Washington. There was little coordination among them.

While the allies recognized the inadequacies of their efforts, there was still a reason for the optimism many exuded at the time. Essentially it rested on the assumption that no Soviet invasion was imminent in 1949 or in 1950. Second, the defense of Europe did not really depend on the numbers of troops gathered or on the quantity of arms at hand. It depended rather on the atomic umbrella that the U.S. commitment gave to NATO: the assumption that American B-29s, flying out of Omaha, Nebraska, and carrying atomic bombs, protected the alliance at all times as they deterred the Soviet Union from hostile action against the West. Beneath this umbrella the allies had breathing space to proceed leisurely. Excessive spending on military budgets to achieve the goals of the MTDP might damage economic recovery. America's own fiscal conservation set the tone, and in the first six months of 1950 there was no compelling reason to jar the allies from complacency. It was hardly noticeable, let alone conceived as a problem, that as of 6 April only $42 million of the $1.3 billion authorized for military assistance had been committed. The first shipment of military hardware did not reach Europe until March. Perhaps then the greatest inducement for European fulfillment of NATO commitments was the need to prove to Congress that they were fulfilling expectations, no matter how slowly, as they took steps toward rearming within an integrated framework.

There were some warning signs of problems ahead in the near future. The German question was inevitably one of them. The Federal Republic in a sense was a by-product of the alliance itself, coming into being one month after the signing of the treaty. Without NATO and the sense of Western solidarity that it created, it is unlikely that the Western allies could have agreed on the establishment of the Federal Republic at this time. If the linkage was not visible in 1949 it was largely because of the specter it would evoke in European breasts of the revival of the German menace.

Yet Germany could not be hidden for long. If a war should break out in Europe it would take place on German soil. What then should be the policy toward the new Federal Republic not only in that eventuality but in the whole preparation for deterrence? As early as November 1949 a position paper by the State Department relating to the potential service of Germany to the organization stated, "the German problem must be viewed and dealt in the total context of general developments. It cannot be isolated. What we do in Germany must not be dictated by considerations of what the Germans demand, or even of our respective national interests, but by a fair appraisal of the indispensable requirements of the Western community of free peoples."[17] Even the French relented as demands for dismantling of German plants were replaced in the spring of 1950 by the European Coal and Steel Community, which would intertwine German and French industry in a supranational structure. This imaginative Schuman Plan, the brain-child of Jean Monnet, would be a means of controlling West Germany while rebuilding Europe and appeasing America's concern for integration. Still, would this be enough to satisfy Americans or Germans?

A more pressing concern for Americans in this first year of NATO's history was how to assess the repercussions of the Soviet acquisition of the atomic bomb. The Russians had broken the American atomic monopoly just as NATO was beginning to put its organization together. The obvious implication was that the atomic umbrella that was to form the prime deterrent to aggression had sprung leaks even before the alliance had become fully operative. To meet this new challenge the Atomic Energy Commission met in October to consider a crash program that not only would expand the atomic stockpile but also explore the building of a hydrogen bomb. The commission's General Advisory Committee debated in secret the wisdom of such an expensive program that would escalate the weapons race. Under the chairmanship of J. Robert Oppenheimer, father of the atomic bomb, the advisory committee decided against the step by a three to two vote. But the pressures for action prevailed. A new special committee of the National Security Council, composed of Dean Acheson, Louis Johnson, and David Lilienthal, formed in November, reversed the Oppenheimer committee's recommendation on the assumption that the Soviets would build a thermonuclear bomb whether or not the United States went ahead with the program.

In accepting the NSC's recommendation, President Truman raised doubts about the limited military budget under which the Defense Department had to operate even as the nation assumed responsibilities for building a European alliance. This alliance was further undercut by a reassessment of the United States military position, made on 31 January 1950 when the president formally approved the recommendations of the special committee. The result was the formulation of the most important NSC paper of the decade, NSC-68.[18] It was the work of the State Department, particularly of Paul Nitze, chairman of the Policy Planning Staff, rather than the Defense Department representative, and it spoke to Dean Acheson's belief that the current budgets were unrealistic in light of the present and future dangers to the nation. In the present were Stalin's achievements with the atomic bomb and with winning China over to communism; in the future loomed a Soviet hydrogen bomb and a massive expansion of Eurasia under monolithic Soviet leadership.

NSC-68 laid out alternatives to massive rearmament to meet these challenges, and found all of them wanting. Neither preventive war, nor withdrawal to isolationism, nor continuing the present slow pace of defense efforts was satisfactory. There was a doomsday quality to the report that feared a Soviet overrunning of Europe as early as 1952 unless the administration considered the expansion of the percentage of the gross national product devoted to defense from 20 percent in peacetime to over half the total. It further claimed that this could be done without destroying the economy. Oddly enough, if there was conflict within the administration over the terms of these recommendations it was between Defense, which was opposed to more than a modest increase in the budget, and State, which wanted to raise it from $13 billion to $35 or even $50 billion. The JCS were more modest in their appetite than the State planners, perhaps because they knew the limits of what the military could assimilate as well as their knowledge of the economy-minded secretary of defense, Louis Johnson.

No action had been taken on these recommendations when the Korean War descended to put into motion many of them. Still, there was an uneasiness in Europe, expressed in the neutralist movement that was stimulated in turn by the Soviet-controlled "peace" initiative of the spring of 1950.[19] Its center was in France, where discomfort with a potential Anglo-American condominium of power already existed and where Communist influence had been strong since the war. Without knowing the secret advice given to the National Security Council, influential French observers such as Jean Jacques Servan-Schreiber recognized a European dilemma stemming from both the American commitment and the Soviet possession of the atomic weapon. On the one hand, it was apparent that the combined forces of Europe and the United States could not contain a Soviet onslaught should war come; on the other, the Soviet atomic bomb would inhibit the United States from responding to Europe's plight. And even if a massive buildup should be completed in time to meet a Soviet military challenge, Europe's economics could be ruined by the effort. In light of such dismal expectations it is not surprising that there was room for growth of neutralist thought.[20]

Despite the foregoing concerns, the Atlantic alliance officially seemed unaffected by the turmoil within the American establishment or by tremors of fear just below the surface of Europe's support of NATO. Nothing seemed to disturb the placid surface of NATO's public life. When the Military Committee and Defense Committee met in late March and early April 1950, they spent little time on examining the implications of the MTDP, beyond putting on paper the pooling of national strengths estimated to be needed for 1954. How forces were to be supplied, paid for, and equipped was never seriously discussed. Their aim, it seemed, was to give the Medium-Term Defense Plan an official stamp of approval for its favorable effect on impending congressional action to extend the Mutual Defense Assistance Act of the previous year. The mood reflected not the new and dangerous world of superpowers controlling one superbomb and preparing to produce another but rather the continued comfort brought by the reality of an American engagement in Europe's security. Beneath this rubric military rebuilding was subsumed under economic recovery and political stability.

Hence, the work of the London meeting of the North Atlantic Council seemed to consist of tinkering with the machinery rather than facing the challenges raised by the NSC-68 report. Steps were taken to work concurrently with the Military Production and Supply Board to examine the financial and economic potential for the allocation of new military expenditures as well as to prepare together detailed estimates of costs with priorities for their application. Reorganization of the council was also undertaken with a council of deputies meeting permanently in London to solve the problems of carrying out council policies and formulating issues to be presented to member governments. But while the deputies council did provide some continuity its authority was limited; it would enjoy no independent powers of its own. When the communiqué of 18 May announced that the council had acted "to ensure the progressive and speedy development of adequate military defense without impairing the social and economic progress of these countries,"[21] it was essentially giving lip service to vague goals while relying for its security on American power and commitment.

THE KOREAN WAR

The outbreak of war in Korea five weeks after the council adjourned in London shook, if not shattered, most of the assumptions on which the alliance had been built. The most fundamental of them was the new American commitment to Europe. It was hardly surprising that as the war intensified on the eastern rim of Asia, America's traditional preoccupation with the Far East would push aside the European orientation in American foreign policy that came with World War II. Asia had never been the bugbear of isolationists that France or Britain represented. It seemed to have fitted into a different covenant, where America could serve as protector of exploited Asians against the machinations of European imperialists. Even World War II was precipitated for the United States not by Hitler's barbarism but by the Japanese attack on Pearl Harbor. Combined with the claims that the Far East had on America's historic memory was apparent transplantation of the Communist menace from Europe to Asia. The enemy was the same; the Soviet Union was perceived to control the People's Republic of China and North Korea as thoroughly as it controlled Poland or East Germany. As anticommunist hysteria reached its peak in midcentury United States, the possibility arose that the lesser danger in Europe would be neglected for the sake of the greater danger in Asia. Europeans legitimately feared that an America arming for combat in Korea would cut back or stop the flow of military aid to Europe. The military setbacks of June and July, with the Republic of Korea in full retreat and American troops confined to a pocket of the peninsula, made these concerns credible.

American response to NATO's problems instead surprised and in some ways relieved and gratified Europeans. Not only could the firm riposte to Communist attack be interpreted as a pledge of America's leadership against Soviet expansionism, but its interpretation of the meaning of the Korea conflict strengthened the commitment to NATO. It was a simple and ultimately mistaken understanding: namely, that Moscow was testing Western, and particularly, American resolve by moving North Korean forces into South Korea. If communism should triumph in Asia, the Soviet leaders would then repeat their victory in the divided Germanies, a European analogue to the divided Koreas. Chancellor Adenauer spoke for the allies when he expressed a conviction that "Stalin was planning the same procedure for Western Germany as had been used in Korea."[22] It did not matter that the action in Korea may not have been a preview of Soviet plans for Europe, or even that Stalin may not have had as much control over North Korea as the Truman administration assumed in 1950. The perceptions of that control governed NATO's reactions, and widespread change in that organization resulted.

The first sign of congressional support for the administration over the defense of Europe arose with the issue of military assistance. The extension of the 1949 act, a modest program at best, passed with ease. Indeed, it was eclipsed by the passage of an additional $4 billion in a supplemental aid program designed to accelerate the buildup of European military forces. It was as if the nightmare visions of the NSC-68 were being realized, and a military budget to cope with its consequences had to be put into effect.

If an attack in Germany was imminent it also meant that the MTDP was inadequate and all the leisurely efforts to meet its terms by 1954 were equally inadequate. The changed circumstances required that each partner raise its defense contribution, but even with new plans that Britain and France had announced in the summer of 1950, the total manpower projected by Europe would be no more than 30 divisions, less than had been projected in the MTDP timetable for 1954 and half the number needed to hold back an invader before that time. In the panicked mood of the summer of 1950 it was estimated that another $20 billion would be required for a credible defense by 1954, and that year itself was no longer an appropriate target date. 1952 would be the critical year.

As the United States pressured its allies to take up the burden of increased expenditures, Europe's relief over America's strong support turned into resentment. By the fall the fears of an attack in Germany had subsided, and the allies claimed to have more to fear from the damage to their economies, to the genuine recovery that the Marshall Plan had generated, from subsuming civilian to military goals. Moreover, the demands of a remilitarized American economy had already set off an inflationary spiral that would undercut Europe's ability both to return to economic health and to make the kinds of military contributions the NATO leadership asked in 1950.

THE GERMAN QUESTION

As uneasy as the European-American relationship was over the problem of burden sharing, however, the Korean War brought to the surface other, even more divisive, issues to exacerbate the alliance. The most troublesome was the creation of a new credible defense force and defense structure in Europe to supplement the deterrent to attack that atomic power was intended to provide. Troops and an organization to direct them were then the primary issue. This meant that the whole facade of regional planning groups, financial and production committees, meeting in separate locations on both sides of the Atlantic in support of what were essentially inadequately equipped and inadequately manned national forces, had to be scrapped. Neither integration of forces nor increases in forces had taken place under the Western Union or in the first year of NATO. Now neither issue could be avoided.

The immediate result was the opening of the German question to a new examination. In the face of the Soviet menace the old problems of denazification, demilitarization, and decartelization seemed irrelevant, at least to Americans. Manpower was needed, and the Germans could provide it; space for maneuvers, for bases, for deployment of troops was all the more vital, and that space was in the Federal Republic of Germany. Rear bases in France or the United Kingdom may have been important, but German soil would be the front line of any assault from the east. Not only was it illogical to omit the German component to NATO, it was also unfair. Why should Americans—and Europeans—labor to defend a West that includes Germany without the Germans participating in the common defense?

Yet the administration was not unaware of the sensitivity of the German problem. Acheson and his colleagues recognized that less than a decade had passed since Nazi barbarism ruled Europe and that the memories of all Europeans, including Russians, could not be erased overnight. The idea of rearming Germany aroused negative emotions throughout Europe, and most notably in France. Although in the month following the Korean invasion the French removed objections to German industries manufacturing war material for the NATO allies and even allowed German police to be used as a surrogate military arm in the event of crisis, there was considerable distance between these actions and explicit sanction for the creation of a German army or a fully independent German nation. There was a way out: namely, to use German troops to fill the gaps in the Medium-Term Defense Plan but to place them under some form of integrated NATO command controlled by the major powers of the alliance. French Foreign Minister Robert Schuman, speaking at the New York meeting of the North Atlantic

Council in September 1950, seemed personally agreeable to the idea then circulating of establishing a European army, modeled vaguely on the recently accepted Schuman Plan, to which Germans could make a substantial contribution.[23]

Within the Pentagon and at Foggy Bottom a German component to NATO was no longer a matter of speculation; the insufficiency of European efforts made it mandatory after Korea. The only question was how to manage it quickly and effectively. The urgency was made even plainer when the availability of German resources was linked to drastic changes in the NATO military structure that would enmesh the United States even more securely in Europe. As Acheson informed the president from New York, "We were prepared to take steps which were absolutely unprecedented in our history, to place substantial forces in Europe, to put these forces into an integrated force for the defense of Europe, to agree to a command structure, to agree to a supreme commander . . . but all based upon the expectation that others would do their part."[24] The extent of America's commitment at this point devolved on the supreme commander, and notably on the specific person involved—the American war hero Dwight D. Eisenhower.

It was a superb choice. Eisenhower's personality and leadership evoked the finest hours of World War II. He was in all probability the one figure who could unite the competitive French and British generals in the Western Union and at the same time win instant support from every American constituency. His choice was a matter, it seemed, of spontaneous consensus. W. Averell Harriman and General Alfred Gruenther hit upon it over a bridge game with Secretary of the Army Frank Pace and ECA Administrator Paul Hoffman as early as 12 September. "At dinner the question of a candidate for a US Supreme Commander for NATO forces came up," Gruenther wrote Eisenhower. "One chap said the selection of Ike for this position is the only way to avoid World War III! Agreement was reached and DDE was selected by acclamation. So get your duffle bag packed."[25] In fact, the official appointment was a matter of such complete agreement that it was difficult to sort out which came first: the council's or the president's designation of Eisenhower as Supreme Allied Commander Europe.

America's expanded service to the alliance, sparked by the anticipated presence of Eisenhower, should have been an irresistible incentive for Europeans to accept German involvement, if not full membership, in NATO. In the long run it was. There were few alternatives in 1950. But in the short run American insensitivity and French intransigence delayed the inevitable. In New York Acheson, against his better judgment, was pushed by the Pentagon to present a "single package": American troops and further American aid would be contingent specifically on NATO accepting a German military contribution, some 10 units of divisional strength under a unified command.[26] The rigidity of this proposal angered the French, while the size of the German presence in that command frightened them. The

New York meeting ended in an exchange of mutual recrimination between French and Americans but without resolution.

Between September and the December sessions of the council in Brussels most of the problems were apparently settled, in large measure by the imaginative behind-the-scenes activity of Jean Monnet, the French economic planner who had inspired the Schuman Plan. In October Monnet adapted that plan to the military sphere in the form of the Pleven Plan, named after France's premier, René Pleven. European members of NATO would create a special European military force to be placed directly under the new supreme command. It would have its own staff system under the direction of a European minister of defense. After this army of some 100,000 soldiers came into being, German contingents would then be admitted in battalion strength.

The Pleven Plan was a means of appeasing American, and even European, pressure, and it worked. Although modified at the council of deputies in the form of the Spofford Compromise, which permitted German units at the regimental level into the army before the European army was completely formed, the Pleven initiative effectively decoupled the single package of September. American aid, the appointment of Eisenhower as supreme commander, and the establishment of a new command structure all could go ahead before the European army or the Germans in uniform would be in place. France's success was accomplished in part by the replacement of Louis Johnson in late September with George Marshall as secretary of defense, a more collegial partner for Secretary of State Acheson. NATO ratified in Brussels the appointment of Eisenhower as head of the new supreme command.

France and Europe won what they had sought—the further commitment of American strength in Europe and an increased deterrent in the form of American divisions permanently stationed in Europe. The price to be paid for these commitments could be put off into the future; a year or more would have to pass before a European defense community, with a supranational council of ministers and a European parliamentary assembly, could be established, and the costs of new defense expenditures might not have to be borne until new negotiations with the United States had eased the terms.

The French device to postpone a German army under whatever guise seemed to succeed with the American partners. There was no public outcry against the Pleven Plan or its amended versions. Instead, there was a sense of progress as the future members of a European defense community were to meet in February 1951 to work out the details of a European army. While Acheson and his colleagues had some serious doubts about the viability, or even the sincerity, of the French proposals, the plans for further action were enough to still congressional critics for the moment. The tortuous negotiations that produced a treaty in May 1952, creating the European Defense Community, and further negotiations for protocols and revisions that led to the French abandoning the community two years later were far from anyone's mind in the difficult winter of 1951.

The war was going badly in Asia, as 300,000 Chinese troops opened up a new phase of the war in Korea. Recriminations in the United States were inevitable, most notably from presidential critics claiming that General Douglas MacArthur's freedom of operation was dangerously curbed in the Far East and that presidential power had been dangerously and illegally expanded by Truman's sending of troops to Korea six months before. Inevitably, it would seem, the troubles over presidential authority would lap over into the changing patterns of NATO's defense in Europe.

They did. What became known as "the Great Debate" devolved on the authority of the president to assign four divisions of American troops on a permanent basis to Europe. This American presence was an integral part of the structural change. Without it Eisenhower would not have an American force to command, and without an American contingent the deterrent would be irretrievably damaged. Such was the immediate issue.

Despite the vital need for troop assignment, as forcefully presented by Eisenhower and other spokesmen, isolationists still were heard. From the sidelines came warnings from voices of an older generation—Joseph Kennedy and Herbert Hoover. For contemporaries such as senators Robert Taft and William Knowland the issue could be joined over the president's authority to send troops without congressional approval. Throughout January and February the debate raged. It was in many ways the last hurrah of isolationism. Ultimately, the Senate approved Eisenhower's command and accepted the dispatch of four additional divisions to Europe. The Senate resolution qualified its approval to the extent that no more than the four divisions be sent "without further Congressional approval, and that the Joint Chiefs of Staff certify that the allies were making appropriate progress in collective defense before the soldiers left the United States."[27]

A NEW NATO STRUCTURE

Once the congressional log jam was broken and Eisenhower's ground forces were accepted, the reorganization of NATO proceeded rapidly. The military phase took place in the early months of 1951; the political a year later, after the triumphant announcements of the North Atlantic Council at its meeting in Lisbon in February 1952. The former was simpler in many ways. The regional planning groups, with the exception of the Canadian–United States regional planning, fell away as planning was replaced by already existing forces. This meant that the Standing Group, the executive agents of the Military Committee, would have under its authority the Supreme Headquarters Allied Powers Europe (SHAPE). The supreme allied commander in turn was responsible for planning the defense of Europe. He was equalled in title by the Supreme Allied Commander

Atlantic (SACLANT), an admiral with headquarters in Norfolk, Virginia, with responsibility for the vital Atlantic sea lanes.

Unlike the Supreme Allied Commander Europe (SACEUR) choice, the Atlantic command was the object of a bitter struggle on the part of the British to secure the leadership for a British admiral, in keeping with the importance of seapower in the British tradition. British pride was not particularly assuaged by the assignment of the command of the English Channel to an admiral selected by the United Kingdom; in fact, the British had two appointments: an allied commander in chief and an allied maritime air commander in chief. Similarly the British fought and failed in their attempts to win a Mediterranean command on the same plane as SACLANT and SACEUR. Admiral Lord Mountbatten did assume a Mediterranean command based in Malta in 1953, but unlike the foregoing commands or even the Channel commands, he would report to SACEUR rather than directly to the Standing Group in Washington.

Complicated as some of the internal jockeying for national preferment was, the arrangements proceeded for the most part reasonably quickly. The most important of the commands, SHAPE, was divided into four inferior commands—Allied Forces Northern Europe, Central Europe, Southern Europe, and the Mediterranean. Integration as such was at the level of headquarters. The mixing of nationalities took place only at the level of headquarters. The bulk of troops represented national forces. They included American forces as well that would be under General Eisenhower's authority.

To complete an important part of the new strategic pattern, Greece and Turkey were accepted into the alliance, raising the number of members to 14. The two Balkan powers, the sites of America's first major commitment in the Truman Doctrine five years earlier, had sought admission to NATO since the beginning of negotiations for the alliance. Greece and Turkey were particularly distressed when the major argument against their admission—their distance from the Atlantic—did not prevent Italy from receiving an invitation. They persisted, however, and although their applications had been rejected in September 1950, NATO's evaluation of their potential role in the reorganization of the military changed circumstances. With the establishment of the Supreme Headquarters Allied Powers Europe in January 1951, their membership became vital to the defense of the southern flank of NATO. Not least of the considerations that were made when Greece and Turkey acceded to NATO at the Lisbon meeting of February 1952 were the 25 divisions they would add to Eisenhower's forces.[28]

The military restructuring of NATO benefited in 1951 as in 1949 from the experience of the Western Union. Its headquarters at Fontainebleau under Field Marshal Montgomery was essentially the prototype of SHAPE and the beginnings of "infrastructure"—the French railroaders term for embankments, tunnels, and other supports prior to laying down tracks—were transferred from the Western Union to NATO's jurisdiction.

The political restructuring followed a year later and was approved also at the Lisbon meeting of 1952. This was more difficult to achieve partly because it meant the jettisoning of the council of deputies that had come into being at the New York meeting of the council, to remedy the difficulties encountered by the inattention of the original council of ministers. The deputies would serve, as Lord Ismay expressed it, "as a permanent civilian body which would be responsible for carrying out the policies of the NATO government in the intervals between the meetings of the North Atlantic Council."[29] The war in Korea demanded more powers than the deputies had; not even their authority, granted in 1951, to speak for all the senior ministers of their respective governments, and not just the foreign ministers, was sufficient. Further changes followed. The old Defense Financial and Economic Committee became the Financial and Economic Board, replacing all NATO groups working in these areas. It was made responsible to the council of deputies. There was also an international secretariat set up under the chairman of the deputies.

Ultimately, the council agreed at Lisbon on 11 February 1952 to appoint a secretary-general, responsible to the council and charged with organizing the work of the council and supervising the work of an international staff/secretariat. The council deputies in turn would be replaced by permanent representatives, and the Defense Production Board and Financial and Economic Board would be incorporated into the activities of the secretariat and staff. Among the important tasks of the secretary-general was chairing the meetings of the permanent representatives and preparing the agenda for the council itself.[30]

A further delay in completing the political transformation of NATO was the delicate issue of moving headquarters from London to Paris, where SHAPE and the secretary-general would be in close proximity. This invoked opposition from Britain, which preferred to keep the headquarters in London. Only after compromises were affected did the British agree. The United States abandoned its attempt to separate the office of secretary-general from chairmanship of the permanent representatives. And both functions would be in the hands of a British official, Lord Ismay, the first secretary-general.

All things considered, the face of NATO from 1950 to 1952 was drastically altered, producing a visage that essentially would be unchanged to the present. There was a sense of accomplishment at Lisbon, where projected force levels, reaching 96 divisions by 1954, reflected the confidence the new NATO exuded in 1952. But how many of these changes were simply new illusions replacing old? The questions of Germany's contributions, the viability of the European Defense Community, the credibility of the atomic arm, and the willingness of the allies to meet the defense production requirements were not answered in the communiqués. Ismay had to tell

Winston Churchill at the end of 1953 that "we had 18 M-Day facing 30 Russian M-Day divisions."[31] This was an improvement over 1950, but the contrast between the reality of the defense accomplishment and the expectations raised by the many changes after 1950 cast doubts on the state of the alliance itself.

chapter 4

NATO AND THE "NEW LOOK," 1952–1958

Dean Acheson had justification at Lisbon for his jubilant claim to President Truman that "we have something pretty close to a grand slam."[1] Compared with the simple promises of 1949 or the sketchy and half-hearted organizational efforts of early 1950, the changes emerging from the Korean War were indeed remarkable. The alliance had been energized by an enormous increase in U.S. military aid; it had created an impressive military and political organization in the forms of supreme commands and a secretary-general secretariat; it had expanded the scope of the alliance through the addition of Greece and Turkey to permit more defensible postures in Europe; and it looked to the future inclusion of West Germany as an inspired way both of increasing the force capabilities of NATO and of ending the long and deadly Franco-German rivalry.

The European Defense Community was to be the crowning achievement of the alliance; the treaty creating the community was signed in May 1952 and would go into effect after ratification by the member states. A special protocol was signed on the same day, 27 May 1952, assuring that an "armed attack on the territory of any of the members of the European Defense Community in Europe . . . shall be considered an attack against all the Parties to the North Atlantic Treaty."[2] A European army, with a German component dedicated exclusively to SHAPE, seemed to be well on the way to realization.

NATO AND THE ELECTION OF 1952

But if 1952 was a year of optimism for NATO, it was also an election year in the United States. Little satisfaction with the progress of the alliance was translated into political advantage for the incumbent Democratic

U.S. delegation to NATO at the thirteenth ministerial session of the North Atlantic Council in Paris, 23 April 1954. Anthony Eden of the United Kingdom stands behind Secretary of State John Foster Dulles. *Courtesy Supreme Headquarters Allied Powers Europe*

administration. The nation's attention was not focused on the putative success of NATO in stopping Communist advance in Europe but rather on the success of Soviet communism in taking China into its orbit, of forcing an unpopular and apparently an unwinnable war in Korea on the United States, and on undermining American institutions through the spread of Communist ideas through Communist agents in the United States. By contrast, the achievements of American statecraft in Europe seemed minuscule. At best the Truman efforts in NATO centered on containment of Soviet power rather than on the defeat of communism and the rolling back of its post–World War II advances.

Aside from domestic problems, including war-borne inflation, the Truman administration had the burden of a deferred public wish for change that had been frustrated in 1948. Truman himself appeared to be a failed leader. Republican candidates confidently anticipated taking over the White House in the fall of 1952.

The war and the Communist menace made foreign relations an issue in the election. Under the leadership of the powerful and respected Senate leader Robert A. Taft, isolationism might rise again. Four years before he had been denied nomination, and the party had lost under Governor Thomas E. Dewey. In foreign affairs the party had followed the advice of Arthur Vandenberg, who had urged a bipartisan policy toward European problems; indeed, as its most important senatorial supporter, Vandenberg had had the policy in the Republican-dominated eightieth Congress. Vandenberg did not live long enough to participate in the election of 1952, but he lived long enough to witness and to denounce the failure of bipartisanship in foreign relations. The Republican party platform of 1952 not only made foreign policy a major partisan issue in the election but also charged "that the leaders of the Administration in power lost the peace so dearly earned by World War II."[3]

Buoyed by Senator Joseph R. McCarthy's sensational accusations of treason as well as of incompetence in the Truman administration, the isolationist remnants made a major case for a renewal of isolationism. In the wings were former President Hoover and former ambassador Joseph Kennedy, celebrating the virtues of an American Gibraltar that could withstand the perils of the outside world only if the United States disentangled itself from alliances. If intervention had any validity, the isolationists believed, it would be in the Far East, a traditional area of American concern. Continuation of the Democratic foreign policy would, the Taft contingent argued, encourage Europe to involve America in its own schemes, wasting the country's resources in military aid and exaggerating presidential prerogatives without defeating the Communist menace. Such was the message of Senator Taft as he battled for the Republican nomination in 1952.

Taft failed. The liberal wing of the Republican party had made its commitment to a Europe-centered foreign policy in World War II and had been a vital element in the establishment undergirding of the Atlantic alliance. It now managed to induce General Eisenhower to retire from his SHAPE command in Paris and to enter the presidential race. His key advisers were Senator Henry Cabot Lodge of Massachusetts and Governor Dewey's shadow secretary of state, John Foster Dulles. Their victory over Taft and his midwestern isolationists was a victory for the continuation of the Truman-Acheson policy toward Europe. But it was not a victory for bipartisanship. In defeating Taft the Eisenhower forces had to make many concessions. If they did not accept explicitly the McCarthy thesis of treason in high places, they professed to share his assumption about the bankruptcy of American foreign policy in its Manichean contest with the forces of communism.

It was easy enough for the Eisenhower forces to distance themselves from the Korean War and its responsibilities. Without embracing General Douglas MacArthur's argument over how to win an Asian war, they joined with him in excoriating the Democratic failure both to anticipate the invasion and then to prosecute the undeclared war successfully. Eisenhower's pledge to go to Korea and clean up the mess personally once he was in the White House implied instant change.

It was more difficult for the internationalist wing of the Republican party to distinguish itself from the Democrats' NATO policy. Eisenhower after all was the very symbol of America's guarantee to Europe's survival. From the winter of 1951 until his return from Europe in the spring of 1952 he could take credit for the resurgence of the alliance in the face of economic, political, and psychological problems stemming from the Korean conflict. If the Lisbon conference represented optimism for the future, SACEUR Eisenhower was a prime mover in generating this spirit.

The way to maintain continuity and still to retain the support of the Republican mainstream was found by John Foster Dulles, the secretary of state designate of the future Eisenhower administration. Success in 1952 would be the fulfillment of a lifetime's preparation for the task. Dulles had been in attendance at the Hague Peace Conference in 1906 as a college student, a protégé of his uncle Robert Lansing, later Woodrow Wilson's secretary of state. In his subsequent career as an international lawyer, he brought to the subject of foreign relations the legacy of the Calvinist clergyman his father had been and a sense of tradition of service reflected in the career of his grandfather, John W. Foster, secretary of state under Benjamin Harrison. As a Republican adviser he had served a bipartisan function as a delegate to the United Nations, as adviser to the Democratic secretary of state at the councils of foreign ministers from 1945 to 1947, and, most important, as Truman's chief negotiator of the peace treaty with Japan in 1951 with the rank of ambassador. If any Republican aside from Vandenberg could symbolize bipartisanship, it should have been Dulles.

From the perspective of the Atlantic alliance Dulles served as a valuable supporter, one of those who welcomed the Eisenhower candidacy. His ambitions helped to rationalize his criticisms of the Truman administration and the Democratic candidate, Adlai Stevenson, for adopting policies he had approved earlier. The Democrats had failed to sustain the moral character of American diplomacy and had allowed themselves to fall into Communist traps. It both fitted Dulles's religiosity and the mood of his party to condemn what he had earlier supported: the doctrine of containment of communism. It had been too negative, too defeatist, and had led to loss of territory in Asia and demoralization in Europe. In a major article for *Life* magazine in May 1952 entitled "A Policy of Boldness," Dulles asked that a policy of liberation replace a policy of containment. It was not enough for NATO to defend the West against a potential Communist attack; NATO must join the United States in serving as a base for liberating the subjugated states of Eastern Europe from the Soviet yoke. Such an objective would be achieved not by war but by successful propaganda, curtailing of trade benefits to the Soviet bloc, and breaking of diplomatic relations with Communist puppet governments.

In many respects Acheson and Dulles shared values derived from their common upbringing in the manse, from a privileged Ivy League education, and from a successful experience in the law. Both men were realists. But as political scientist O. William Perlmutter has observed, "Dulles was prepared to accommodate himself to the McCarthy influences and to accept office upon conditions that would have been utterly repugnant to Acheson. On the other hand, Acheson was much better prepared to accept the ideological differences between the United States and the Soviet Union [and China] than was Dulles." While both men attempted to bring Christian principles into the life of a statesman, Acheson would apply them only to private affairs; he was a realist on public affairs. By contrast, Dulles's realism on the private level led him to overlook his moral scruples, even as he was less ready than Acheson to make "an uneasy peace with secular principles of power politics."[4]

THE STATUS OF FORCE AGREEMENTS

The landslide victory of General Eisenhower catapulted the Republicans back into office after 20 years of Democratic government. For the first time in this period both houses of Congress were controlled by a Republican majority. The new president, it seemed, was now in a position of authority that his predecessor never achieved. It was enhanced by the glow of his remarkable military career.

The mood of the 1952 presidential election affected relations with the entire outside world, not just the Soviet bloc. A primary motif was the accretion of presidential powers in foreign affairs, originating in and expanded further in the Korean conflict. Since 1951 Senator John Bricker, an Ohio isolationist and Republican candidate for vice president in 1944, had been advocating with increasing stridency and increasing support an amendment to the Constitution that would negate the authority of any treaty that would deny or abridge a right enumerated in the Constitution. Additionally, it would subject executive agreements between the president and a foreign power to the same limitations that applied to treaties. Here was the congressional revenge for the Yalta agreement that was made without congressional approval. The Eisenhower administration, which had made the modification of constitutional provisions regarding the treaty powers of the president a central theme in the presidential campaign, was faced with living the implications of its promises. Once in office Dulles understandably refused to accept even a watered-down Bricker amendment. Scores of executive agreements coming under congressional scrutiny would have paralyzed the operations of the State Department. Bricker never forgave Dulles for his defection.

While the amendment would have affected relations with foreign governments everywhere, a less publicized Bricker initiative would have affected the NATO allies specifically. This was the Bricker reservation to the NATO

Status of Forces Agreement, dealing with criminal jurisdiction over the forces of one NATO power stationed in the territory of another. The issue would never have arisen had the Truman administration not succeeded in winning the Great Debate of 1951, after which four U.S. divisions would be stationed indefinitely in Europe. Prior to that time American troops in Germany represented an occupying force that would manage offenses of every kind under the military court-martial system. After 1951 American troops in foreign territory would be stationed by a contractual arrangement that involved appeasing the national sensibilities of the host nation. Otherwise, American forces in Europe would be in the position of occupiers of defeated nations or of privileged auxiliaries to inferior allies. The situation would be intolerable in the long run, inflicting mortal wounds on the body of the organization.

To resolve the question the Truman administration had begun a series of agreements as early as 1951 that would remove from contention the charge of extraterritoriality for Americans on NATO territories. Under the status of forces agreements, Americans accused of criminal offenses in the host country while away from their official duties would be subjected to the jurisdiction of that nation's laws. This meant that the provisions of the Constitution—trial by jury, or right to a public trial—would be denied to American offenders abroad. These agreements would be, as Under Secretary of State Bedell Smith put it, "unprecedented" in the history of American foreign relations but vital to the future of the alliance.[5]

It required courage for presidents Truman and Eisenhower to face down the disapproval of Bricker and his supporters. It was all the more difficult for Dulles because the reservations were made by his own party and touched on the issue of European relations that went to the heart of the differences between the isolationist and internationalist wings of the Republican party. But as in the Bricker amendment, the administration in 1953 refused to follow the congressional leadership. The reservations asked by Bricker would have the United States maintain "exclusive jurisdiction over the members of its force or civilian component and their dependents with respect to all offenses committed within the territory of the receiving state." The agreement otherwise, he asserted, would "reflect a callous disregard of the rights of American armed forces personnel."[6]

Bricker and his allies regaled the Senate with scenarios of cruel and unusual punishment that would be meted out to American servicemen. They ranged from losing their hands for petty thievery to losing their liberty in substandard foreign jails. It did not matter to the critics that mutilation was not practiced among NATO countries or that military courts-martial would impose in most cases more severe sentences than would foreign tribunals. Their point was that American sovereignty was being infringed on by status of forces agreements and that constitutionally guaranteed rights of Americans were at stake. The defeat of the resolution, like that of the

Bricker amendment, was the result of a collaboration of Democratic senators and a sobered Republican establishment. The Senate approved the NATO Status of Forces Agreement on 15 July 1953, by a vote of 75 to 15, with a resolution much more moderate than that of Senator Bricker's.

There was no doubt the steadfastness of the Eisenhower-Dulles position on NATO. Yet it was not surprising either that the general criticisms of the Truman administration would have yielded these serious challenges to the ability of its successors to honor the commitment to the alliance, and even to manage foreign relations at all.

THE "NEW LOOK"

If the troubles of the Soviet bloc after the death of Stalin gave some breathing space for the new administration to work out its self-inflicted difficulties, it also permitted NATO an opportunity to take stock of where it had evolved in the four crowded years of its existence. The Lisbon meeting of the North Atlantic Council with its triumphalism and the European Defense Community treaty with its expectations of a new order in Europe did not gratify initial hopes. In some ways the euphoria of the past year could not have been sustained under any guise.

The Lisbon accomplishments had been preceded by the establishment of a Temporary Council Committee only four months earlier at the Ottawa meeting of the North Atlantic Council in September 1951. Its function was to come up quickly with a solution to the problem of ends and means: namely, how to reconcile massive requirements of NATO's buildup with the ability of the member nations to contribute their appropriate share. The United States was devoting some 14 percent of its gross national product to defense, while many of the allies were doing no better than 3 percent. To meet this crisis, and to take into account the strains that the shortfalls in raw materials after the outbreak of the Korean War placed on the intraalliance balance of payments, "Three Wise Men"—W. Averell Harriman of the United States, Jean Monnet of France, and Sir Edwin Plowden of the United Kingdom— were deputized by the council. They were supposed to determine just what the economic resources of each member were and how much they might expend for the common enterprise. And they had to do this in a few short months.

They completed their task in time for the Lisbon meeting. At best there would still be a shortfall of some $6 billion to meet the full defense require-ment for the MTDP by 1954. As for the pressure put on allies for more sacri-fice, Lord Ismay understated the opposition when he observed, "It should be recorded for the sake of accuracy that not all members were happy about the TCC conclusions."[7]

Reality intruded even before the Truman administration left office. Neither force goals nor equitable burden sharing would be realized within the time span of the defense plan. The necessary financial and economic resources were not politically available in 1952 or 1953, and the Eisenhower administration had to face the implications from the moment it came into office. The issues were complicated by election pledges to wipe out waste as well as corruption and to reduce the cost of the inflated Truman defense budget. This was the mandate of the new secretary of defense, Charles E. Wilson, formerly chairman of the board of General Motors.

The ending of the Korean War and the struggle of supremacy in the Kremlin permitted some room for working out a "New Look" at American foreign military policy that would reflect both the realities of NATO's current defense posture and the imperatives of the Eisenhower priorities. These were accomplished by first stretching out the period of maximum danger and ridding the alliance of the "magical critical year of 1954," as the president put it.[8]

But the New Look was not simply a retreat from aspirations. The administration could argue first that excessive military expenditures in the alliance could endanger the economies of alliance countries and achieve the Kremlin's objectives of destroying the West through economic collapse. More significantly though, Dulles could envision a defense of the West through the development of the tactical and strategic nuclear weapons that would be cheaper than conventional equipment and more effective in deterring the Soviets from attack. A reduced defense budget could be justified by increased allocation of resources to the nuclear arm. Such was the inspiration of the Wilson slogan, "greater bang for the buck." Such also was the origins of the so-called doctrine of massive retaliation.

These shorthand terms were for the same objective: maintaining and even improving the deterrent strength of the West at more manageable costs than had been projected in the Truman period. In a series of speeches in December and January 1953 and 1954 the secretary of state and the chairman of the Joint Chiefs of Staff made clear that the United States would want flexibility and mobility for emergency deployment of U.S. forces and that it would expect that the allies would fill such gaps as may be left. But their critical message was that deterrence would "depend primarily upon a great capacity to retaliate, instantly, by means and at places of our own choosing." Lest this mean that any act of aggression would mean an atomic bomb dropped on Moscow, Dulles in the April 1954 issue of *Foreign Affairs* explained that by "massive retaliation" he was thinking that the "free world must maintain the collective means and a willingness to use them in ways which most effectively make aggression too risky and too expensive to be tempting."[9]

That fewer troops could perform NATO's mission was reinforced by the development of compact and comparative low-yield nuclear warheads suitable for tactical military targets. As early as September 1952, General J. Lawton Collins, army chief of staff, could claim that while tactical nuclear weapons might not decrease initially the total number of troops needed for the defense of Europe, it would eventually permit defense to be accomplished by fewer divisions than had been anticipated.

Optimism over the potential for technology to solve manpower shortages was perhaps expressed best not by a European ally but by an American, Admiral Arthur W. Radford, chairman of the Joint Chiefs of Staff from 1953 to 1957, who recommended the cutting of the armed services by 800,000 men in 1956, limiting armies to civil defense missions and to token presence for morale reasons. No Korean-scale war would again be possible if the result would be massive retaliation. The result inevitably was a letdown in the tempo of arms buildup, dramatized by France's transfer of four divisions to Algeria in 1954 and Britain's later withdrawal of two divisions in 1957.

There was always some uneasiness about this celebration of new and cheaper shortcuts to security. General Omar Bradley, chairman of the Joint Chiefs of Staff from 1949 to 1953, seemed to counter Collins's optimism by warning that the weapons were not advanced sufficiently to warrant any slackening of efforts to meet the MTDP goals. The warning of General Matthew B. Ridgway, Eisenhower's successor as SACEUR, was more alarming when he pointed out a year later that the new tactical nuclear weapons might turn out to be even more expensive than conventional weaponry and require more troops to manage them. There were other, even more serious, reasons for worry over the impact of the New Look on NATO that centered on the reliability of the American commitment to Europe, on the credibility of the nuclear deterrent, and on the vulnerability of Europe itself. Many of them came to the surface before the end of the first Eisenhower administration.

In 1953 and 1954, however—the years of maximum danger earlier—NATO could accept the idea that some stabilization had been achieved, even if the stated U.S. goals of "liberation" were not likely to be achieved. Pronouncement from military headquarters seemed more dutiful than minatory. General Alfred M. Gruenther, on the eve of succeeding Ridgway as supreme allied commander, did declare that the Soviet forces "as of today, Monday, 18 May 1953 are stronger than any force we have. They have a significant advantage over us."[10] He went on to note that the Soviets had 175 infantry divisions and a capability of expanding to more than 300 divisions within the first 30 days of hostilities.

These listings of numerical superiority of the potential adversary represented reasonably accurate figures, and they contrasted sharply with the alliance's strength on paper in the mid-1950s. Yet the stretch-out seemed not to exacerbate NATO's anxieties. In June 1954 General Gruenther could list 90 to 100 divisions in varying degrees of readiness and could make this accounting without a sense of inferiority to the Soviet forces. There was a disposition to contrast the sorry conditions of 1949 or 1950 with the changes a few years later, even when these changes fell short of the MTDP goals. Each year, for example, the European NATO countries had increased their contributions by 120 percent. And from the United States the trickle of military aid that had begun in the spring of 1950 had turned into a steady flow as the passage of years shortened the lead times between appropriations and expenditures on the one hand and deliveries on the other. The total value of the end products was close to $2 billion by the spring of 1953.

Whatever discomfort the disparity in troop numbers might still present was dissipated by the increasing acceptance of tactical nuclear weapons introduced into Europe in this period. Maneuverable rockets and missiles, such as *Honest John, Corporal,* and *Matador,* arrived in Europe in 1954. Confidence was displayed over the alliance's ability to keep a forward shield strong enough to force the enemy to attack in concentration, particularly the anticipated German contingents. An attack would result in a nuclear response, in which the allies would play their role. For the moment the question of how far the McMahon Act of 1946 prohibiting collaboration with any foreign power on atomic weapons would be relaxed was deferred. An Atomic Energy Act of 1953 did permit sharing certain information on the size or weight and other characteristics of systems, but it insisted on nuclear warheads remaining under American control at all times. Such difficulties as this might make with the allies were still in the future, however.

Guided by the New Look, Gruenther's SHAPE had sent to the NATO Standing Group in 1954 a three-year plan for reorganizing NATO's military forces based on the availability of nuclear arms. Lower manpower thresholds reflected the substitution of nuclear for some conventional forces. In the form of MC 70—a plan with 30 combat-ready divisions, armed with tactical nuclear weapons—the Lisbon goals were revised downward formally by 1957. The shield became thinner in manpower, almost, if not wholly, symbolic. The enemy would not have to be defeated on the ground; the attack, if it should come, would be a tripwire, unleashing nuclear response that would presumably defeat the enemy. More important, it would inhibit the enemy from acting. In this context the American physical presence was a vital element in the deterrence, both to assure Europe of America's involvement and to squash Soviet temptations to transgress.

The changing military picture of Europe was reflected in the elliptical language of the North Atlantic Council communiqués. While always putting the best face on any issue, the council in December 1953 "invited the Military Committee to continue its re-assessment of the most effective pattern of military forces, for this long term . . . due regard being paid to the results of studies of the effect of new weapons." A year later the emphasis was on improvement of efficiency and quality of NATO forces by means of effective combined exercises and "from the supply of large quantities of new equipment." Without formally abandoning the numerical buildup of the early 1950s, the December council meeting in 1956 made clear that the results of the studies of nuclear weaponry led to a directive that future military plans would take into account "the various types of new weapons available for NATO defence." Not until the December 1957 meeting did the ministers actually identify nuclear weapons in their communiqué, and when they did it was made more specific than any early reference to defense measures. "NATO has decided to establish stocks of nuclear warheads, which will be readily available for the defence of the Alliance in case of need."[11]

These statements exuded an air of confidence. The coexistence policy of the Soviet Union that followed Stalin's death, no matter how sinister its ultimate purposes, has deterred Soviet aggression in Europe and indeed "contributed to the adoption by the Soviet Government of the so-called policy of co-existence." So the North Atlantic Council asserted in its May 1956 communiqué.[12]

NATO AND GERMANY

Yet the road to coexistence, real or imaginary, in the Eisenhower era was rarely seen as a success story in the United States, particularly by Secretary Dulles. Whatever the council might say about "coexistence" as a Soviet admission of failure, whatever the SACEUR might point to as a record of achievement in infrastructure or in the rise of military assistance, whatever satisfaction the secretary-general might take in the "NATO Method," the system of consensual decision making that moved all the allies in concern, was spoiled for Dulles and for many of his colleagues. Were achievements truly meaningful? How could they be when the Soviet's wish for coexistence was a trap for unwary Westerners?

Not all the American concerns were evidence of paranoia. Many of NATO's wounds stemmed from two very real problems, both internal and both in many ways self-inflicted. One was the inflammation of the German question from 1952 to 1955; the other was the divisiveness that out-of-area questions, notably over British and French colonial interests in Africa and Asia, imposed on NATO from 1953 to 1956. Together they almost ripped apart the fabric of the alliance.

Germany was the more critical because its role was at the heart of the alliance and at the heart of the defense of Europe. As observed earlier, German manpower was essential for the defense of Europe; German territory was the site of the forward front, the main boundary between East and West. By contrast, the northern sector, where Norway is contiguous with the Soviet Union, or the southern sector, where Turkey borders on the Caucasus, remained peripheral fronts. If the Soviets should attack, it was expected it would be in Germany. Equally important was the necessity for a Franco-German rapprochement if Europe was to be saved. The internecine European conflicts representing the nationalism of the past had to end.

For all the foregoing reasons the rapid ratification of the treaty creating the European Defense Community was anticipated at the time of the U.S. presidential election of 1952. Everything should have been in place by this time. The Pleven Plan itself was already a year old. In Paris and in Bonn in May 1952 the fear of a German army and of German rearmament in general should have been allayed. It seemed that all ramifications of the community had been explored: the number of German units involved (12 out of 43 divisions), the authority of the European Defense Community, the nature of the association of the United States and the United Kingdom, the relationship to SACEUR.

The Truman administration had given increasing weight to the EDC in 1951 and 1952, particularly as Acheson sought unsuccessfully to bring Britain into the community. The arrival of Dulles on the scene intensified American pressure for completion of the process.

American intervention both hastened and delayed action. Dulles's fast-warming friendship with Chancellor Konrad Adenauer was a major factor in Germany's resolving its reservations about the arrangement. There was doubt among Germans about the wisdom of the EDC, particularly if it inhibited opportunity for reunification. This was a theme taken up both by right-wing nationalists, disturbed as well by the blurring of a German identity in the EDC, and more forcefully by the Social Democrats, led by Erich Ollenhauer, with its inherent dislike of German rearmament. Spurred by this new friendship, Dulles sought acceleration of ratification. He was responsible for the statement in the communiqué at the North Atlantic Council meeting in April 1953 that pressed for the inclusion of the EDC as soon as possible in a closely united Europe and threatened to "give a little re-thinking to America's own foreign policy in relation to Western Europe" if the treaty failed to be ratified.[13]

For Americans, the issue was in part the fulfillment of a European commitment to defend itself. It was also a chance to end once and for all the crippling divisions that plagued the world in the past and now damaged the progress of the alliance. The intimidation was heavy-handed and did not take sufficiently into account the still lively fears of the French and other Europeans of a new, possibly dangerous, departure. Worried about congressional impatience and the fortunes of his friend Adenauer, Dulles shook the council and his auditors at a press conference on 14 December 1953 by the vigor of his demands for final ratification of the treaty. He later admitted that his widely publicized statement "about an agonizing reappraisal" was designed as "a means of breaking into the consciousness of the French assembly."[14]

It was the wrong signal. Rather than jarring the French into action it increased their concerns about their isolation from the United States—and from Britain—as they stood more alone than ever in a Europe that would be dominated by the Germans. World War II after all was less than 10 years into the past. But the long debate triggered other factors in the retreat from the treaty. Gaullists and other nationalists railed at the loss of freedom for French troops in the community. These considerations were all the more powerful when the Indochina War was included in the debate. France had to be free to maintain its out-of-area commitments, threatened as they were in 1954 by disaster in Southeast Asia.

No French government could go before the country without then demanding new guarantees from the United States and Britain. These included new military aid as well as the integration of the EDC and NATO on matters of command, tactical support, and logistics. They were granted, and still the French were not satisfied. The unwillingness of the Americans and British to come to the aid of France after Dienbienphu's fall in May 1954 underscored France's negative judgment.

The last scene was played out in August 1954 as a new French premier, Pierre Mendès-France, in office since June 1954, made the removal of France from Indochina a matter of higher priority than the incorporation of France into the EDC. A new protocol was introduced on 16 August in Brussels that would have downgraded the authority of the Board of Commissioners and in effect would have made the United States and the United Kingdom full partners in the EDC. These were rejected. Eleven days later a vote on a procedural motion, that the occasion was not suitable for deliberation, removed the issue from the French Assembly without a vote on the EDC itself. As Edward Fursdon put it, "the EDC was dead, without even having been accorded the honour or the dignity of a funeral oration."[15]

If there was nothing but silence in France it was more than compensated for by the vehemence of the reaction among France's NATO allies. Dulles sounded a cry of betrayal as he appeared ready to engage in that "agonizing re-appraisal" that he had threatened in December 1953. Its essence would be to write off France as a partner in the defense of the West or substitute it for a bilateral alliance with Germany. Congress appeared to be in full agreement. Only a month before, the Senate Armed Services Committee had recommended that all aid to France be cut off if the EDC was not ratified by the end of the year. And on 31 July the Senate gave the president virtually a blank check, by a vote of 88 to 0, to grant Germany sovereignty unilaterally in the event of the collapse of the community.

None of these threats was carried out. On the contrary, by putting to rest finally the question of the EDC the alliance was faced with a crisis of survival and passed it with remarkable speed and confidence. Dulles's anger may have been genuine. The annoyance and frustration of the European allies were not much less in evidence than the American, but the idea of either banishing France or building up a fully independent Germany was anathema.

To resolve this dilemma British Foreign Secretary Anthony Eden articulated Mendès-France's plan—embodied in the London Nine Power Conference of 28 September and the Paris Conference of 2–22 October—to satisfy French, German, and American anxieties about the future of the alliance. It was simply an exhumation of the buried but not quite lifeless body of the Western Union, changing its name to the Western European Union (WEU), including both Germany and Italy in its membership and using this organization as a means of bringing Germany into NATO. Its virtues from the French point of view were at least twofold: first, the organization would be able to restrict German manufacture of nuclear, biological, and chemical weaponries, as well as of warships and strategic bombers; second, the strengthened European union that would oversee these arrangements included the United Kingdom. For Germany, the WEU would be the vehicle for achieving its sovereignty, even if somewhat qualified, and its membership in the Atlantic alliance. There would be German rearmament with an army wholly dedicated to the SHAPE command. In addition, the long-standing Franco-German conflict over ultimate control of the Saarland was settled in a Saar Statute attached to the Paris Agreements. It permitted a referendum that ended the Saarland's semiautonomous status under France in 1955 and opened the way for its incorporation as a German state in 1957.

The rapid succession of events in September and October centered on Eden's almost instant intervention with the silent support of Mendès-France. Within a week of the French Assembly's decision on the EDC, new meetings with new proposals were in motion. The point of departure was the restoration of German sovereignty, but with the understanding that safeguards satisfactory to its neighbors could be provided. The unacceptable supranational character of the EDC was now removed, overcoming earlier British inhibitions and satisfying French nationalist concerns. If the agreements succeeded, it was largely because there was no alternative to a NATO solution.

Given these circumstances, the American reaction had to be articulated with care. Dulles was able to bring himself to say to the president as early as October that if the plans materialize "we will have saved most of the values inherent in EDC,"[16] although American sentimental pressures for European unity remained a problem for him. Moderation worked, if shakily. After the French initially voted against rearming Germany in December, the State Department prepared alternate statements based on the final judgment of the Chamber of Deputies—one congratulating France on its decision, the other speaking of "concerted action" excluding France.[17] Drawing on the awful alternative to failure, Mendès-France staked his ministry on a final vote and won. As James Reston expressed it, "Premier Pierre Mendès-France got his vote of confidence from the French National Assembly, but France herself got no vote of confidence here."[18]

Chancellor Adenauer, for his part, had to cope with opposition from the right and from the left, who saw in the Federal Republic's adherence to the West loss of bargaining power with both blocs, permanent division of Germany, and subordination to French controls. To his critics he countered in the January 1955 issue of *Foreign Affairs* that "I believe that the only concrete possibility of bringing about a relaxation of the conflict in Europe, and thus of achieving German reunification, lies in an attempt by the Western European Union and the Atlantic Community, acting jointly, to seek a solution of the pending problems with the Soviet Union sooner or later."[19] The

United States and its allies had weathered a difficult crisis and emerged at the end of 1954 far stronger and far more united than any observer would have anticipated.

NATO AND THE THIRD WORLD

Concurrent with the crisis over the European alliance, however, were issues relating to the Third World. Surfacing in 1954 and continuing throughout the Eisenhower administration, these issues offered few grounds for complacency. Particularly disruptive was the long simmering French colonial war in Indochina and its effects on French policy toward the United States and toward the alliance generally. Broadly construed, this has been known as "out-of-area," and later "Third World," relations. From the beginning the geographic scope of the alliance was a matter of great importance, largely because the United States had identified itself as the leader of anticolonialism while its major European allies were also the world's leading colonial powers—Britain, France, Belgium, and the Netherlands—with territories scattered throughout Asia and Africa. European colonialism had been a major barrier against America's breaking with its isolationist tradition. Trouble among allies had broken out even before the treaty had been signed, as the United States lined up on one side and the Europeans on the other in the Indonesian war for independence against Dutch control. As the treaty was being formed, the United States had opposed the inclusion of Algeria into the alliance because of the precedent Algeria might make for the responsibilities of the alliance. It was a sensitive question on both sides, settled by the acceptance of the Algerian "departments" of France, which would be the southern boundary of NATO at the Tropic of Cancer in Article 6 of the treaty.

The onset of the Korean War blurred the edges of American anticolonialism, particularly with respect to its position on France's colonial posture in Southeast Asia. Previous pressure against the French in favor of Indochinese nationalism dwindled and ultimately disappeared as the enemy in Asia was perceived to be part of the same Communist conspiracy that induced Moscow to use North Korean and then Chinese Communist troops against South Korean and U.N. forces. French assertions that their war against communism in Asia was America's war as well struck a responsive chord in Washington. Should the French withdraw in Indochina the United States position on Korea conceivably could be endangered. "Holding the line" in Southeast Asia became as vital to America's national interest as to France's. This perception softened American complaints over the lagging French efforts in Europe, since troops and supplies drained from Europe, did serve containment elsewhere. It was no problem for the Dulles worldview that held a more expansive conception of containment than Acheson had in the previous administration.

Still, this new understanding of colonialism did not heal wounds inflicted by out-of-area issues. Throughout the 1950s the American public and Congress seemed to continue their visceral support of nationalist sentiment. If it was blunted in Indochina, it broke out in full flower in Algeria, where Senator John F. Kennedy of Massachusetts was an eloquent spokesman for a new African policy. Unlike Indochina, Algeria and Tunisia were far removed from the Soviet Union or China, and American advocacy for their independence could be identified with preventive measures against a future Communist takeover. Anticolonialism was still alive. Even Indochina was not untouched. As the Viet Minh rebels grew stronger, French clamor for American aid met with rumbles that France had invited its own destruction and that if Americans were in charge of the military campaign the results would have been much different.

In 1954 the fall of Dienbienphu and the Geneva conference—at which the French washed their hands of Indochina—proved to be even more troublesome to the alliance and Franco-American relations than the German question had been earlier that year. France believed that America betrayed French forces in Indochina with promises for intervention that were not kept. Moreover, there was a deep suspicion that the indecent haste with which the Eisenhower administration inserted an American presence in place of the French after France's departure was proof not only of America's unreliability but of perfidy as well. The grand design of Secretary Dulles in which new security organizations, on the order of NATO, would ring the Soviet world with a bond of allies was an object of suspicion among many French officials. A Southeast Asia Treaty Organization, which would encompass South Vietnam through a special protocol, was a mask for a Pax Americana that attempted to contain if not destroy the Soviet bloc, but at the expense of the interest of the Atlantic allies.

Britain shared some of these attitudes two years later in the Suez crisis of 1956. After pressing for removal of British troops from the canal on the grounds that Egypt would then be moved to join an anticommunist bloc in the Middle East, Dulles was only able to secure from President Gamal Abdel Nasser an Egyptian arms deal with the Soviet Union in 1955. Dulles's answer was to deny Egypt funds for the ambitious Aswan Dam project, which in turn led to Nasser's illegal nationalization of the canal. The Americans then protested without effect. The confusing messages to allies and enemies alike led to an Anglo-French-Israeli assault on the canal, without the United States' knowledge. The NATO allies' distrust of American motives induced them to conceal their plans for recovery of the canal; and when they failed, they witnessed the United States sharing an unwelcome position with the Soviet Union in denouncing British and French imperialism against a country that Dulles hoped would be one of the major pillars of his worldwide containment policy.

NATO was in serious trouble when its three major constituents were so mistrustful of each other, and at a time when their disunity underscored their impotence in the face of the Soviet repression of Hungary's rebellion against its domination. There was an element of hypocrisy in the American posture that was almost as obvious as the atavistic gunboat diplomacy of the French and British. While President Eisenhower summoned familiar isolationist and anticolonial sentiments to denounce the allies, the administration's concern was more over the damage that the abortive Anglo-French invasion did to anticommunist unity than over the integrity of Third World territory.

The rising level of hostility among the Big Three of the alliance was a particular burden for Lord Ismay, the able first secretary-general of the alliance. As Churchill's chief of staff and colleague of General Eisenhower in World War II, he could draw on both wartime experiences and wartime friendships to ease relations among the powers and at the same time to expand NATO's policymaking role. He found his niche as conciliator and facilitator in issues ranging from Germany to Cyprus. Although the North Atlantic Council played no official role in the former and failed to conclude agreement over the latter, he could look for the most part with satisfaction to his role in following the path of quiet diplomacy. The Suez debacle symbolized a breakdown in political consultation that Ismay had identified earlier and that he had attempted to solve through a committee of three foreign ministers, the "Three Wise Men" (Lester Pearson of Canada, Halvard Lange of Norway, and Gaetano Martino of Italy), established at the council meeting in May 1956. The committee's functions were to broaden the nonmilitary aspects of NATO and to strengthen operation and consultation among the allies in every area. The committee's report was submitted to the council two months after the Suez affair, in December 1956. It recommended among other things that consultation be initiated in the planning stages whenever the interests of the alliance were involved, and by implication it included out-of-area activities. The secretary-general was empowered to form a committee to settle the kind of disputes that had erupted in Indochina and Egypt.[20]

Shortly after Ismay resigned in early 1957 his more political successor, Paul-Henri Spaak, the former Belgian prime minister and founding father of NATO, pursued even more vigorously a stronger NATO role in decision making. His strategy was influenced by the committee of three's advice that "the present need . . . is more than simply broadening the scope and deepening the character of consultation. There is a pressing requirement for all members to make consultation in NATO an integral part of the making of national policy."[21]

The advice did indeed reflect the wisdom of the statesmen who composed the report, but it also reflected the interests of the smaller nations worried over the direction the larger members could take the alliance. While lip service was given to the ideals, Secretary Dulles made it clear that the United States had global responsibilities that might require the United States to respond to a crisis outside the treaty area without waiting to consult its NATO allies.[22] Dulles was thinking of China primarily, but U.S. unilateral action might have to be applied to any part of the world outside NATO. The question of consultation outside NATO was not solved even when the allies saw the consequences of their division over the Suez; it remained to plague them repeatedly over the next generation.

GENEVA AND DISENGAGEMENT

In all these contretemps of the mid-1950s, the Soviet Union continued to loom in the West as a menacing force, an evil manipulator waiting in the wings to destroy the allies collectively or singly. While the brutal subjugation of Hungary was obscured by the Mediterranean imbroglio, Soviet threats of nuclear destruction against Britain and the tanks on the streets of Budapest served to heal some breaches within the alliance. In the Middle East the United States' presence after Suez was accepted as the Western pacifier in place of the British. When a Communist-Progressive coalition government had threatened to oust American troops from Iceland and leave NATO itself in 1956, an appeal from the NATO council based on Soviet behavior in Hungary helped to change Iceland's mind. A more cynical explanation for Iceland's removing the leftist government devolved on the implications for the nation's economy in the departure of the American dollar along with American troops.

The sword that hung over NATO in the mid-1950s was not to be found in tanks or planes or in nuclear missiles of the Soviet Union, however. As Dulles saw it, the danger after the Communist failure to prevent the allegiance of the Federal Republic to NATO lay in a new, deceitful but peaceful face that the Kremlin under Nikita Khrushchev was prepared to show to the West. If they could not remove American troops from the Continent by force, they might do so by a new mix of threat and blandishment to Europeans, particularly to Germans.

Their weapon was a new Communist organization, the Warsaw Pact. The admission of Germany into the Western bloc was matched by the admission of East Germany into an Eastern bloc, the Warsaw Pact organization, that came into being on 14 May 1955, nine days after West Germany formally became a member of NATO. The Warsaw Pact in many ways appeared to be a counter-NATO, a distorted mirror image of the West. The responses to external attack, consideration of mutual aid, the establishment of a political council, and the 20-year term of life all point to the model of the Atlantic treaty. In the words of Andrej Korbonski, "one might venture to guess that those responsible for the final version of the Warsaw Treaty had a copy of the NATO text at their elbows."[23]

Despite the gathering of all the Soviet Union's Communist neighbors—in addition to Albania, the only noncontiguous power—none of the

Western allies betrayed new fears of additional military dangers as a consequence of this alliance. It simply put on paper what had been in practice since the cold war had begun. There would be no new Communist divisions on the field. In fact, the pact was interpreted as a symbol of Soviet failure to break up NATO. It contained in Article 11 a plea for its own dissolution, "should a system of collective security be established in Europe." The signing of the treaty was belittled in Western newspapers and barely appears in the correspondence or memoirs of Western policymakers. Both the U.S. secretary of state in his report to the president on the events of "an historic week" and the president in his memoirs emphasized the remarkable Austrian State Treaty of 15 May, not the Warsaw Pact of 14 May, and the anticipated Soviet pilgrimage to Belgrade.[24] The Kremlin had agreed to a treaty that would remove Soviet troops from Austria in return for neutralization of that country; Khrushchev appeared prepared to visit the Yugoslav leader Marshal Tito in Belgrade in the self-effacing spirit that the Holy Roman Emperor Henry VI visited Pope Gregory VII in Canossa. The Soviets spoke optimistically of a harmonious meeting of the Big Four powers at a summit meeting at Geneva in July. Small wonder that the Warsaw Pact was in the welter of what seemed to be more significant events of the day.

To many observers on both sides of the Atlantic, the policy of Western firmness, of containment, had succeeded. The Communists were in retreat. Harrison Salisbury of the *New York Times* speculated as early as November of 1954 that Kennan's prediction of Communist mellowing was about to be realized.[25] Europeans were more optimistic than Americans for the most part. Prime Minister Anthony Eden floated the idea of a "zone of equalized armaments" in Germany stretching 60 miles on either side of the internal frontier. Even Chancellor Adenauer was sufficiently carried away by the spirit of the moment to inform British Foreign Minister Harold Macmillan one month before the Geneva meeting that the Soviets were seeking a détente and might even abandon East Germany to achieve it.[26]

This kind of language brought chills to Dulles's heart. He saw in the Austrian treaty or in proposals for collective security not a Soviet retreat but only a tactical withdrawal in the face of Western unity. If NATO should relax its guard because of these soothing notes, dangerous consequences could result. There was danger of entrapment in meeting the Soviets at Geneva, but the meeting itself could not be avoided. The president had committed himself as early as 10 May to "do anything, to meet with anyone, anywhere, as long as . . . there is the slightest idea or chance of furthering this great cause of peace." He was convinced that "Foster and I should be able to detect whether the Soviets really intend to introduce a tactical change that could mean, for the next few years at least, some real easing of tensions."[27]

Dulles was by no means as confident as Eisenhower seemed to be. He exposed traps everywhere. Remembering how President Wilson's stature as head of state had been diminished in 1919 by the equality given to his European colleagues who were just heads of government, Dulles even agonized over the president accepting an invitation to dine with the French premier at Geneva. Dulles deplored "the respectability that would be given to the Russians by being photographed in social gatherings, or group photographs with the president and with the French and British heads of government."[28]

What followed in Geneva seemed to confirm the secretary's worst nightmares. The Soviets took every advantage of the "spirit of Geneva" to pursue their plans to divide the United States from its allies. Their smiles were more unnerving than their scowls. They refused to allow or accept on the agenda any discussion of the subjugation of Eastern Europe; they proposed a security pact that would have removed the United States from the equation; and they would consider German unification only after the military organizations—NATO and the Warsaw Pact—had been dismantled.

Yet for all Dulles's gloomy predictions, the Soviet gains at Geneva were limited. None of their goals was met. The president was as effective as Khrushchev in exuding a spirit of goodwill, and he very likely was looked on as more sincere when he recorded his "great satisfaction in telling him [Khrushchev] that the entire western world would cheerfully abide by the decision of the German electorate, regardless of the outcome."[29] When Adenauer was invited to Moscow to meet with Soviet leaders, it resulted in Soviet recognition of the Federal Republic, not West German withdrawal from NATO or West German recognition of East Germany's legitimacy. Conceivably, Soviet acceptance of Adenauer meant that the Kremlin, despite its harsh language, would rather have West Germany, armed, inside the bosom of a NATO that would protect East as well as West from the specters of a Fourth Reich. The Geneva summit meeting may have been a testament to the limits of Communist power in the post-Stalin era.

Such realism did not mean that the Soviet power would not be exercised (witness its behavior in Hungary and Poland in 1956) or even that it would not engage in adventures outside Europe to frustrate the Western alliance system (witness its policy in Egypt in the same year). But the Soviet Union's primary effort in this period was expressed in the language of peace, of disengagement, of neutralization, of nonaggression, of dissolution of all pacts. There was constant worry on the part of the secretary of state that one or more of the allies would succumb to temptations from the East. The lure of "disengagement" was a durable by-product of the Geneva summit. Even with full knowledge that nothing had been accomplished over German reunification, Adenauer was continually plagued by demands from the right that the East be played off against the West, and from the left that neutralization and disarmament were not only desirable pacifist goals but also the only means of securing reunification.

One of the more influential voices in favor of disengagement was that of retired American diplomat George Kennan. In radio lectures delivered for the BBC in 1957 on six successive Sundays beginning on 10 November and published the following year, Kennan advocated a Soviet withdrawal from Central Europe, matched by a compensatory withdrawal on the Western side, perhaps even by the withdrawal of all American forces from Europe. Once the Soviet Union was freed of its fears over NATO and Germany, Kennan wagered, presumably liberalization of controls would follow in the East. NATO itself would not be dismantled necessarily, but its reduced functions might cause it to atrophy. Kennan, who had never been fully convinced of NATO's worth, was not worried over its fate. "We must get over this obsession," he asserted, "that the Russians are yearning to attack and occupy Europe, and that this is the principal danger."[30]

While there was no orchestration between Kennan's position and the Soviet's, there was a confluence of pressures as the Polish Foreign Minister Adam Rapacki presented before the United Nations on 2 October 1957—and renewed in a formal note to the United States on 14 February 1958 after Kennan's radio talks—a proposal for an nuclear-free zone in Central Europe embracing both Germanies.[31] From the American perspective, the Rapacki plan omitted too much that was essential to genuine denuclearization, such as a system of inspection of existing nuclear stocks and a plan for discontinuing production of nuclear weapons. Less directly, but with equal clarity, the United States criticized the plan for its implicit removal of America's presence from Europe while the Soviet Union remained a menacing neighbor to a still divided Germany by its geopolitical position alone.

Disengagement never materialized in the 1950s. Its failure was ensured in part by Dulles's conception of the inner workings of the Communist world—a conception that was supported by much of the American establishment. Dean Acheson led the attack on Kennan and Rapacki, warning of the dire consequences to the security of the West in the departure of American forces from Europe. The exclusion of nuclear weapons, according to Acheson, would yield enormous advantages to the numerically greater mass of Soviet troops stationed within easy distance of Western Europe.[32] The unacceptability of inspection of stockpiles to the Soviet Union inevitably bred distrust in the United States. Kennan himself felt the full brunt of disapproval. Abuse, he recorded, came in from all sides: "My punishment was not long in coming. I had, after all, offended all the leading statesmen now in power and some who were not."[33]

While attractions of détente and the inherent instability of continuing confrontation in Central Europe haunted all the allies, the sacrifice of the Western alliance would be even more destabilizing than the recommendations for change. The judgment of NATO statesmen was that implementation of plans would undo the sense of security that had permitted the renascence of Europe over the past decade. Concurrent with the defense of NATO after all was the *Wirtschaftswunder* of their economic revivals, most notably in West Germany but shared by other European allies. Under the NATO umbrella the Europeans moved toward a European community, at least a common market, as reflected in the Treaty of Rome. On 25 March 1957 six of the NATO allies—France, Germany, Italy, and the Benelux countries—created the European Economic Community (later called the European Community—in 1993 changed to the European Union). The question then was whether Europe would defend itself without an American presence on the front line or without a nuclear deterrent as a vital source of psychic as well as material support.

NATO's answer in 1957 was negative, but by the end of that year its rallying behind the American position was tinged with new fears rather than a wholly reasoned rejection of plausible Soviet peace proposals. At the very time the Soviets invoked a new era in Europe, they unveiled a new terror as well: on 4 October 1957 they announced the successful launching of the first earth satellite, *Sputnik*, with its intimations of Soviet superiority in the area of intercontinental ballistic missiles (ICBMs). *Sputnik* raised fears that the Soviet Union could dominate the world from outer space.

The scenarios projected by this remarkable technological achievement indeed spoiled the propaganda value of peaceful coexistence and forced the allies to look to the leader once again for protection. But what they saw set in motion greater doubts than in the past about the reliability of the American connection. For it suggested the ICBMs would make the United States as vulnerable to Soviet attack as the Soviet Union was to American strikes through medium-range ballistic missile bases in Western Europe. Nuclear weaponry, it appeared, placed the United States and the alliance in an entirely new light. The response to this threat would preoccupy the allies for the next half-dozen years as they sought ways to revitalize their collective defense system as well as to maintain the credibility of American participation. *Sputnik* wonderfully concentrated SHAPE's and the North Atlantic Council's mind on the military dimension of Europe's future as no other action from the East could have managed to do in that decade.

chapter 5

NATO AND THE DÉFI FRANÇAIS, 1958–1966

Unlike the Brussels Pact, which stipulated a 50-year period before any party might legally leave the alliance, the North Atlantic Treaty was more modest in its expectations. Article 13 mentioned a 20-year span, while Article 12 provided for potential review of the treaty after 10 years. These arrangements were in deference to America's residual suspicions of permanent alliances and were based on an assumption that the purposes of the transatlantic association would have been accomplished in 20 years' time if not in 10.

Ten years after the signing of the treaty many of the expectations of the 1940s seemed to have been reached, or to be within reach. The enormous problem of German integration into the West was solved by the London and Paris agreements of 1954. The creation of a European community, while not completed, was in the process of coming together. Or so the Treaty of Rome—which established the European Economic Community, later called simply the European Community (EC) and now referred to as the European Union (EU)—promised in 1957. The division between the Inner Six, the members of that community, and the Outer Seven, a looser economic union led by the United Kingdom, would be terminated when Britain joined the EC. The defense of Europe, developed within an elaborate military machine, was linked intimately both to the presence of six divisions of American troops and to the nuclear weaponry the United States would wield against an aggressor.

No matter how indistinct the relationship may have been, an Atlantic community blossomed alongside the European community. The American connection was firmer than ever. Not only was there no sign of thinning out or of removing the American military from Europe, but the powerful military

"Parley at the summit," Palais de Chaillot, Paris. Meeting of 15 NATO governments, with President Dwight D. Eisenhower heading the U.S. delegation, 16 December 1957. *Courtesy National Defense University Press*

establishment was largely an American instrument. American generals dominated the alliance as "supreme" allied commanders in SHAPE and in SACLANT. Names such as Eisenhower or Gruenther or Norstad were more visible to the NATO publics and carried greater weight than the European civilian secretaries-general. Ismay, Spaak, and Stikker were men of distinction in Britain, Belgium, and the Netherlands, respectively, but they were not in the rank of their military counterparts.

Whether the activities of SHAPE were a European or an Atlantic accomplishment, progress was undeniable. The infrastructure system had resulted in the addition or improvement of 140 airfields, 5000 miles of fuel pipeline, and 15,000 miles of land telephone and telegraph lines that helped to link depots and airfields from northern Norway to eastern Turkey in the first decade of NATO's history. Such was the erosion of national sovereignty that the internecine wars of 1914 and 1939 were unthinkable at the end of the 1950s. Europe had arisen, with America's help.

Was there then an opportunity to reassess the cold war in accord with the provisions of the treaty? The Soviet Union of Nikita Khrushchev was not the same threat as Stalin's Kremlin. The language throughout the mid-1950s had been "peaceful coexistence," the termination of blocs, the neutralization of Germany, the need for nuclear-free zones. Indeed, in July 1958 test-ban negotiations between the United States and the Soviet Union was begun. The need for dramatic action to outlaw war was the theme of Khrushchev's triumphal tour of the United States in the summer of 1959. The Soviet premier was ready to abolish all weapons, both nuclear and conventional, he claimed before the United Nations on 18 September.[1]

If Europe's economy and morale had been restored and if the Soviet Union had recognized limits to its Communist ambitions, why should American troops remain in Europe? Why should the North Atlantic Treaty not be amended if not discarded?

The answers to such queries may be found in the 15 years of U.S. hysteria over the issue of communism in the world and certainly over the behavior of the Dulles State Department until his death in 1959. Distrust was too deeply ingrained in the West to allow acceptance of a new image of the Soviet relationship. Khrushchev's offer of disarmament was seen as another version of Soviet attempts to dismantle the alliance, weaken America, while proceeding to build up intimidating power. The Soviet leader's offer did not include provision for inspection or supervision of nuclear tests or of military bases. Another answer was to be found in the fragility of the institutions established over the decade. The allies made it clear that military effort would not survive the removal of American troops. Adenauer's efforts to identify Germany with the West would be lost if NATO ceased to exist. French rapprochement with the former German enemy was dependent on the presence of the NATO umbrella.

SPUTNIK AND BERLIN

These considerations were in place even before the impact of the *Sputnik*'s burst into the stratosphere. Its announcement was accompanied by a reckless display of Soviet truculence as Khrushchev boasted of Soviet superiority over the West. Whatever advantage the United States may have enjoyed in the nuclear race, from the atomic bomb in 1945 to the hydrogen bomb in 1953, the monopolies had been broken and the lead lessened over the decade. Now it was not just a question of the Soviets catching up with American technology but rather their moving ahead and using their new lead to taunt the West. Even the rate of growth of the gross national product of the USSR between 1950 and 1958 was 50 percent higher than that of the United States, sufficient to encourage the Russians to talk about "burying" the United States in economic competition. The effect of these advances was to shake the alliance rather than to harden its resolve. Despite Dulles's preference for the open challenge, the allies wondered about the credibility of the American nuclear umbrella and about NATO's usefulness in assuring them security. The intercontinental ballistic missile was "the ultimate weapon," Khrushchev claimed.[2] Would the United States invite disaster to itself, as the new ICBM capabilities promised, by initiating nuclear war to meet aggression in Europe by conventional arms?

By December 1957 the United States had its own version of *Sputnik* and was prepared to close the missile gap. Actually, it was a gap that never existed. Khrushchev cleverly exaggerated the capabilities of Soviet nuclear capacities by having the Soviet media quote hysterical Western accounts of the threat. The Soviets were capitalizing on a false lead to panic the Western allies.

They succeeded up to a point. The insecurities that had plagued U.S.-European relations rendered the allies vulnerable to the new threat. U.S. attempts to calm passions by supplying its NATO partners with intermediate-range ballistic missiles (IRBMs) to offset the effects of the new Soviet rockets were not sufficient. Only Britain seemed to welcome them; Turkey and Italy accepted them with less enthusiasm, while France looked with some apprehension at the prospect of their installation in Germany. Nor were the efforts of SACEUR Lauris Norstad of themselves enough to restore the psychological balance. Norstad emphasized the linkage between sword and shield, with renewed emphasis on a shield that would protect the NATO forces until a sword—nuclear power—could be wielded. In support of Norstad's theme, Henry Kissinger's *Nuclear Weapons and Foreign Policy* in 1957 popularized the idea that nuclear weapons need not spark an all-out war but could serve as a further deterrent to Soviet adventures in the central sector. With the first of 12 German divisions reporting to NATO on 1 January 1958 and with the prospective return of French divisions from Algeria, Norstad would have 30 divisions on the ground to reinforce the shield. In Norstad's words, a "stout shield" would complete the deterrent.[3]

None of these efforts seemed to go to the heart of the question in the late 1950s: namely, the willingness of the United States to apply strategic retaliation in the event of a Soviet attack in Europe, as opposed to a direct attack on the American continent. It seemed to many of the allies that the Soviet ability to strike directly at the heart of America might inhibit American response in Europe. "Massive retaliation" now had a hollow ring.

Even Secretary of State Dulles seemed to move away from the strategy identified with him. In an article for *Foreign Affairs* that appeared just before *Sputnik* orbited, he sounded appreciative of the Kissinger emphasis on the tactical use of nuclear weaponry, in a manner that would distance the United States from the use of strategic weaponry.[4] It put more emphasis on the possibilities of defense on the ground—and that ground would be in Europe. When the ailing Dulles stepped down in April 1959, his successor, Christian Herter, sounded all the more frightening to Europeans because of his casual statement at confirmation hearings that he could not "conceive of any president engaging in all-out nuclear war unless we were in danger of all-out devastation ourselves."[5]

The loss of confidence in the United States and in the alliance itself was reflected in a special heads-of-government conference in Paris in December 1957, where most of the allies, except Britain, displayed their reservations about accepting intermediate-range ballistic missiles. They expressed more interest in resuming negotiations with the Soviets even on terms that might be damaging to NATO interests.

The United States had little choice but to explore at least possibilities for détente. President Eisenhower, who had been an eloquent advocate of control of nuclear weapons at the first Geneva conference in 1955, was more than willing to advance another version of his "Open Skies" proposal. Then he had proposed "to give to each other a complete blueprint of our military establishments, from beginning to end" and "to provide within our countries facilities for aerial photography to the other country."[6] In 1958 the Soviets agreed to a new meeting in Geneva to deal with a comprehensive test ban, less ambitious than the talks three years before, but all the more pressing as the nuclear race accelerated. They failed. A voluntary moratorium, which lasted three years, preceded the meetings on 31 October. But the Soviet leaders had no more intention of allowing a serious inspection system than they had in the past.

It was obvious that they felt no need to appease the West given the tremors in the alliance and the effect on the United States. Even while the Geneva talks were proceeding, Khrushchev purposely set in motion a new crisis. On 10 November he announced that the Soviet Union intended to sign a separate peace treaty with East Germany. Later in the month he said that they would do so within six months if a negotiated solution to the Berlin problem could not be found. Once a peace treaty had been made, East Germany would have sovereignty over Berlin. The allies then would have to make their arrangements for remaining in Berlin with a regime they did not recognize. The deadline was 27 May 1959.

Few actions on the part of the Soviets could have been more provocative than reviving the Berlin issue, which had been dormant since 1949. It was far more effective than the Rapacki Plan, with its nuclear-free zone, or unification of Germany on the basis of neutralization, or any other variation of the softer language that had characterized the spirit of Geneva. Buoyed by nuclear advances, the Soviet Union's plan would have nullified the Yalta agreements, wherein the three wartime allies agreed to a joint occupation of Berlin. In essence it informed the allies that British or French or American access to Berlin would be a matter of negotiation with the German Democratic Republic. Should the West fail to respond to this proposal, the Soviets then would turn over the supply routes to the city to the East Germans. If the Kremlin had carried out its intentions, it might have broken the Atlantic alliance in its tenth year. By one major action it would have exposed the hollowness of the benefits Adenauer had been promised from NATO; it would have exacerbated France's and other European powers' ambivalent feelings about Germans; it would have revealed the unreliability of America's leadership; and it might have stampeded fearful allies into accommodation with the Soviet Union on other matters—and on Communist terms.

Khrushchev miscalculated. Meeting in Paris in December 1958, the North Atlantic Council and West Germany rejected the Soviet plan for Berlin without qualification. In its Declaration on Berlin the council considered "that the denunciation by the Soviet Union of the inter-allied agreements on Berlin can in no way deprive the other parties of their rights or relieve the Soviet Union of its obligations."[7] For the moment NATO marched more resolutely together than before. The installation of IRBMs went ahead as General Norstad's message of firmness urging the use of nuclear weapons in case of aggression was recorded with approval. At the same time the council, and the United States in particular, agreed to open discussions over Berlin as long as no ultimatum was in effect. Eisenhower would even sweeten negotiations by agreeing to forego on-sight inspection teams for nuclear tests. But if after making their positions clear the United States and NATO were willing to deal flexibly with an abnormal situation, without going to the brink, so was Khrushchev. The risks in winning a permanently divided Germany by what would have to be force must have been more than he had expected or would bear. The deadline passed without Soviet action.

Not that the Soviet Union admitted that the stakes were too high. Khrushchev, for all his bluster, retreated in the face of the uncertain results that a military route would take. Based on his appraisal of their vulnerable connections to Berlin and on the divisions within the alliance, Khrushchev hoped that the allies might cave in. But Eisenhower, without the help of his fatally ill secretary of state, kept options open; he claimed that the United States had no plans "to shoot our way into Berlin" or "to fight a ground war in Europe."[8] A nuclear response was left in doubt. Prime Minister Harold Macmillan attempted to serve as middle man in reporting to Washington that the deadline would be called off if a new summit conference convened.[9] While Eisenhower hesitated to accept such a quid pro quo, Dulles's funeral on the day of the deadline provided an occasion for the deadline to be neglected.

The waning days of the Eisenhower administration saw no resolution to any of the problems facing the alliance. The president himself occupied a more central role in policymaking in the absence of Dulles. Secretary of State Herter was crippled with arthritis, and while this disability affected in no way a sharpness of mind and brightness of spirit, it added to the image of a more halting policy than had been identified with his predecessor.

The troubles in part stemmed from the Soviet Union's continuing interest in exposing weaknesses in the alliance and in its intransigence over critical points in the new Geneva talks that had begun just two weeks before Dulles's death. Deadlock continued and was not seriously modified by a meeting in Washington between Khrushchev and Eisenhower after the Soviet premier's spectacular cross-country tour of the United States in 1959. Berlin was not forgotten; even as a new summit meeting was planned in Paris for the spring of 1960, Khrushchev renewed his threat to sign a separate peace treaty with East Germany. Although no time limit was demanded, it was obvious that the meeting would suffer from duress, in the event it failed to solve either the Berlin issue or come up with a test-ban treaty.

The summit meeting never took place. The so-called U-2 affair—the downing of a high-altitude intelligence overflight on 1 May deep in the heart of the Soviet Union and the confused response of the United States to the charges of spying—offered Khrushchev an opportunity to cancel the forthcoming meeting in Paris. The cover story of a weather plane accidentally straying into Russian territory was blown by the capture of its pilot, Francis Gary Powers, and the president accepted the embarrassment of confessing to a lie.

It was a difficult moment for Eisenhower. Yet, as in so many times in the past, the Soviets may have overplayed their hand. If the intention was to destroy the credibility of America's leadership in NATO, it failed miserably. The incident did not have a damaging effect on the United States; rather, the knowledge among the allies that such Soviet activities as the construction of an operational ICBM base east of the Urals had come under direct American scrutiny through reconnaissance planes with extraordinary technological capabilities increased rather than diminished respect for U.S. leadership. There was no immediate rush to expel Americans from the base in Adana, Turkey, where the U-2 plane originated, or for Charles de Gaulle or Macmillan to make a pariah of the president when he arrived in Paris on 14 May to meet with Khrushchev. In fact, de Gaulle, so obstreperous on most occasions, seemed to relish his backing of wartime colleague Eisenhower. He countered the Soviet shock over being "overflown" by saying that the most recently launched Soviet satellites overflew French skies 18 times without his permission. If there were reservations about the management of this contretemps it was over a streak of American naïveté in permitting the president to take responsibility on himself for what nations normally do and disavow. De Gaulle made it clear to Eisenhower, "I do not know what Khrushchev is going to do nor what is going to happen, but whatever he does or whatever happens, I want you to know that I am with you to the end."[10]

As the year ended, North Atlantic Council members, in Spaak's final meeting as secretary-general, deplored the lack of progress during the past year on disarmament, welcomed American maintenance of nuclear weapons available to NATO, and "in face of the recent Soviet threats and harassing tactics, . . . they once again declared their determination to protect the freedom of the people of Berlin."[11] In brief, the Soviet record was too soiled for the world to take seriously Khrushchev's histrionics over the U-2. Like Dulles's death a year before, the U-2 provided a diversion to avoid a summit meeting in which the allies would not budge over Berlin. The U-2 incident also inspired a reaction that underscored NATO's solidarity, at least on this issue at this time.

KENNEDY AND KHRUSHCHEV

In the winter of 1961 NATO and its enemies listened to the sound of a new administration that spoke of a "New Frontier." A youthful John F. Kennedy announced in his inaugural address the onset of a renewal of American vigor to be expressed at home and abroad. The goals would be the same as those of the Truman and Eisenhower administrations; the difference would be in the clarity of their program and the strength of their resolve: "Let the word go forth from this time and place, to friend and foe alike, that the torch has been passed to a new generation of Americans— born in this century, tempered by war, disciplined by a hard and bitter peace, proud of our ancient heritage."[12] For Western Europe, Kennedy wanted to infuse a tired alliance with the vigor he had promised to America. The New Frontier would be translated as the "Grand Design," to use the words of Joseph Kraft,[13] wherein an old military alliance—well into its second decade—would be transformed by a twofold reconstruction: first, a recognition of NATO as a genuine partnership in which Europe and America would meet as equals rather than one serving as a ward of the other; second, an effort to subordinate the dominant military emphasis of the alliance to political and economic purposes.

Or so it was proclaimed. Kennedy's plans for a reconstructed alliance were founded on a conception of a broad community of interests resting on two great pillars standing astride the Atlantic, each indispensable to the other. "The future of the West," asserted Kennedy in 1963, "lies in Atlantic partnership—a system of cooperation, interdependence, and harmony whose peoples can jointly meet their burdens and opportunities throughout the world."[14] The Atlantic Convention of NATO Nations issued a Declaration of Paris in 1962 that formally claimed NATO as an Atlantic community. The seeming success of NATO diplomacy in reconciling the interests of Britain, Greece, and Turkey with the Greek Cypriote demands for union with Greece symbolized the communal emphasis of the alliance. Secretary-General Spaak, following Ismay's initiative, helped to arrange the Zurich agreements in 1959 and the independence of Cyprus in 1960. Under this compromise the British retained two bases, and the Greeks and Turks stationed 950 and 650 troops, respectively. It soon broke down with unhappy consequences for NATO and American policy in the Mediterranean, but its temporary viability opened up the possibilities available to NATO as a peacemaker.

These changes were not expected to end the American link with Europe but to recognize the end of the cold war. Such a vision was identified with the Atlantic ideologues, such as Under Secretary of State George Ball, and its theme of Atlantic partnership could be credited to Ball's mentor, Jean Monnet— "le père de l'Europe," as Denise Artaud has observed.[15]

Yet another view of the Grand Design would have Monnet's language inspiring it but would deviate considerably from any Monnet plan. The Grand Design was also intended to compensate for the relative decline in American power. The balance of payments deficit, the slowing rate of U.S. economic growth, and the European pressures for nuclear sharing all might be remedied by tapping European power. Economically, the Grand Design included a Trade Expansion Act to ensure a free market for American goods in the West. European unification—the eastern Atlantic pillar—would be a means of containing Germany as well as developing an economy that could pay for American troops. A carefully calibrated multilateral force, operating nuclear weapons, would satisfy European demands for access to weapons while keeping in American hands the essential control of their use. This would also mean antagonizing the three major allies if the calibrations were incorrect.[16]

The dimension of NATO's problems inherent in this conflict suggests that the Communist menace of the past could be placed on a back burner, that the Soviet Union had become essentially normalized. Nevertheless, headlines from 1960 to 1962 were still filled with threat, and the by-products of nuclear power were found in a variety of Soviet activities.

Nowhere was this more evident than in the Third World. The Mediterranean in particular was an area of historic interest for the Soviets. Communist support of Nasser's ambitions for Arab leadership or of Algerian struggle for independence was an issue that concerned more than just the southern flank of NATO. Yet Soviet efforts were marked more by failure than success. Even while Britain and France were humiliated in the Suez crisis of 1956, American, not Soviet, influence increased in the Middle East. With all their hopes for a Mediterranean presence in the 1950s, the Soviets went for a few years without any vessels even stationed in the Mediterranean after Albania defected from the Warsaw Pact and roughly turned the Soviet Union out of its submarine base at Valona in 1958.

Khrushchev was less successful in Latin America despite the temptations that Fidel Castro's Cuba provided. His morbid language was put to use again when he announced at a news conference in the Kremlin that the Monroe Doctrine was dead and that "the remains of this doctrine should best be buried as every dead body is so that it should not poison the air by its decay."[17] Such sentiments were intensified when the aborted invasion of Cuba at the Bay of Pigs revealed a bungled CIA collaboration with Cuban exiles based in Florida. A year and a half later Khrushchev was emboldened to install ground-to-ground missiles on Cuban territory with capacity to fire ballistic missiles at a range of 1,000 miles. The secret preparations of airstrips were challenged by a U.S. "quarantine" on ships carrying offensive military equipment to Cuba. In this confrontation, which could have been a casus belli, the Soviets removed their missiles, though not before demanding a reciprocal dismantling of U.S. Jupiter missiles in Turkey and a pledge against the invasion of Cuba. These missiles in Turkey as well as Italy were subsequently withdrawn on the grounds of obsolescence. As in Berlin in 1959 and 1960, Khrushchev backed away from the brink.

Berlin itself was an issue too in the Kennedy administration. In August 1961, after an apparently inexperienced president made something less than a triumphal tour of Europe in the spring, immediately after the Bay of Pigs incident, Khrushchev threw down a gauntlet in Berlin for a third time: he erected a wall separating East from West Berlin.

The wall itself took some time to complete, but its symbolic effect was immediate. On 13 August just after midnight, East German troops installed roadblocks and barbed-wire barricades at most of the crossing points between East and West Berlin. This action was, inter alia, a symbolic challenge to the Yalta agreements. It may have reflected Khrushchev's contempt for what he considered Kennedy's immature behavior and a belief that he could challenge JFK's leadership of the alliance in a manner he would not have dared to do under Eisenhower. Despite favorable comments in his memoirs, Khrushchev had sized up Kennedy's abilities at the meeting in Vienna, and the verdict was not flattering. There in June the Soviet premier had demanded in an aide memoire the end to the allied occupation of West Berlin.

The wall was a solution, and one that could cause rifts in the alliance. The allies seemed stymied by the action. Mayor Willy Brandt of West Berlin condemned the feeble reaction. Indeed, it took four days before a note of protest was delivered to Moscow. When Vice President Lyndon Johnson visited West Berlin, he was greeted by hecklers claiming he had come too late.

Given that the wall was erected in East, not West, Berlin territory, there was no violation of wartime agreements, no matter how provocative the manner of its execution. NATO's fear was that the wall might be a prelude to aggressive action. On the same day, 18 August, that Johnson was sent to "show the flag," Kennedy ordered reinforcements for the 5,000 U.S. soldiers stationed in Berlin. By January 1962, 50,000 reached Europe to raise U.S. troop levels in Europe to the record number of 434,000.

But this was the extent of the American response, which for all practical purposes was the total response of all the allies. Once the shock of the wall wore off, it was recognized on all sides that the walling off of the East was not the first step in a larger Soviet design but a defensive act to shore up a faltering East Germany. In 1962 over 150,000 East Germans had escaped to the West via Berlin, almost half of them under the age of 25 and many of them skilled workers. The wall remained, as Arthur Schlesinger put it, "a shabby obscenity straggling across the face of the city."[18] But it was not a sign of bellicosity on the part of the Soviet Union.

In retrospect, the repeated failures of Khrushchev in Berlin, in Cuba, and in the Belgian Congo, where Soviet-supported Patrice Lumumba and Antoine Gizenga led abortive campaigns, were fixed subliminally in the minds of NATO and the Warsaw Pact. Soviet weakness, while never officially celebrated, was felt in many ways. The disappearance of the missile gap was one of them. In mid-1961 Defense Secretary Robert S. McNamara revealed that only a few of the Soviet ICBMs were operational. And in the glow of a new recognition of U.S. superiority in nuclear weapons capability, a limited test ban of nuclear weapons in the outer atmosphere was agreed to in 1963. The ouster of Khrushchev from power in 1964 may have had domestic causes such as agricultural policy, but these causes rested on a failure of foreign and military policies as well.

"THE END OF THE ALLIANCE"

If containment was the sole function of the Atlantic alliance, it may be claimed that the mid-1960s saw the realization of stability—even if it was only a balance of terror. The terms were not necessarily Acheson's or Dulles's. Communism had not collapsed; the Soviet empire remained intact; Europe was divided; nuclear power remained untamed and uncontrolled; and there were clear limits to American power. Those limits, combined with the arrival to potential superpower status of a potentially united Europe, turned out to be a new threat to the survival of NATO. For Germany and for Adenauer in particular, it meant that his promise of reunification had been a deceit; for France, it meant that subservience to the United States was no longer necessary; for Britain, America's "special partner," it meant being caught—thanks to the Kennedy-McNamara sophisticated military machine—between the Continent and the United States, and in uneasy conjunction with both.

In this situation it was understandable that from all flanks of NATO calls would be heard for the dismantling of the alliance. The presence of NATO forces standing watch, with nuclear arsenals in many of the nations, seemed less necessary in the 1960s than in the 1950s. Fissures seemed deeper than before, and the argumentation less restrained. Greeks and Turks fought once again over Cyprus.

Turkey had been increasingly upset with American policy after President Lyndon B. Johnson wrote to Prime Minister Ismet Inönü in 1964 that if the Soviet Union attacked Turkey as a result of the latter's behavior in Cyprus, there would be no automatic NATO support for his government.[19] Scandinavians, always cautious about the SHAPE connection, felt justified in the policy of keeping nuclear forces out of the area and refusing to accept foreign bases on their territories in peacetime.

In the United States a spate of important publications appeared in the mid-1960s, with a common theme: NATO had outlived its usefulness. It had served its purpose when the Soviet threat had intimidated Europe. Now that Europe had revived, the need for the alliance had gone. In fact, the alliance itself would become a detriment to the keeping of peace in the world and to keeping America's democratic traditions intact.

Senator J. William Fulbright, the powerful chairman of the Foreign Relations Committee, in a major address to the Senate in 1964, entitled "Old Myths and New Realities," called on his countrymen to recognize that Europe had changed since 1949, and so had communism: "The myth is that every Communist State is an unmitigated evil and a relentless enemy of the free world; the reality is that some Communist regimes pose a threat to the free world while others pose little or none." Granting that the Soviet Union was no longer a formidable adversary to the West, he urged that its hostility should not be put into the language of theology or of demonology. The Soviet Union at last, as in the Kennan prognosis of 1947, had reached normality as a nation and was as beset by the Chinese challenge to its suzerainty as the United States was by the French challenge. Some forms of mutually advantageous arrangements between East and West were not unreasonable. He observed that the NATO allies had implicitly recognized change through the steadily increasing trade with the Communist bloc. Without saying explicitly that NATO should dissolve, he implied that the organization certainly, and possibly the alliance as well, had lost its mission.[20]

Other commentators, such as Ronald Steel, Richard Barnet, and Marcus Raskin, were less hesitant in their judgments about NATO than Fulbright and far more radical in their recommendations than Kennan had been in the 1950s. The titles of their major works—Steel's *The End of the Alliance: America and the Future of Europe* (1962) and Barnet and Raskin's *After 20 Years: The Decline of NATO and the Search for a New Policy in Europe* (1966)—explain their case. NATO was irrelevant, or worse, in the 1960s. Rather than criticize the French rejection, British resentment, or German restiveness in the alliance, the United States should recognize that Europe had recovered its powers and wished to remove itself from the wardship implied in NATO: "The old order has broken up." While Kennedy may have given lip service to this understanding, his administration—like its predecessors—had not acted on it. According to Steel, "As the Crusades were to medieval Christianity, so NATO has been to American diplomacy under three administrations: the instrument by which all incongruities would be subsumed in the quest for a higher moral order."[21] The alliance had become sanctified as a symbol of American power.

This "arrogance of power," as Fulbright was to call it in a subsequent speech, was in itself unwittingly destructive of America's own freedom. The price paid for a Pax Americana would be that which every imperialist regime had experienced. For those such as David Horowitz, who saw NATO as an instrument of world domination, the result would be the shrinking of liberty at home and abroad as the military-industrial elite assumed control of the global economy on behalf of the few against the many. Marxists and the new revisionists, who would win larger audiences after the Vietnam War had gone sour, found in the NATO of the 1960s a useful example of American aggression—from beginning the cold war to consolidating capitalism at home. So, argued Horowitz, "far from being responsive in character or directed towards negotiating a settlement of Europe and the cold war, U.S. postwar policies of containment were designed, basically, to translate a military and economic *superiority* of power into an absolute *supremacy* of power, meaning the ability to dictate terms to the Soviet Union."[22]

That there would be a period of self-examination, even self-denigration, with respect to the American participation in NATO 15 years after the treaty was signed was not of itself surprising. The circumstances seemed to lend themselves to such a reaction. The problems of the postwar era seemed relatively remote in the 1960s. The Soviet military menace so much touted in the past, and as recently as in the *Sputnik* accomplishment, proved to be a paper tiger of sorts. The Kremlin repeatedly moved away from crises it provoked, and the gap between East and West appeared to be in favor of the latter. Europe, far from needing American protection, seemed to chafe at its constraints. De Gaulle's reaction won considerable understanding from such knowledgeable observers as Robert Kleiman of the *New York Times* and Henry Kissinger of Harvard. While both men in their books of this period— *Atlantic Crisis: American Diplomacy Confronts a Resurgent Europe* (1964) and *The Troubled Partnership: Reappraisal* (1965)—recognized the necessity for NATO's survival, they also urged reforms that sympathized with the French behavior in the de Gaulle era.

Yet there was considerable hyperbole among the critics concerning the terminal state of NATO. It was in trouble, but in this period the trouble was not a crisis but a malaise that sapped the vitality of the alliance rather than cut it asunder. For all the rhetoric expended on the eschatology of NATO, there were continuities that were more striking than changes. Not even de Gaulle's withdrawal from the organization in 1966 led to France's or any other nation's, denunciation of the alliance itself. Without a formal invocation of Article 12, the allies did take steps, however, to accommodate the conditions of the 1960s. But they did so on an assumption that the purposes of 1949 were still valid half a generation later. The Soviet Union as a superpower remained a standing threat to Western security.

DE GAULLE'S CHALLENGES

Sputnik was the catalyst that drew reactions from the major members, each somewhat different from the other, that forced NATO and the United States to pay attention to dissatisfactions with the management of the organization. France was the most vigorous dissenter over the course of the alliance and over the leadership of the United States. Long before de Gaulle had come to office in 1958, France had been out of step. From the beginnings it had been suspicious of the Anglo-American condominium; it had been a center of leftist sentiment, with a large Communist cadre and an even larger body of opinion sympathetic to neutralism in the cold war; the wartime traumas had created a paranoid reaction to the revival of Germany that was expressed in France's opposition to the European Defense Community. Above all, there was resistance to the decline in grandeur. French civilization was, arguably, the standard for the world, and its decline in any aspect—linguistic, military, economic—was too painful to bear. It was made all the more insufferable by the apparent replacement of France with Anglo-Saxon superiority.

This aperçu in some ways was more difficult to accept than the might of the East. The Soviet Union, inferior in strength and in culture to the West, might be managed more easily than the United States and its junior partner, the United Kingdom. A popular metaphor of the de Gaulle era, drawn from Shakespeare's *Tempest*, was of a sensitive, cultured, and intelligent Ariel civilizing the two clumsy, brutal, and stupid Calibans. Western Europe, with its capital in Paris, was the civilizing force, while the two monsters, the superpowers, were superficially stronger. They could be tamed by the missionary activity of the West. While other Europeans might contest the location of the capital, they shared a conviction that the Soviets and the Americans were culturally their inferiors.

There was hardly an issue in the first decade that did not offend French sensibilities, if not disturb their sense of national interest or security. The obsession with America displaced even their concerns over Germany, particularly after the admission of the Federal Republic into NATO and the settlement of the Saar issue. The United States rubbed French nerves raw in regard to Indochina, the Suez Canal, and the Algeria crisis. It was under Guy Mollet, not under de Gaulle, that the *force de frappe*, an independent nuclear deterrent, was initiated. It was France's way to assert its independence from America and a base from which to claim leadership of the Continent.

For the French, *Sputnik* was simply the final proof that the Americans could not be counted on for the defense of Europe. If the Soviet Union could reach the United States with its missiles, the former invulnerability of America was destroyed; the last shred of "massive retaliation" was also destroyed. Would the United States unleash its nuclear arsenal in the event of an invasion of the Continent if by doing so it would risk destruction of its own cities? The French answer was no. Hence the imperative to provide one's own deterrent. This was the conclusion of such military intellectuals as General Pierre Gallois, who found that "since the United States itself is vulnerable to Soviet ballistic missiles, the automatic nature of American intervention is less certain."[23]

When de Gaulle's Fifth Republic shoved aside the ineffectual rotating governments of the Fourth, the strategic argument was joined by a powerful political imperative that combined security with grandeur. The *force de frappe* was only one of many elements in that mixture. To become the pre-eminent power in Europe, France had to take positions different in part from those of the past. First was the exclusion of Britain from the European Community on the grounds that its special ties to the United States would compromise its independence. De Gaulle's veto of British application to the EC was predictable. Second was a special relationship of France's own making with Adenauer's Germany that would make the Germans a loyal but inferior ally in the making of a new Europe. Germany's return to full membership, if not full equality, would be dependent on the evolution of a French-dominated EC. Third was the assumption that the cold war was over and that the United States rather than the Soviet Union was the chief challenger to France's leadership.

De Gaulle's opposition to the principle of an integrated NATO command, to American predominance in the alliance, and to a common nuclear policy was a prelude to his dramatic departure from SHAPE itself in 1966. His dissatisfaction with his allies may have had its roots in the humiliations he and France suffered vis-à-vis the "Anglo-Saxon" in World War II, but he cannot be accused of repressing them until the 1960s. In the wake of American opposition to French intervention in the Suez Canal in 1956, he had been ready to scrap the North Atlantic treaty: "We should have told the Americans this is what we want to do and if you do not accept it, the Atlantic pact is no more. They would have gone along. Today we are threatened with a stoppage of gasoline supplies. Well, I would say: 'As of midnight tonight, American troops can no longer travel on French highways and there are no longer any American bases in France.'"[24] Ten years later these recommendations were acted on.

But more than pronouncements, public or private, heralded de Gaulle's direction. On assuming office he in effect gave the United States one more chance to alter its course. On 17 September 1958 he wrote to Eisenhower and Macmillan proposing a Franco-Anglo-American triumverate that would bypass NATO channels and consult on global and nuclear issues. When this plan was summarily turned down, as it had been in other forms since the alliance was established, de Gaulle went ahead with his dual-tracked moves to detach France from the organization and to replace American leadership of Europe with his own.

While his pronouncements often had a casual air about them, as if they were impromptu affairs, his plans in fact were carefully prepared and brilliantly staged. Timing was of the essence. De Gaulle could not act until all the pieces were in order: a nuclear capability must be in place, the Algerian war had to be concluded, the alignment of Germany had to be assumed, and—as important as any consideration—the essential neutrality, if not benevolence, of the Soviet Union had to have been achieved.

Although the French rejection of the North Atlantic Council's decision to deploy nuclear weapons in Europe was made in the last days of the Fourth Republic, it was carried out fully and enthusiastically under de Gaulle. IRBMs could be placed on French soil only if shared under a dual-key arrangement, like Britain's, and then only if France received the necessary technical assistance to produce its own missiles. When negotiations finally collapsed in 1959, General Norstad moved 250 American Supersabre fighter-bombers from French to British bases, where they would have access to tactical nuclear weapons.

Similarly clear signals were given to the Soviet Union. To dramatize the idea of excluding superpowers and the cold war from the Mediterranean, de Gaulle removed the French fleet from the Mediterranean in 1959. The code language, *"la Mediterranée aux Mediterranéens,"* was a way of asserting a French preeminence in the area and of pushing out both American and Soviet warships. Four years later he removed the French Atlantic fleet from SACLANT's authority as well, simply by eliminating France's Atlantic ships from an Annual Review Questionnaire that would have listed vessels available to NATO in the following year.

In all his actions political issues were related to military. When France refused ostentatiously to participate in "Fallex '66," a military exercise for allied general staffs, it did so because the exercise seemed to implement the new American flexible response strategy to potential attack that had replaced "massive retaliation" under Kennedy. This opposition to flexible response centered on building up conventional resistance before nuclear weaponry would be used. It reflected, among other things, a retreat from instant U.S. response to Soviet aggression, and as such disturbed the Germans as much as it did the French. Perhaps more. De Gaulle countered on this discontent with the new American doctrine that presumably deprived Germans of nuclear protection without altering the agreements that denied Germany nuclear capabilities of its own. Not that de Gaulle or any Frenchman would change this. Rather, Germany could look now to France for both nuclear and other protection that the Anglo-Saxons would not provide. The exclusion of Britain in 1962 from the EC invigorated the de Gaulle–Adenauer alliance just as it deepened the isolation of Britain and America from the Continent.

Under other circumstances the overt hostility of France to the United States might have strengthened Anglo-American ties. The British after all had interpreted the significance of *Sputnik* differently from the way the French did. Under Prime Minister Harold Macmillan, Eden's successor, the British committed themselves to revive and repair the damage done by the Dulles-Eden split in the Middle East and to take advantage of Macmillan's wartime intimacy with Eisenhower to integrate British policy into America's. Unlike the Continental members of NATO, the British possessed their own nuclear force, primitive as it may have been compared with those of the superpowers. Indeed, the debacle at Suez made the British more convinced than before that the key to British security rested on a nuclear deterrent. As much as possible it would be an independent nuclear force, "juju, an amulet," as Colin Gordon saw it, "that would restore British self-confidence badly shaken at Suez."[25] The nuclear route would also elevate Britain's status in the partnership with the United States, entwining Britain even more closely in an Anglo-American defense system.

As a pledge of confidence to the United States, the Macmillan government accepted 60 Thor ICBMs to be installed in four British bases under a dual authority. In return the British anticipated American aid in modernizing their nuclear weaponry. And with good reason. Little more than a year after Suez, Eisenhower succeeded in having the McMahon Act of 1946, which had forbidden collaboration on atomic weapons with any foreign power, amended to liberalize access to nuclear weapons data. The resulting Anglo-American solidarity was at French expense. De Gaulle's France was excluded; no help would be given to the *force de frappe*. In fact, the offer to France to install IRBMs on French soil would keep control under the authority of the SACEUR, while the British-based IRBMs would be under bilateral U.S.-British command. Small wonder that the French rejected the U.S. offer in 1959.

For the British, the lure of "special relationship" obscured the damage done to their Continental relations, at least until the actual rejection by the EC took place. Macmillan seemed to have found the solution to Britain's weakness. It was not in accepting a new place for itself as a leading Continental power. Nor was it in waving the banner as head of the Commonwealth, which had loosened both political and economic ties to Britain. Rather, it may be expressed in Macmillan's words, "We are the Greeks in this American Empire. You will find the Americans much as the Greeks found the Romans—great, big, vulgar, bustling people, more vigorous than we are and also more idle, with more unspoiled virtues but also more corrupt. We must run [this headquarters] as the Greek slaves ran the operations of the Emperor Claudius."[26] In brief, the British will continue to rule behind the scenes by manipulating their American partner.

Macmillan's expectations were too extravagant. His hopes—and even his career—were shattered in the Kennedy years and ostensibly over nuclear matters. The difficulty began in the era of good feeling, in the last year of the Eisenhower administration, when the British came to the United States for help. Britain's silo-based missile program, known as Blue Streak, had developed technical and financial troubles that forced its cancellation. The British turned to an air-to-surface missile, Skybolt—then in an early stage of development—that would give their Vulcan bomber fleet stand-off capability to strike strategic targets in Soviet territory. In a loosely phrased agreement at Camp David, Eisenhower agreed to sell Skybolt missiles for the independent British nuclear deterrent force and not to cancel production without prior consultation with the British.

Less than three years later a new American administration embarrassed Macmillan and antagonized Britain by cancelling Skybolt without adequate notification. The action was not taken out of any Anglophobic sentiment; the Skybolt development simply did not meet the standard of cost-effectiveness set by Kennedy's secretary of defense, Robert McNamara. In full public view at the Nassau summit meeting in December 1962, Macmillan was exposed to ridicule by the abrupt American decision and by its awkwardly presented substitutes.

Kennedy certainly intended none of the obloquy that resulted from the cancellation of Skybolt. He realized the extent of Eisenhower's commitment and the meaning of an independent nuclear deterrent to the British. As an Anglophile and admirer of Macmillan as well as a devotee of the European connection, he produced a substitute in the more effective Polaris missile for British submarines. It was too late. France spurned a similar offer: namely, that they must be dedicated to a NATO force but with an escape clause in the event of national emergency. The Skybolt fiasco was another proof to de Gaulle that the United States' promises could not be trusted and that Britain occupied a special subordinate role in American military planning. Britain would be America's Trojan horse inside Europe. De Gaulle's veto of British membership in the EC followed a month later, in January 1963.

Britain's bitterness was almost as deep as France's, and it was caused in part by what Alistair Buchan has called a "central fallacy." The Greek-Roman relationship no longer applied. The United States had become "Greeks to their own Romans by mobilizing the vast intellectual resources of their continental state."[27] The crisis did not break the ties; an Anglo-American "special" relationship continued, and occasionally with considerable emotion in the subsequent years, but the British were rarely again under the illusions that had governed Macmillan. The Continental connection was to have greater significance for Britain than in the past.

It was the third major power in Europe, West Germany, that preoccupied America's NATO planning in the early 1960s. British sensibilities could be ignored, and French disaffection endured, but German adherence to the alliance was a matter of more anxiety than anything caused by tears in a Franco-American or Anglo-American fabric. One explanation stems from the centrality the United States had given West Germany in its conception of a united Europe, extending back to the need for German resources in 1950 and to the war ties between Adenauer and Dulles in succeeding years. Another was the always lively uncertainty over the direction Germany ultimately would take in or out of the alliance. Its long borders with the Warsaw Pact countries, its divided homeland, its special contributions to the traumas of both the Soviet Union and France, all made the German satisfaction with NATO important to every ally, and most especially to the United States.

The dependence was mutual. Chancellor Adenauer staked his own career and his vision of Germany on an American connection. Only an American army standing guard on German borders would assure Germans of security against a hostile superpower in Berlin and in what Adenauer always considered the occupied territories of eastern Germany. Only the threat of massive retaliation would give him confidence. Beneath this rubric he could proceed to bury the ugly German past inside a new Europe, one that would find permanent reconciliation with France and with Germany's other western neighbors.

To achieve these goals, Adenauer had to contend with opponents from left to right. By claiming that adherence to NATO would force the Soviet Union ultimately to accept reunification on Western terms, he made a commitment that obviously could not be fulfilled in his lifetime. The Social Democratic party attacked him for accepting rearmament, for provoking the Soviet Union, and for foreclosing opportunities for insulating Germany from the cold war. Erich Ollenhauer, the leader of the Social Democratic party, felt that German membership in NATO would embitter relations with the Soviet Union, revive the spirit of militarism among Germans, and leave the country permanently divided. The right wing, Deutsche Reichspartie, complained of Germany's inferior status in NATO and of the requirement that its armies be dedicated to SHAPE. Both ends of the political spectrum deplored the loss of opportunity to play off the superpowers against each other.

Adenauer's dominant personality helped him to win out over all opponents, and the economic recovery of Germany under him and his successor, Ludwig Erhard, sustained German loyalty. The 12 German divisions became the most important European contribution to the alliance. Yet uncertainties abounded. As early as 1955 a NATO maneuver called into question whether German forces served the other allies rather than Germany. Operation Carte Blanche hypothecated a German death list of 1.7 million and shocked German public opinion into a realization that even a victory in a nuclear war would bring disaster of an order worse than the two world wars. These questions did not affect Adenauer's resolve. But they did force him into an embrace of "massive retaliation" that *Sputnik* shook loose.

The consequences were disturbing. By the end of the Eisenhower era Adenauer's friend Dulles had departed, and the United States was considering new unsettling strategic approaches to NATO defenses. First, tactical nuclear weapons, while attractive from an American vantage point, not only would be employed in German soil but suggested a retreat from an instantaneous American nuclear response to attack. Second, the approach of a more flexible system, welcomed by the Kennedy administration, was a further retreat from the Eisenhower-Dulles system. It meant ground warfare, with German troops as the major actors, German civilians as the major victims, and German territory as the major battlefield.

Under these circumstances de Gaulle's approach to Adenauer for a Franco-German understanding that would reflect a Continental community was attractive. It was true that de Gaulle obviously expected a superior position for France and that this nationalistic emphasis was an uncomfortable aspect of France's friendship. Open acceptance of the Oder-Neisse line and a divided Germany was even more difficult to agree to. It contradicted Adenauer's promises of 1954. But these dampeners were counteracted by the apparent decline in West German enthusiasm for reunification, partly through acceptance of Soviet power and partly as a result of complacency generated by economic prosperity. They were reduced in significance also by a shared dislike of the flexible defense strategy now openly accepted under Kennedy and by a shared distrust of British dealings with the Continent. At the same time, the United States was pressing Germany for more financial support for American bases and reducing the number of its troops in Germany.

The Franco-German collaboration expressed in a treaty of cooperation of January 1963 signified that Adenauer had found in de Gaulle a new Dulles. Their joint rejection of Britain's application to the Common Market could be construed as a rejection of the United States as well. As Kennedy sardonically observed to Arthur M. Schlesinger, "From a strictly economic viewpoint, we have known all along that British membership in the Common Market would be bad for us; so now we are better off. On the political side, our chief object was to tie Germany more firmly into the structure of Western Europe. Now de Gaulle is doing that in his own way."[28] France's success at America's expense in both organizing Europe along its lines and in incorporating West Germany into its *Europe des patries* was by no means complete. The Germany of Ludwig Erhard and Kurt-George Kiesinger, while resolutely Christian Democratic and firmly attached to rapprochement with France, had none of the Carclinginian emotions that united Adenauer and de Gaulle. A return to Charlemagne's conception or even to the Holy Roman Empire was not in their plans. A Europe of nations, with France as the preeminent leader, had limited attractions in the long run. And the protective mantle of the United States always appeared more sturdy and more durable than the Gallic links.

THE MULTILATERAL FORCE, 1960–1964

These caveats gave heart to American attempts to recast the defense structure of NATO in ways to appease the requirements of the Germans, the British, and the smaller members of the alliance. General Lauris Norstad was the key figure in the initial efforts. A protégé of Eisenhower, he had been SHAPE's first air deputy and assumed his functions with the Eisenhower accolade of being "the best organizer" he had ever met. Norstad's dominant personality and his devotion to NATO made his voice in NATO councils politically as important as Spaak's or Spaak's successor, Dirk Stikker of the Netherlands. He epitomized "the new generation of United States soldier-statesmen-diplomats."[29] Using his position as Supreme Allied Commander Europe and his reputation as pro-European, he devised a plan of appeasing German restiveness over nuclear forces and of arresting French movement toward disengagement from SHAPE.

The solution was to be the Norstad Plan, which would make NATO a fourth nuclear power by having its own nuclear component. In this way the fears emanating from *Sputnik* would be dissolved; the Europeans would have their own nuclear capability; the French would be relieved of the burden of Anglo-American hegemony and could give up their independent nuclear deterrent; and the Germans and other Europeans would have a role in defense they had not played before. In many ways the dumbbell idea of Kennan in the 1940s and the future Grand Design of Kennedy, with its twin transatlantic pillars, were implicit in Norstad's thinking. The idea appealed to Spaak, and the U.S. proposal of what the North Atlantic Council communiqué identified as "an MRBM [medium-range ballistic missiles] multilateral force" was taken up and placed under study at the December 1960 meeting of the council. The council also accepted more reluctantly and implicitly the language of flexible response, which Norstad and other American leaders had been moving toward in the last Eisenhower years: "There must be a proper balance in the forces of the Alliance of nuclear and conventional strength to provide the required flexibility."[30]

McNamara was to emphasize in an influential speech at the Athens meeting of the council in May 1962 the linkage of conventional forces, flexible response, and a European MRBM force. The latter never materialized, but flexible response strategy finally became NATO doctrine in December 1967.

The Norstad Plan as such never had much chance for realization. The smaller nations, which earlier had rejected missile bases, had no more interest in assuming new burdens than they had the old. Their identification with NATO was with America as the shield and sword; they were as restive with the abandonment of massive retaliation as they were with new initiatives. France for its part was going its own way. Unless the "fourth nuclear partner" was France, Europe was not interested. Nor was Britain listening very closely; in 1960 the "special relationship" dealt with America, not with Europe. What was most important, however, was Congress's resisting any serious effort to gut the McMahon Act. Even the concessions to the British had been too much. The prospect of having 15 fingers on the button was unacceptable. Even if the supreme allied commander would be wearing his American hat, as commander of the U.S. European Command, the concept of NATO as a nuclear power was still unacceptable. The "two-key" system for control of NATO's land-based medium-range missiles went too far.

But if the Kennedy administration did not rally to the Norstad Plan for a multilateral force, it was neither because of congressional opposition nor the

mixed feelings of the European allies. It was more because of the philosophi-
cal outlook of the new administration and the commanding position of
Secretary of Defense Robert McNamara. McNamara, rather than Secretary
of State Dean Rusk, would be the dominant American figure in the 1960s.

His caveats were at least twofold. One was the danger of too much
authority in nuclear affairs going to Europe, or more specifically to a
German-controlled Europe. Too much access for West Germany to long-
range nuclear weapons would exacerbate both Franco-American and Soviet-
American relations. The other was a new rationalization of NATO defense
that conflicted with the views of Norstad. Influenced by JCS Chairman
General Maxwell Taylor, flexible response was fully developed. The best
deterrent now resided in the threat to respond "appropriately" to whatever
aggression the enemy would launch: conventional defense, tactical nuclear
weapons, and strategy weapons all had a role, depending on the level of escalation imposed by the enemy. The development of the Polaris missiles on
unassailable submarines revived confidence in strategic weapons, particularly
in a second-strike counterforce. Centralized decision making must remain in
American hands; the Norstad plans seemed to decentralize authority excessively.

But there was a third element in the Kennedy consideration. Norstad was
too popular, too independent, and too closely associated with Eisenhower to
continue in his post. He was replaced by General Lyman L. Lemnitzer in
1963, a dedicated supporter of NATO, whose association with the alliance
went back to his service as U.S. liaison officer with the emerging Brussels
Pact organization in 1948. Lemnitzer was also less political, less likely to offer
a challenge to the Pentagon's wisdom with respect to NATO policy.

It was Lemnitzer, not Norstad, who was called on to accept a new version
of the multilateral force (MLF) that flourished from 1962 to 1964. The combined pressures of German restlessness with a military posture that did not
reflect new economic power, the continuing inexorable steps on the part of
France toward independence, and the commitment of Polaris missiles on
British submarines to a NATO multilateral force all contributed to resuscita-
tion of the MLF. Additionally, the force would be a surrogate for missiles dismantled in Italy and Turkey after the Cuban crisis.

The MLF would no longer be land-based. Instead, a proposal that originated with Robert R. Bowie, head of the Policy Planning Staff in the
Eisenhower administration, envisioned the MLF in the way believers a
decade before had viewed the EDC: namely, as a means of converting Europe
into a unified entity ultimately equal to the United States. These State
Department "theologians" wanted the MRBMs in Europe to be part of a collective force inhibiting development of national nuclear capabilities. The
nuclear missiles, as recommended by Secretary of State Christian Herter in
1960, would be moved from land to sea, with 25 surface vessels of different
nations carrying eight Polaris A-3 missiles with a range of 2,500 miles or

more. The fleet would be assigned to SACEUR and the NATO fleets in the Atlantic, Mediterranean, and the Channel, with mixed manned crews and nuclear warheads under joint ownership and custody. Every participating nation could veto the use of the nuclear weapon. American responsibility of sole custody of stockpiled warheads on the Continent would be neutralized under the new arrangements, although the United States would still have the final control of the weapons. Germany remained the key to the MLF's success, not only because participation would divert attention from French and British nuclear capabilities but because it would be a vehicle to push Germans and other allies into helping to finance the MLF and paying more for U.S. troops stationed in Europe.

None of these plans ever materialized, despite their attractiveness to American Europeanists such as Under Secretary of State George Ball, who found European unity in itself a virtue, and to such military organizers as McNamara, who envisaged a quick solution to a variety of problems in the success of the MLF. It could not work. De Gaulle would not be lured out of a *force de frappe* and into a NATO force; the MLF was another means of Americanizing Europe. Macmillan's Britain, suffering from the bruises of the Skybolt fiasco, would not exchange its problematic nuclear deterrent for a loss of identity inside an MLF. As Macmillan once commented to Ball about the prospects of a mixed crew, "You don't expect our chaps to share their grog with the Turks, do you?"[31] Only the Germans welcomed the program— a stance that created of itself more problems than it solved. German access to weapons, no matter how carefully insulated, still could send tremors down European spines and agitate the Soviets as well.

Apart from the true believers in European unification or the supporters of a quick fix, the MLF never really captured the imagination of the Kennedy administration, and it seemed much too muddled for the Johnson succession to manage. It was too much a sleight of hand, with too many unanswered questions. When Secretary-General Spaak had asked Norstad "who in NATO" would control the nuclear weapon, the SACEUR responded that the alliance "succeeded as well as it had without answering unanswerable questions."[32]

Some efforts were made to keep the idea alive. The British proposed in June 1964 an alternate MLF plan based on a force of land-based aircraft. And when Prime Minister Harold Wilson took office in the fall of that year he came up with another alternative that would set up a separate nuclear force with American MRBM weapons already in Europe and Britain's V-bombers and Polaris submarines joining an allied force of surface ships. The Atlantic Nuclear Force (ANF) would involve an advisory group composed of France, Germany, and Italy to participate in American conventional as well as nuclear planning.

The potential for even more confusion was obvious in the ANF. By the December 1964 North Atlantic Council meeting Belgium, Norway, and

Denmark voiced their objections, partly over a French point that no meaningful negotiations could be made with the Soviet Union on the reunification of Germany if Bonn had a significant share in the control of strategic nuclear weapons.

The MLF was not vetoed; it simply disappeared in an ever vaguer rhetoric, without satisfaction to any party. The MLF or ANF appeared in none of the NATO communiqués of December 1964 or through the year 1965. The closest a communiqué came to touching on the subject was when the defense ministers on 31 May–1 June 1965 "agreed that further consideration should be given to a proposal for ways in which consultation might be improved and participation by interested allied countries extended in the planning of nuclear forces, including strategic forces."[33]

END OF THE GRAND DESIGN

The various evasions did not mean that the problem went away by itself. NATO's attention, led by the United States, was directed increasingly toward conventional defense of Europe, which always was the heart of the flexible response. If conventional forces failed to check aggression, then options for nuclear weapons, tactical and strategic, would be available. The threat of escalation would be the primary element in recasting the deterrent. If the MLF could not satisfy Europeans' discontent with the nuclear part of the package, other devices could be substituted.

A special committee of NATO defense ministers met in June 1965 to deal with nuclear consultations. After some hesitation in Germany over Gaullist reactions, a Special Committee of Defense Ministers was established in November of that year. A year later this committee was institutionalized both in the Nuclear Defense Affairs Committee (NDAC), open to all allies, and in the Nuclear Planning Group, composed of the United States, Great Britain, Germany, and Italy. Three other members of the NDAC would be represented in rotation. Within these units all the many complications of NATO defenses were heard, from problems of target selection and warhead allocation to coordination of commands.

These activities in pursuit of a more effective deterrent strategy gave comfort to planners and papered over some of the rips and tears in the NATO skein. They reflected an ongoing recognition that Soviet power was still a formidable entity that could, as in the Berlin or Cuban crises, give rise to specters of aggression against the alliance. They also reflected the need for sharing both authority and costs in an alliance where the balance had changed over 15 years. America was not as powerful relative to Europe as it had been in 1949; Europe was not as weak or fearful as it had been after World War II.

If the Grand Design had failed, it was because Europe was not strong enough or united enough to become an equal partner or confident enough to abandon the American connection. Yet if the alliance still had meaning for most of its members, it rested on the importance of maintaining a balance of power between East and West. But the European perception of an East-West standoff not only gave rise to discontent with NATO in America among critics who deplored its imperial character but also permitted the Johnson administration to give Southeast Asia priority over Europe in the mid-1960s.

Conversely, the taming of the superpowers opened a path for the most traumatic moment in NATO's history: de Gaulle's eviction notice of 1966. In the foregoing achievements France was conspicuously absent. It had rejected the MLF, and it would take no part in the Special Committee on nuclear consultation. The way had been prepared. If the ensuing expulsion of American forces from France and France's dissociation from NATO were a surprise, it may have been "because de Gaulle had said it so often without doing it." That he was able to disengage his nation without special penalties was partly, as Under Secretary of State Ball angrily recorded, because he knew that "whatever he did, his country would be protected by American power."[34] The United States could not defend Germany and the other allies without defending France as well. But de Gaulle's success was also a consequence of a conviction that the Soviet threat had moderated and that the Soviet Union, like the United States, could be manipulated with impunity for the advancement of French interests.

Whatever the workings of de Gaulle's mind in the winter of 1966, his actions had immediate and powerful effect on the machinery of NATO. From an organizational perspective the watershed in NATO history has been 1966; its structure was considerably altered when the political and military headquarters moved from France to Belgium.

chapter 6

DÉTENTE AND THE NIXON DOCTRINE, 1966–1974

Crisis has been an endemic factor of NATO's life since its inception, and milestones in its history can be located in any one of the many crises that erupted in the first 15 years. None, however, has had greater resonance than France's withdrawal of its forces from the integrated command of SHAPE in the winter of 1966.

On the most obvious level it forced immediate changes in both the military and political structures of the organization. SHAPE was physically removed from Rocquencourt to Casteau, near Mons, in Belgium. Allied Forces Central Europe (AFCENT) headquarters was relocated from Fontainebleau to Brunssum in the Netherlands; the U.S. European Command (EUCOM), headed by the SACEUR, along with all U.S. army and air force installations had to find new bases in Europe, mostly in Germany. And all these moves had to be completed within one year's time.

Changes in the political arrangement of the organization were less dramatic but probably more profound. At American insistence, and with France's reluctant compliance, the secretary-general's office transferred to Brussels in October 1966. More important, with France removed from the deliberations of military planning, the surviving 14 members reorganized the Defense Planning Committee (DPC) as an instrument under the secretary-general to direct military affairs. Similarly, a Nuclear Planning Group, without France, took on the challenge of nuclear involvement of the allies in NATO. Again with France out of the scene, the old Standing Group in Washington was supplanted by an integrated International Military Staff in 1966 with its headquarters in Brussels. The Military Committee itself was also transferred to Brussels from Washington. All of these changes emerged from the French decision and represented a liberation of the alliance from

French negativism. The DPC was the new vehicle for decision making, and the International Military Staff, with its broader representation, had a primary role in military planning.

Undergirding these changes were important and pervasive assumptions about the course of the alliance, not all of them a product of de Gaulle's behavior. France's act was a proximate, not the fundamental, source of change. First was a recognition that the stability of the West still required a continuation of the alliance. Second was an unease with American leadership on the part of the smaller nations of the organization. Third was a sense that the Soviet threat had altered its character, that a détente between East and West was possible in the age of Leonid Brezhnev even more than under Khrushchev.

The fact that no nation followed French leadership out of the organization and that even France made it clear that it would remain in the alliance underlay all the shifts of command locations and decision-making machinery. The enhanced position of the smaller nations in the recasting of the NATO machinery was less a reproach to French negativism than to American dominance. And the North Atlantic Council decision of December 1966 to commission a new task force to examine the future problems of the alliance "in order to strengthen the Alliance as a factor for a durable peace" was a message to seek more consultation within NATO and détente between NATO and the Warsaw Pact.[1] Without the dual continuity of U.S. involvement and the new relaxation of East-West relations, de Gaulle's expulsion of NATO would have destroyed the Western alliance.

DE GAULLE'S IMPACT

For the United States, the potential for positive changes in the alliance was not immediately apparent in 1966. Instead, long pent-up emotions over the continual provocations spilled over into every level of reaction. Not only was de Gaulle's action insulting, but its effects were humiliating: the United States was to pack up its men and material and get out of France with an insultingly short deadline to accomplish the task. In 1966 the French made it clear that they would not denounce the alliance but instead would separate participation in the organization from membership in the alliance.

De Gaulle's letter to President Johnson was presented on 7 March. Similar letters were presented to heads of states or governments in Britain, West Germany, and Italy two days later. At the end of the month memoranda to all the allies announced that France was withdrawing from the organization and expected prompt removal of NATO forces from its soil. In these memoranda, on 29 March, but not before this occasion, the French specified for the first time a timetable for the transfer of American and NATO com-

mands out of French territory as well as for termination of all French personnel in SHAPE posts.[2]

American reactions were vehemently expressed from all parts of the political spectrum. For critics of NATO, such as Senator Mike Mansfield and
others who fretted about Europe's negative reaction to America's Vietnam
War, the challenge was a welcome reminder that something was wrong with
NATO. Changes should be made, particularly with respect to the presence
of American troops, not only in France but in the rest of Europe as well.
Indeed, as Mansfield was reported to have said, de Gaulle may have per-
formed "a needed service" by providing an occasion to reduce American
obligations and placing greater responsibility on the European allies for the
defense of Europe.[3] Within the Pentagon there was an echo of this sentiment
from McNamara's circle, which felt that the prospective loss of French participation was of limited military significance and hence could be used to
streamline, with cost savings, the NATO defense system.

But neither was the dominant emotion in Washington. Others in the
Pentagon wished to challenge the legality of de Gaulle's cancellation of
bilateral agreements that provided for two years' notice before termination,
as U.S. ambassador to France, Charles Bohlen, discovered when he returned
from Paris for consultations. This position was strongly supported by
Europeanists in the State Department, like Under Secretary of State Ball,
who purportedly informed allies in Paris that the United States would challenge the legality of eviction, ignore deadlines, and deny France access to
intelligence sharing and to the NATO Air Defense Ground Environment
(NADGE) system.

President Johnson's response, however, turned out to be remarkably mild,
considering the provocation and the advice he received. Ambassador Harlan
Cleveland, U.S. permanent representative on the North Atlantic Council,
noted that while Johnson's "private references to General de Gaulle
stretched his considerable talent for colorful language, he imposed an icy
correctness on those who had reason to discuss French policy in public."
John M. Leddy, assistant secretary of state for Europe, recalled the draft of a
stiff letter of protest prepared by Rusk with the advice of Bohlen, Acheson,
and Ball. The president altered its tone on the grounds that de Gaulle was
not going to change his mind whatever arguments may be made: "He's asked
us to get out of France. We'll get out of France." Leddy also recalled an
ambassadorial lunch—without the French ambassador—where Johnson said,
"Well, when that old man talks I just tip my hat. When he comes rushing
down like a locomotive on the track, why the Germans and ourselves, we
just stand aside and let him go on by, then we're back together again."
General Andrew J. Goodpaster suggested that Johnson's composure was not
shaken because he was not personally engaged in a confrontation with de
Gaulle; it was a confrontation between two nations.[4]

The 14 allies ("les Quatorze"), chaired by André de Staercke, Belgium's dean of NATO's diplomatic corps, complied, coming up with a public statement concerning NATO without France after a series of formal and informal meetings. In Cleveland's judgment the 14 produced, on the basis of a British draft, "a declaration of admirable clarity and, considering it was produced by diplomats and politicians, remarkable brevity"—fewer than 150 words.[5]

Rather than emerging demoralized and divided by the experience, NATO political leaders appeared energized. Bohlen perceived a manic quality in their reaction, as if the allies had foiled the French by not begging for delay, dragging their feet, raising objections at every turn, or in short behaving "in a rather bitchy fashion," which the occasion might have warranted.[6]

The 14 could afford some self-congratulation in their restraint. Punitive measures might not have been easily achieved in light of barely repressed sympathy for de Gaulle's behavior on the part of some of the smaller allies. Acceptance alone could win consensus. Besides, the challenge from France was not directed against the secretariat or the council itself. Those offices were carefully exempted from de Gaulle's wrath. The French did not initiate the removal of the council or the secretary-general from Paris to Brussels. When Secretary-General Brosio departed for Brussels in October 1966, it was a consequence of NATO's—particularly America's—initiative, not France's. On this occasion NATO was given no deadline to leave Paris. On the contrary, the French reluctantly went along with the council's decision.

No such leisurely reaction was available to General Lemnitzer as supreme allied commander. As leader of SHAPE and EUCOM he had only one year, until 1 April 1967, to meet de Gaulle's deadline for the final removal of NATO's and America's military presence in France. While the choice of a new host country for SHAPE was settled on 21 June, when the Belgian House of Representatives approved its transfer to Belgium, the specific location of military headquarters and the conditions under which it would be built took the entire summer of 1966 to complete. The removal of the major subordinate headquarters, AFCENT, from Fontainebleau was even more problematic, since it was not known as late as 1 July whether its destination would be the Netherlands or Germany. On that date the SACEUR said he "was getting very concerned about the delays that are being imposed, because it would be most difficult to move either one of these headquarters in a year, and now we only have nine months left before April 1, 1967."[7]

The removal of SHAPE and AFCENT from France was not Lemnitzer's only concern. As commander in chief of all American forces stationed in Europe (EUCOM) he had to find a new home outside of France for EUCOM and for the U.S. Communications Zone headquarters. EUCOM found spacious and comfortable facilities (then used by the Seventh Army) in Stuttgart, although it was Lemnitzer's view that economic reasons had dictated a move to a location that would be "much too far removed from SHAPE in Belgium."[8]

But if Stuttgart was considered to be too far from SHAPE, the ultimate location of SHAPE itself was too far from the political headquarters in Brussels. The SACEUR's first choice was a military base in Evère, an eastern suburb of Brussels neighboring the international airport. This suitable facility, however, became the home of the secretary-general and the permanent representatives, not SHAPE. The Belgian government offered two sites far from the capital and unsatisfactory in most respects. Both were in southern Belgium and were available because they were among the few acreages belonging to the state that had some basic infrastructure already in place. While the Belgian ministry claimed that it would be politically unpalatable to place SHAPE in an urban area, it was obvious that the depressed Hanaut province where Casteau was located would benefit from the installation of 1,700 NATO families. This issue was more to the point than Belgium's professed fear of SHAPE as a possible lightning rod for enemy attack.

These negotiations exacted a toll in time and patience. SHAPE had to settle for a headquarters, outside Mons, some 30 miles from the airport—a concession that not even the Belgian promises to spend $500 million readying Casteau for occupation and building a modern road system to Brussels could fully mitigate. Despite all these disabilities, the deadline, was met successfully. The new headquarters opened on 31 March 1967, one day ahead of schedule. Much of the construction was done in the winter, but even with a reasonably mild season, it was an impressive accomplishment.

Besides the NATO infrastructure, there was the matter of U.S. bases. To pack up and ship the billion dollars and more worth of supplies and equipment from American bases required what a House investigating committee called a "herculean" effort.[9] Not that Congress was happy either with the French behavior, particularly the putative profiteering over reimbursement for American expenditures in France, or with the State and Defense departments that had permitted too much of common NATO infrastructure, with its vital center in France, to come from American dollars. Still, the congressional committees shared a conviction that General Lemnitzer had understood and surmounted the variety and complexity of the problems he had faced as an American and a NATO commander. A little over a year after the move the SACEUR could report with justified satisfaction to the North Atlantic Assembly at its meeting in Brussels "that these tremendous relocations have been completed successfully without the loss—even for a moment—of the command and control so vital to the security of all Allied Command Europe."[10]

Unquestionably, one reason for NATO's ability to cope with what could have been a critical shock to NATO's military system was de Gaulle's shrewdness in easing some of the transitional burdens. The expulsion order was not categorical. He allowed special provisions to be made allowing the United States to continue the use of the vital oil pipeline from Donges on the Atlantic to Huttenheim in Germany. He also extended an offer to the Federal Republic to maintain the stationing of French forces in that country, not under SHAPE's provenance but under the London-Paris agreements of 1954, wherein Germany was allowed to enter NATO.

The most important French concession was agreement after some petty harassment to permit NATO planes en route from Britain to southern Europe to fly over France. Had de Gaulle kept a ban on all bilateral overflight rights that had been given to France's NATO allies, the linkage of France with Switzerland and Austria would have created a neutral belt of nations—or an "Elysian Curtain," as C. L. Sulzberger called it[11]—splitting NATO into two parts and thereby reducing flexibility of troop dispositions. For a time after May 1966, authorization for 39 categories of American overflights was subjected to monthly, and then almost daily, clearance. The problem was satisfactorily resolved in November of that year in a meeting between General Lemnitzer and General Charles Ailleret on the future status of military relations between France and its allies. Overflight privileges were subsequently extended to all allies.

In exchange for well-calibrated arrangements, the French military made sure that it would enjoy the continuing benefits of the NATO air alert system. NATO Air Defense Ground Environment (NADGE) would be an integrated as well as improved defense system, but it was important enough for French security to justify France's contributing a share of the costs (12 percent of the total) and having a French company as a member of the consortium chartered to construct the system.

Similarly, French national interests determined the future of the French military presence in Germany. While the West German leaders were unwilling to accept the 1954 agreements as the basis for permitting French troops to remain in place, neither the Germans nor the other allies could accept the French alternative: full withdrawal from Germany. Rather than persist in their claim that France could station troops in Germany only within a NATO context and under NATO authority—a claim that would invoke the unpalatable French alternative—the Germans were ready to compromise.

The result was an interim agreement allowing the temporary stationing of French forces in Germany after 1 July 1966, pending a permanent understanding. This was satisfactory to the French as long as the NATO mission they served was not integrated within the Allied command. The matter was settled through an exchange of letters on 3 December 1966 between France's foreign minister, Maurice Couve de Mourville, and Willy Brandt, foreign minister of the new German coalition government. The legal snarl was untangled by a recognition that the 23 October 1954 convention on foreign forces in Germany did not rule out the continued presence of French troops.

Having won its point, France permitted the flying of both German and French flags over the bases and consented to inform German liaison officers with the French forces 14 days in advance of any troop movements at or above the regimental level.

France therefore was able to keep its troops in Germany on its own terms free from alliance obligations and free, for that matter, to leave whether or not the Germans or the Americans wished them to go. The North Atlantic Council, in turn, became an unwilling witness to this understanding, and no clearcut military plans resulted that would bring French contingents under a NATO command in the event of a war alert. The most that Lemnitzer was able to extract from Ailleret was assignment of French troops in the event France decided to participate in NATO's common military actions. Joint contingency plans could be made, but these would imply no automatic commitment by the French.

While France's deft tactics lessened the impact of damage done to the structure of European defense, they could not change the fact that damage had been done. Nor could the skill and efficiency of Lemnitzer and his staff in meeting the deadlines imposed on the alliance and on the United States by de Gaulle's ambitions for France do more than minimize the short-run weakening of the alliance's security in Europe. The SACEUR was responsible for implementing a policy of forward defense and a flexible strategy that long had been part of America's thinking and was finally accepted by the allies formally at the December 1967 meeting of the North Atlantic Council in Brussels.[12] For Lemnitzer it was an unhappy irony that the council adopted finally this combined strategy at the very time he felt NATO defenses to be most vulnerable. Maintaining a defense at the frontier of West Germany involved a commitment of manpower and equipment at a level belied by the reduction of U.S. troops in Europe—caused primarily by the demands of the Vietnam War and by the reluctance of European partners to sacrifice more for the common cause than they had already done—a reluctance fostered primarily by a growing sense of détente with the Soviet Union.

The positive thinking predominant in 1967 was postulated on the assumption that the removal of France from SHAPE would "be in no way disabling" to the military posture of the alliance. French territory, according to Secretary of Defense McNamara, was not necessary for the defense of NATO: "Neither the United States nor its allies have ever contemplated a war in which falling back upon French soil through the battlefield of Germany was an acceptable strategy for the alliance."[13] The key term, "forward defense," meant Germany, not France. So while French cooperation was obviously desirable, it was not vital.

The U.S. response in the Pentagon was so positive that it seemed almost as if de Gaulle's act were a blessing in disguise to the alliance. At one point Lemnitzer was moved to comment that "one more benefit of this sort and we will be out of business."[14] For the planners in Casteau—American and

European—the reaction was frightening. NATO ministers talked blithely of forward defense—indeed, of a five-year force plan—at a meeting of the North Atlantic Council. At this same meeting, attention focused on a report made by Belgium's foreign minister Pierre Harmel to the North Atlantic Council that asserted, "Military security and a policy of détente are not contradictory but complementary."[15] Détente could mean the unravelling of NATO without prodding from outside.

The issue of the oil pipeline, which military leaders considered to be vital, was not resolved by French concessions. Those could be changed by a Gaullist whim. From a westward flow from France to Germany, the infrastructure had to be changed to a north-south axis, as supplies from the United States were transferred to German in place of French ports. Even more painful was the realization that the Berlin crisis of 1961 had revealed the vulnerability of the old north-south military supply line; hence, the decision earlier in the decade to locate as close to the Atlantic as possible. Even if communications dislocation was only a temporary problem, the men on the field felt that they had a major challenge ahead in redeploying combat garrisons without damaging their effectiveness.

To maintain credibility in the face of altered circumstances, General Lemnitzer tried to force NATO to recognize that it had to be prepared to cope with the consequences of France's actions and that the relative ease of the move from France to Belgium should not lull the allies into a false sense of security. In an address to the North Atlantic Assembly in November 1967 the SACEUR noted that potential enemy military capabilities remained substantial and were growing. What would happen to deterrence, he asked, when allies reduced their terms of military service, redeployed troops to the United States, and cut back on military budgets and still expected the armed forces to conduct an effective forward defense in the event of aggression? He responded to this rhetorical question by noting two alternatives: to thin out already marginal resources in Central Europe, and accept earlier use of nuclear weapons, or to provide more units for conventional defense. France's withdrawal of its forces, even under the strong likelihood of its return in a crisis, still reduced the flexibility of the Allied Command Europe to carry out its operational missions. "This potential loss," he concluded, "is from a vital area—one in which I considered the existing forces to be of marginal strength before this action was taken."[16]

TOWARD DÉTENTE

Less than a year later Lemnitzer's forebodings seemed to have been confirmed by the Warsaw Pact's brutal suppression of the liberal Alexander Dubček regime in Czechoslovakia. While the Soviets had sent sufficient signals to the West to quiet fears of conflict with NATO, there was always the possibility of miscalculations and misunderstandings. The SACEUR had to place "immediately and covertly," as he expressed it later, allied installations and forces on emergency alert without giving pretext to the Warsaw Pact to threaten invasion of NATO territory in the guise of protecting Czechoslovakia from Western armies. At this moment of tension he looked to Brussels for advice and received no answer. Lemnitzer's explanation was that, "being August, Europe's holiday time, no political guidance was forthcoming from the NATO Council." This silence in Brussels, he felt, was "one of the most serious breakdowns in the political-military mechanisms of the Alliance that occurred during my tenure as SACEUR."[17]

The SACEUR's exasperation was understandable but not wholly justified. NATO was sobered by the severity of Soviet repression in Prague. The Brezhnev Doctrine, trumpeting the right of the Soviet Union to preserve the indivisibility of the Warsaw bloc against internal subversion, was a setback to the principle of détente and a reminder that military force remained a major element in the geopolitical life of Europe. The Defense Planning Committee claimed that the Warsaw Pact's invasion of Czechoslovakia had forced NATO to reassess its defense positions, and the committee promised to add funds to the NATO force plan for 1969–73. This statement followed an agreement not to withdraw any troops from the NATO command structure in the immediate future.[18]

There was a concerted NATO response to Soviet naval expansion throughout the late 1960s and early 1970s. The most publicized was the establishment of a Maritime Air Force Mediterranean in Naples to coordinate surveillance throughout the area. This new unit developed from recommendations made at the council meeting in Reykjavik in June 1968.[19] Also in Naples, AFSOUTH replaced the Mediterranean Command, formerly based in Malta. The decline of British power in the area, marked by the independence of Malta in 1964, placed greater weight on the readiness of the U.S. Sixth Fleet, itself located near Naples.

None of the foregoing activities should be dismissed as lip service to the common defense. The anxieties were genuine, as were most of the efforts to remedy perceived weaknesses. The abrupt ending of the "Prague Spring" did have meaning for the allies. But the sense of menace that in turn required maintenance of serious defense efforts was subordinated to the growing consensus among the members that the Soviet Union and its allies had achieved a state of normality in international relations. While the Czech crisis revived ugly memories of the recent past, most of the allies found comfort in the Warsaw bloc's explicit signals to the West that its concern was with one of its members, not with one or more of its rivals. It is worthy to note that the December 1967 council meeting that accepted flexible response as NATO doctrine also approved the Harmel Report, which called for the encouragement of détente, and that the June 1968 meeting of the North Atlantic Council, which called for the establishment of an air surveillance command in the Mediterranean, also adopted a resolution in favor of mutual and balanced force reductions between NATO and the Warsaw Pact nations. After years of studiously snubbing the Warsaw alliance, NATO communiqués, beginning in December 1970, routinely mentioned it as a negotiator in talks that would complete a détente. By 1972, as Secretary-General Joseph Luns revealed, the phrase "bloc to bloc" implied not just normality but respectability.[20] The cold war appeared to be at an end, even if some forms of vigilance would have to be maintained.

That the juxtaposition of measures for defense and détente emphasized détente more than defense was not surprising. Pressures toward this outcome had been building over the decade. They came particularly from the smaller members of the alliance but were supported for a variety of reasons at this point by the larger members as well. Gaullism required a period of relaxation for it to flourish; Germany under the Socialists saw it as a means of winning a special relationship with East Germany in *Ostpolitik*: Britain, with its declining power, looked to a new European relationship in the Common Market; and the United States, beset by the growing troubles of the Vietnam War, had less time and money for its European commitments.

Manlio Brosio, as secretary-general in this period, symbolized the new direction and spoke for the lesser powers in the alliance. An Italian diplomat with well-known French sympathies, he lacked the political stature of his predecessors but was arguably the most successful of NATO's secretaries-general to date, as Robert Jordan has noted.[21] Ismay had won attention as a wartime associate of Churchill, while Spaak and Stikker had been foreign ministers of Belgium and the Netherlands, respectively. But Brosio's diplomatic talents were perfectly suited to the tasks before the North Atlantic Council and the alliance at large. His tenure coincided with that of General Lemnitzer's, a coincidence that permitted the secretary-general greater latitude than would have been the case with Lemnitzer's more political predecessor, Norstad. Brosio's cautious responses to de Gaulle's action were based on the importance of keeping the door open for France's return to SHAPE— a stance that suited the allies more than the Americans. Moreover, his steadfast support of détente, even in the face of the Czech crisis, was more successful than Lemnitzer's warnings about military preparedness.

While the SACEUR may have accomplished his mission in 1966 with distinction, the move to Brussels marked a relative decline in the political weight of his office. Under Norstad the supreme allied commander was at least the equal of the secretary-general and superior to the American representative in NATO. This was not the case with Lemnitzer. Partly the change was a consequence of his more traditional conception of his duties. His authority, he felt, rested on his military expertise, and in this area he was authoritative and occasionally confrontational when necessary. But he shied away from the political role that former SACEURs had enjoyed.

There was still another element in the change. The abolition of the Standing Group and the transfer of the Military Committee from Washington to Brussels—in fact, to the same building the political headquarters reoccupied—subtly changed the relationship between the SACEUR in Casteau and the chairman of the Military Committee in Brussels. It led to the secretary-general consulting with the SACEUR only on operational matters, while dealing with the Military Committee on the coordination of military and political affairs.

This did not mean that American power would be confined to SHAPE. Harlan Cleveland, the U.S. permanent representative on the council, was a figure of considerable stature. The council continued to suit America's purposes. No matter how active the secretary-general was in his role as chairman of the council, he remained primarily a "decision-ratifier" as William T. R. Fox and Annette B. Fox have observed.[22] The so-called NATO Method, a rule of unanimity, effectively prevents the council from making decisions, and this has hampered coordination of efforts. While special committees, such as the Committee of Three in 1956 and the Committee on the Future Tasks of the Alliance in 1967, had urged greater consultation among the allies, the United States was unwilling to be bound by constraints imposed by its allies when its own responsibilities were global rather than regional.

Yet the organizational changes of 1966 and 1967, made with the collaboration of the secretary-general, opened the way for the voices of smaller nations to be heard more clearly than in the past. While American Atlanticists were venting their anger against de Gaulle, Brosio noted and respected the mixed signals he received from the 13 other nations. Portugal, for example, acclaimed the note of "realism" in de Gaulle's behavior, according to *Diaro de Noticias*. It was likely that this was the indirect way of the government of Antonio Salazar of pressing its annoyance with the allies' unsympathetic views of Portugal's colonial policies in Africa. Similarly, Canada, inhibited by French Quebec, attempted to behave as if nothing had happened. Belgium—and Germany as well—looked for hopeful signs in de Gaulle's recognition of the value of the treaty itself.

Once the decision was final the visibility of smaller nations was obvious. It was André de Staercke who chaired "les Quatorze" and who served as a liaison to France when the secretary-general felt himself unable to provide this function. With France absent from deliberations, the Defense Planning Committee created in 1963 became a vehicle not only for carrying on military affairs of the alliance but, under the chairmanship of the secretary-general, also for serving as the voice of the majority. The result was an enhanced role of civil officers over the military and an increased stature of smaller nations vis-à-vis the larger. Similarly, the establishment of the Nuclear Planning Group in 1967 brought nuclear problems under the wing of the secretary-general and as such narrowed the gap at least semantically between the United States and its allies. Conceivably, a better version of a multilateral force would emerge.

The most visible expression of a European entity, where smaller powers would be heard, was the EUROGROUP, formed in 1968 and consisting of all the European members except France. Its importance was expected to be twofold: it was to be a means for the coordination of defense efforts and a forum for harmonization of European views on major political or strategic questions affecting the defense of NATO Europe within the alliance framework.

Had France been present in these activities, the movement toward integrated efforts would not have taken place. Its momentum, however, was a product of some of the same spirit that permitted France's freedom to dissent: it was recognized that the Soviet menace, while still lively, had been tamed and that American participation, while still necessary for the security of Europe, could be reduced from its former significance.

Détente was not a code word for anti-Americanism, although understandable resentments would be aired under its rubric. The growing Common Market could see itself in the near future as an entity removed from the United States as from the Soviet Union. Some of its policies, notably its economic aims, were competitive with those of the United States. Britain's resolute decision to join the European Community and France's willingness in the post–de Gaulle era to accept Britain in 1973 were evidence of a new European spirit that inevitably would be pitted against the Atlantic or American ties. After 20 years none of the allies, including France, had been willing to accept the invitation of Article 13 of the treaty and give a notice of denunciation to the United States, yet all would share in one fashion or another a wish to denounce one aspect or another of the American connection. Witness Pierre Trudeau's Canada striving to reduce the NATO commitment because of its function as an instrument for exploiting its North American neighbor; or Turkey's nursing a continuing grudge over President Johnson's threat in 1964 to cut off aid if American equipment were used for Turkish intervention in Cyprus. Witness also Brandt's Germany wishing to reshape its future by making a special relationship with East Germany and by coming to terms with its eastern boundaries irrespective of American concerns.

The key to the allies' behavior was not simply rejection of American tutelage. Rather, it was the opportunity that détente offered Europe. The fact that relaxation from tensions in Europe coincided with the rise of tensions in Asia, generated by the American war in Vietnam, simply made a European initiative in NATO all the more imperative. American leadership could not suffice alone, if at all. The Harmel Report, with its leadership from the smaller countries of NATO, was a fitting symbol of the direction the allies, including the French, desired. Like the report of the Committee of Three in 1956, it called for greater political consultation among the allies, but this was not its thrust. Nor was its specific listing of defense problems in exposed areas such as the Mediterranean flank its significant component. It was "an active pursuit" of an effective détente, to be made firm by steps toward disarmament and balanced force reductions.[23]

This resolution dominated NATO councils over the next half dozen years. It was reinforced by the "Reykjavik signal,"[24] a declaration for mutual and balanced force reductions, and translated into action by a spate of confidence-building measures taken with the Warsaw Pact bloc. The results were considerable. In August 1970 the Federal Republic signed a treaty with the Soviet Union recognizing the Oder-Neisse frontier between Poland and East Germany, followed by a treaty with Poland itself. The United States did not lag behind in the movement toward détente. An Antiballistic Missile Treaty and a Strategic Arms Limitations Talks (START) agreement were signed in 1972. But the apparent triumph of détente was the ongoing tasks on mutual and balanced force reductions (MBFR) held in Vienna beginning in 1973 and the Conference on Security and Cooperation in Europe (CSCE). The latter resulted in the apex of détente, the Helsinki Final Agreement of 1975, essentially a declaration of coexistence on the part of East and West, a mutual recognition of the lines of demarcation settled at Yalta.

Reasons for European enthusiasm for promoting détente were obvious: it would lessen the need for U.S. interference, it would minimize the threat of the Warsaw Pact, and it would, most importantly, bring long-term prospects of peace to countries that would be battlefields in war. For Germans, it was worth repressing the promises of Adenauer that NATO would bring reunification. *Ostpolitik* was the best that could be achieved, a normality that would establish a nexus of economic and cultural ties between East and West Germany that would render political separation less important. For France, détente perpetuated its freedom to separate itself from Europe or NATO as freely as under de Gaulle, but without generating the resentments he had raised. For Britain, as a new European nation, it provided affiliation with the EC to provide the prosperity that no "special relationship" with the United States had been able to bring.

But what of the United States? It collaborated in every phase of the changing posture of NATO, even at the expense of its authority in the alliance and even with the knowledge won by contests with the Soviet Union outside NATO, in Cuba and in the Middle East, that the Soviet Union had not accepted détente in the way America's European allies had assumed. The major explanation stems from the American involvement in the Vietnam War, and with it an understanding that its relative power in the world had diminished since the 1940s.

American decline was masked in the mid-1960s by an attitude prevalent in McNamara's Defense Department more than among Dean Rusk's diplomats: namely, de Gaulle's expulsion order had given the United States an opportunity to regroup and reshape American forces in Europe, to make them more cost-efficient. Waste and artificially high equipment costs in Europe were a chronic concern of the Pentagon in this period. But wittingly or otherwise, the underlying problem was the overextension of American commitments. Could the United States conduct a full-scale war in Asia while bearing the financial costs and provision of troops in Europe? The answers in part were to redeploy American troops from Germany as a cost-saving device and as a cautionary measure in the event of emergency in Vietnam. The parallel with French withdrawals of support in Europe for the sake of their Indochinese position in the 1950s was stark. Yet the United States could say that removal of 35,000 military personnel would not involve a lessening of its commitment to NATO. Even after the 24th Infantry Division was returned to the United States, at least one brigade would remain in Germany at all times.

These activities disturbed Europeans, particularly German leaders encountering American and British pressures for financial help to offset American foreign-exchange costs of its forces in Germany. Agreements were made that ameliorated the tensions, many of them hastily concocted and circuitous in their aims. For example, the German government agreed on 2 May 1967 to have the Bundesbank invest in a $500 million program of special medium-term U.S. government securities in lieu of paying directly for the costs of American troops in the Federal Republic. This arrangement earned the scorn of Senator Mike Mansfield, the majority leader, who felt that rather than bearing their fair share of expenses Germans would be winning new profits from their loans.[25] American demands for help did not abate; nor did their threats to reduce troops from Europe unless a fairer distribution of the burdens were made. In the next few years the Federal Republic, under duress, signed more direct offset accords. In 1971 a revised arrangement provided for over $2 billion in benefits to the United States, amid grumbling from Germany that the United States had undervalued the increasingly important military forces placed under NATO command over the past decade.

The issue was not efficiency or quality control. It was Vietnam. The war diverted American attention from Europe, identified Secretary of State Rusk with Asian, not European, affairs, led McNamara to resign his office over his disapproval of the course of that conflict, and ultimately drove President Johnson from the White House in 1968. Europe became a lesser theater as Asian concerns predominated. When NATO did surface as an issue in the late 1960s, it appeared as an irritant both because of Europe's ostentatious lack of support for the U.S. efforts in Vietnam and because it demanded of the United States far more money and manpower than the alliance seemed worth at the time. The annoyance and willingness to act on it were exacerbated by relative Soviet passivity, by its obvious wish for accommodation and détente. But outside the Six-Day War of 1967 between Israel and its Arab neighbors, which was not of Soviet making directly, the Warsaw Pact did little to take advantage of America's problems in Asia by initiating crises in Europe.

Perhaps the Soviets did not need to act. Vietnam's effect on European relations was dramatically exhibited in a series of resolutions offered by Senator Mansfield as early as 1966 and reaching a climax in 1971. They called for massive troop cutbacks of U.S. military personnel assigned to NATO defense duties in Europe. The reasons were clearly presented as the excessive costs of American involvement in NATO as a consequence of the war in Vietnam and the changed conditions in Europe, which made a high level of troop force unnecessary. In short, Vietnam was a factor in American interest in détente.

THE NIXON DOCTRINE OF 1969

The advent of Richard Nixon to the presidency in 1969 was the occasion for reconceptualizing America's role in the world—something that the preoccupation with the Vietnam War had prevented earlier. As the prime mover in European—and other—affairs in the Nixon administration, Henry A. Kissinger functioned first and primarily as adviser for National Security. He used the National Security Council much as McNamara had used the Pentagon or Dulles the State Department, as a pied-à-terre for affecting policy in all parts of government. Until Kissinger was appointed secretary of state in 1973, that office was less visible under Secretary William Rogers in NATO issues than it had been under Rusk. Kissinger, a Harvard professor and Nelson Rockefeller's protégé, had been in and out of government since the appearance of his influential *Nuclear Weapons and Foreign Policy* in 1957. As a scholar with a European background, he had both a sense of history and a particular understanding of Europe to shape his weltanschauung. In 1969, despite their differences in background, he and Nixon made an effective team. They recognized the need to end the war in Vietnam and the limitations in American power that this recognition entailed, and they wished to do so without destroying the credibility of American leadership in Europe or unleashing neoisolationism at home. With Metternich—the subject of his doctoral dissertation—as one source of inspiration, Kissinger wished not to restore the Pax Americana of the postwar world but to use the still vast American power shrewdly, amorally, and secretively if necessary to bring a better order to the world.

His answer with respect to Europe was expressed in the Nixon Doctrine, the first major revision of the Truman Doctrine in almost a generation. Containment was redefined. On the one hand, it was to reflect an idea raised by the British historian Denis Brogan during the Korean War:[26] namely, that there were limits to American power and that the way to success lay in the realignment of objectives to resources. The failure of American policy in Vietnam in a war that made a mockery of containment was the price of ignoring this wisdom. Rather than be comforted by American backing of allies in Vietnam, Europeans were appalled over American errors in judgment and alarmed over the resulting drain on its energies. The Nixon Doctrine would retreat from limitless support of anticommunist regimes everywhere.

On the other hand, the United States would identify priorities of attention, assuming that some parts of the world were of greater concern than others. If southeast Asia was placed in a lower category of priority, there would be justification for American involvement. This would not be translated into precipitate abandonment of commitments. America's blessings and some material support would continue. But the message was that the South Vietnamese would have the primary responsibility of defending themselves. Kissinger, in an important article in *Foreign Affairs*, published in 1969 and written just before he entered government service, mingled "Vietnamization" with what was to be the Nixon Doctrine. The president himself gave his imprimatur during a visit to Guam in the spring of that year.[27]

Whether the Nixon Doctrine was conceived primarily as an artful device to extract the United States from the Vietnamese morass, from accepting defeat without having to confess to it, is immaterial to the NATO scene. The ending of a divisive war and the establishing of Europe as the first priority should have been welcomed in the alliance. It was Nixon's answer to much of the criticism emanating from the alliance in the 1960s about lack of consultation by the United States. Presidential candidate Nixon had lashed out at the Johnson administration the year before for ignoring NATO, particularly for making no mention of it in his State of the Union of 1968. According to Nixon, "Actions have been taken by the United States which vitally affected the security of our European partners, without even the courtesy of prior consultation. It's time we began paying Europe more attention. And if our ideals of Atlantic independence are to mean anything in practice, it's time we began lecturing our European partners less and listening to them more."[28]

As president, Nixon made a point of visiting Europe a month after his inauguration to dramatize his desire for "genuine consultation." In a speech before the North Atlantic Council he informed a responsive audience that the cold war, "the era of confrontation," was in the past and that an "era of negotiation" had taken its place.[29] His pledge, it seemed, applied to relations within the alliance as well as with the Warsaw bloc.

Kissinger participated fully in this spirit. He had written widely on European affairs, most notably in his book *Troubled Partnership* (1965). He even displayed considerable understanding for Gaullist sentiments as he urged the United States to accept the full implications of an equal partnership. His aim, however, was not to accept Gaullist nationalism but the equally daunting challenges implicit in a supranational Europe.

After the neglect of the Johnson years, Europe seemed to have found sensitive and supportive friends in Washington. Repeatedly over the next two years the Nixon administration gave assurances of its concern for Europe in ways that should have melted even the most suspicious allies. The handling of the vexing Mansfield resolutions that emanated annually from the Senate since 1966 was more vigorous than under his predecessor. Substantial reductions of American forces stationed in Europe gathered more advocates as resentment built in the United States against the Vietnam War and against the large dollar gap in foreign exchange, $1.5 billion a year that the half million personnel in Europe cost the United States. The intent of the resolutions was to induce the allies to make greater contributions to NATO. It was not a criticism of the NATO structure itself, Mansfield claimed. He was convinced that the size of the American contribution could be pared "without adversely affecting either our resolve or ability to meet our commitment under the North Atlantic Treaty."[30]

Nixon held firm against any reductions. His arguments were cogent, certainly from a European perspective. Any unilateral withdrawal of forces would create an imbalance in Europe that risked Soviet adventures there and would undermine the deterrent that had kept the peace for a generation. America's credibility too was at stake. Such action could trigger a neo-isolationist reaction in the United States. Withdrawing troops from Europe, despite every assurance, would be seen as a consequence of withdrawals from Asia. The precedent in one continent could be applied to another.

The Senate response in 1971 was to mount the strongest attack on troop policy since the Vietnam War began. And the issue was not simply that a dollar gap was excessive, or that European economies could provide more funds, or that NATO's stability would not be damaged. It related more to domestic anger over the "imperial presidency" as the Congress attempted to restrict presidential prerogatives on the use of troops in Cambodia or in Southeast Asia generally. Europe would not be exempted. The spirit that animated senators Taft or Bricker when they opposed the dispatch of troops dwelled in the Democratic—and Republican—opposition to Nixon's long, circuitous, and duplicitous disengagement from Vietnam.

Senator Mansfield proposed an amendment to a bill in 1971 extending the Selective Service Act that would require U.S. forces in Europe to be halved to 150,000 men. Given the widespread popular support it enjoyed, the administration was forced to mobilize the NATO's American friends, including former SACEURs Gruenther, Norstad, and Lemnitzer, along with such prominent Democrats as former Secretary of State Acheson and Under Secretary of State Ball, to oppose the Mansfield Plan. Even former president Johnson was recruited for the full-page advertisement in the *New York Times*[31] warning the nation of the dire consequences for the alliance if American troop strength in Europe were cut back so drastically.

At the same time the administration was beating back this most dangerous assault on its European policy, Nixon and Kissinger were helping Europe more subtly by averting their eyes from activities that in the past would have elicited loud positive or negative responses. French critic Raymond Aron noted approvingly "the ostentatious silence"[32] of Americans when Britain maneuvered—this time successfully—to enter the Common Market in 1973. Moreover, the United States chose not to articulate its uneasiness about the *Ostpolitik* of Chancellor Willy Brandt despite doubts about the terms the Warsaw bloc would demand in return for improved relations with East Germany. This decent respect for Europe's sensibilities seemed to fulfill the promise of the Nixon Doctrine to treat as equals, not as minions, the European partners as they pursued their special interests.

1973—"THE YEAR OF EUROPE"

For all his circumspection President Nixon earned little credit and less thanks from his European partners. Perhaps he brought too much baggage from the past with him into the White House. The image of Nixon, the McCarthyite hatchetman of the Eisenhower administration, was not easily dimmed. Europeans looked for angles in his Nixon Doctrine that would expose his benevolence toward Europe as a fraud.

Implicit in its projection was a détente with the Soviet Union, a relationship the European allies had been working toward for years. But under the Nixon-Kissinger tutelage it became an object of suspicion. Détente for Americans, Europeans feared, was essentially a confession of weakness, no matter how elaborately Kissinger might proclaim its relativity. When the presidential adviser spoke of multipolarity replacing bipolarity, this was not an awakening of American sensitivity to a changed world but another justification for abandoning the American commitment in Vietnam. By extension, an American détente with the Soviet Union might include the abandonment of Europe as well as Southeast Asia. The newfound respect for a European entity might be an approach to the "Europeanization" of NATO's defense of the West, parallel to the "Vietnamization" of the war in Asia. To build its new "structure for peace," America might sacrifice the interests of its European allies. Such were the fears that emerged from European suspicions about American foreign policy.

If the limits of American power impelled the United States into negotiations with the Soviet Union, bilateral results could be dangerous to European interests. Hence, mutual restraints on the part of the superpowers effected through antiballistic or Strategic Arms Limitation Talks (SALT) agreements could mean that the United States was seeking to protect itself from the potential enemy while leaving its allies exposed. De Gaulle may have departed from the scene in the 1970s, but his assertion that America would not sacrifice its security for the sake of Europe's was given new currency by the Nixon Doctrine. The American call for Europeans to do more for themselves seemed to have stemmed less from a respect for equality than for a barely repressed desire to minimize American responsibilities from commitments abroad.

The Nixon Doctrine was seen as a sinister way of making a virtue out of weakness, by retaining leadership and at the same time reducing obligations, or reassigning them. "Its purpose," in the words of James Chace and Earl Ravenel, "was to assuage domestic opposition to costly interventionist wars through a limited military retrenchment, yet at the same time remain politically engaged throughout the globe."[33] From this skeptical angle of observation, Nixon's visits to Moscow for the signing of arms limitation agreements in 1972, or his even more striking visit to the People's Republic of China that same year, symbolized more than a new American flexibility; it concealed a loss of confidence that could seriously damage NATO's sense of security.

The SALT I negotiations in particular were a matter of some anxiety for the European allies. While the substance of the talks devolved on the limitations of strategic weapons that could hit either the Soviet Union or the United States, the definition of which weapons were strategic affected the allies directly. The Soviet interpretation would identify tactical nuclear aircraft in NATO as strategic weapons, while IRBMs and MBRMs located in the Soviet Union would be excluded from this category, and hence unregulated. The Soviet IRBMs were obviously a threat to Europe, and the Soviet success in relabelling tactical weapons as strategic was bound to generate friction between America and Europe. The United States would be seen once again making bilateral arrangements with the other superpower to protect itself at the expense of its allies.

Europeans could point to other actions to sustain their judgments of the untrustworthiness of the Nixon administration. At the very time it was congratulating itself over turning back congressional attacks on U.S. troop assignments in Europe, and over its quiet backing of *Ostpolitik* and European unity, the administration turned a hostile eye on the activity of the enlarged Common Market. While giving formal endorsement to unification as it had for a generation, the genuine prospect of an active competitor in a united Europe, particularly as Britain, Denmark, and Ireland joined the Inner Six, had a frightening aspect. The flattering image of a United States of Europe in the American model always had a dark side; there was always a hidden fear in every administration that the American Frankenstein would create a monster he could not control. As an economic study noted, "In the long run we could be confronted by an 'expanded Europe' that . . . will account for about half of world trade, compared with our 15%; it would hold monetary reserves approaching twice our own; and it will even be able to outvote us constantly in the international economic organizations."[34]

There followed charges that Europeans, with their preferential trade agreements, constituted an economic rival that would beggar the American producer. Their behavior was all the more offensive when it accompanied an American dollar weakened in part by the drain of the Asian war that Europeans did not support. Worse still, the dollar gap in exports could be blamed on the expenses the United States continued to bear on behalf of ungrateful Europeans. While the administration did not follow the advice of one government official who wished to bring home 20,000 troops from Europe for every Florida or California citrus grower "put out of business by Common Market policies,"[35] Nixon did follow the advice of Secretary of the Treasury John Connally and suspended the convertibility of the dollar in 1971. A 10 percent surcharge was imposed on all imports. The resulting devaluation of the dollar had an immediate and harmful effect on the European allies. Aside from the damage to their economies, the unilateral action seemed to expose the hollowness of the administration's proallied sympathies.

Actually, the Connally initiative was short-lived. An agreement signed at the Smithsonian Institution in Washington later that year created a floating exchange rate that helped to restore a temporary equilibrium to a monetary system that depended on the stability of the dollar. The surcharge was lifted. American troop levels abroad were not lowered. Yet considerable psychological damage had been done. At the beginning of the second term, Nixon's doctrine was less credible in the eyes of Europeans that it had been four years before.

It was obvious, if ironic, that there was greater need for repair of linkages within NATO in 1973 than there was between the United States and the Soviet Union. To meet this problem as squarely as possible the president determined to express his concern by at least a rhetorical gesture: 1973 would be "the Year of Europe" in American foreign policy, as he called it in a January news conference. Secretary of State Kissinger intended to highlight Europe in the "year" with a proposal in April for a new Atlantic Charter, a rededication of the Atlantic Alliance. Phrases such as a "fresh act of creation" and "a revitalized Atlantic partnership" punctuated his speech.[36]

Europe's reaction was cynical. Kissinger's grand speech on 23 April was made as the Watergate disclosures were beginning to shake the underpinnings of the Nixon administration. In mid-April the president was forced to dismiss his key aides, H. R. Haldeman and John Erlichman, leaving Kissinger in an even more prominent role than he had occupied before. Was the Atlantic Charter then a diversive act to push aside the ongoing Watergate follies, or was it an attempt, as Richard Barnet suggests,[37] on the part of the presidential adviser to establish himself as the George Marshall of the 1970s? Did he intend to cast himself as an FDR or Churchill, authors of an earlier Atlantic Charter in 1941?

Despite Kissinger's professed intentions, the proposal was awkwardly managed. His overtures contained many of the elements that had contributed to European suspicions from the beginning of the administration. The speech had been made without sufficient consultation at home or abroad. Delivering it from New York was one measure of the problem. More critical was the message itself: "The United States has global interests and responsibilities.

Our European allies have regional interests." The style has been character-ized as "the royal-court model of foreign policy making," and it could only grate on European sensibilities.[38] The language and tone accentuated the separation of America and Europe and, by implication, the new bilateral relationship between the United States and the Soviet union.

Not all the difficulties arising from this speech derived from Kissinger's lordly manner of presentation or from the seeming arrogance of his assump-tions. Some of them were the by-product of Europe's own aspirations and pretensions. With the United Kingdom as a member the newly expanded European Community achieved a growth and a confidence that encouraged once again a European entity to think of itself as an equal, if not superior, partner to the United States, much as the Western Union had wished in 1949 or the Council of Europe had sought in succeeding years. With the Nixon administration in disarray, the importance of European unity was never greater. Kissinger took for granted that Europe indeed might be ready to take care of itself; greater burden sharing was a vital aspect of his design, particularly as American balance-of-payments problems continued. Wishful thinking on both sides of the Atlantic exaggerated the reality of European unity. President Nixon specifically referred to it in his State of the World Address in May.[39]

Superficially, projection of a new Europe was not unreasonable. Its appearance was impressive. The population of the Europe of Nine was 260 million in 1973, as opposed to 210 million in the United States, and 249 million in the Soviet Union. The community's gross national product in that year was almost twice that of the Soviet Union and was only 20 percent less than that of the United States. But figures did not tell the whole story. There still was no United States of Europe, and there was little prospect for such organized community in the foreseeable future. There was no method for Europeans in 1973 to raise their own troop levels, to exact taxes, or to develop a credible nuclear force on their own in the manner of the United States of America. The role of the NATO superpower was still vital, for the alliance's well-being in general and for the achievement of such pressing objectives as the MBFR in particular. As long as Europe's defense rested on the flexible response doctrine that NATO had accepted, no matter how reluctantly, in 1967, the allies remained dependent on American nuclear protection.

So while they chafed at the condescension of "the Year of Europe," the allies stances in the North Atlantic Council meetings reflected swallowed pride. Attention was paid to steps toward détente. SALT I may have created uneasiness, but at Copenhagen in June 1973 the ministers expressed hope that SALT II might address their grievances. They even gave some obei-sance to "the Year of Europe." Watered down though the effort was, one might recognize its presence in a reaffirmation "of the principles and objec-tives of the Alliance established a quarter of a century ago." It was coupled, however, not with a rededication to greater financial obligations toward defense but with an exhortation for greater efforts at improving East-West relations.[40] But communiqués could only smooth over, not dispel, the mood of suspicion that hung over the alliance in "the Year of Europe."

Grievances on both sides ultimately burst into the open over an out-of-area issue, the Arab-Israeli War of October 1973. As in 1956, the Middle East, rather than an internal problem or an action on the part of the Soviet bloc, triggered destructive centrifugal movement that split the alliance. Former Assistant Secretary of State Eugene V. Rostow called the Arab assault on Israel "the most basic thrust against the Atlantic alliance since 1945, far more serious than earlier crises over peripheral points like Cuba, Berlin, and Korea."[41] Whether Rostow had unfairly trivialized the Berlin crises, or whether the Soviets really intended to use the war to outflank allied forces in Central Europe and drive the United States out of the Mediterranean, is arguable. What is beyond question is American anger at Europe's distancing itself from its NATO ally. The Arab attack initially inspired an "arm's-length" position toward the war on the part of Britain and France, according to President Nixon.[42] When American military aid was rushed to the scene, the NATO partners, with the reluctant exception of Portugal, denied the use of their territories or air space for the resupply of Israeli forces. While there was no obligation to provide stopping off points for transshipment of supplies, as Portugal did with the Azores, Europe's hostility to America's role in this crisis had emotional and political undertones in NATO more significant than a pro-Arab bias.

The latter was certainly a factor, as so many NATO members carefully nurtured their special relations with Arab powers: France with Algeria, Greece with Egypt, Italy with Libya. Support for the Palestinian cause was a cheap price to pay for economic benefits the Arab connections supplied. Their economies were dependent on secure access to Middle Eastern oil in a way that Americans could not appreciate properly. While the North Atlantic Council could not express this sentiment adequately, the EC, where the NATO partners comprised the dominant majority, issued a communiqué of its own in the midst of the war endorsing the Arab interpretation of U.N. Security Council Resolution 242 of 1967. In effect it endorsed Egypt's and Syria's concerted attack on Israel.

A deeper political issue was also at work. America's support of Israel was seen as a frightening example of disregard for European interests and sensibilities. Europeans blamed the higher value that the administration placed on domestic politics at the expense of their own vital interests and convinced themselves that American softness toward Israel was responsible for the turmoil in the Middle East. The October war, as Kissinger observed, released the allies from restraints that had prevented them earlier from venting their frustrations with American leadership over their inferior position.[43]

It was hardly surprising that this attitude received scant sympathy from most Americans. According to Irving Kristol, "the plain fact was that the United States found itself on the brink of a confrontation with the Soviet Union, and in this circumstance our European allies deserted us."[44] Congress was not slow in making its resentment heard, through the Jackson-Nunn amendment, a rider to a vital military appropriations bill. Public Law 93-155, sec. 812, which required the president to reduce U.S. forces in Europe by the same percentage as Europeans, failed to offset costs in the balance of payments of American troops in Europe for fiscal year 1974.[45] Once again an out-of-area conflict, the Middle East in place of Southeast Asia, provoked retaliatory acts on Europe. The president underscored the national feelings when he asserted in March 1974 that "the Europeans cannot have it both ways. They cannot have United States cooperation on the security front and proceed to have confrontation and even hostility on the economic and political fronts."[46]

Small wonder that as the twenty-fifth anniversary of the alliance approached predictions of an early demise surfaced again. A Gallup poll revealed that internationalist views in 1974 had reached the lowest figure since 1945. Only 48 percent of those polled approved the use of force to help Western Europe in a crisis. Another measure of the alliance's distress was the reluctant equality the official NATO Review gave to the "Downs" in an essay on "Twenty-Five Years of Ups and Downs." Still, the editor remembered that NATO was always in one state of distress or another and that if it survived the rancor of the Suez crisis, the shock of the Berlin Wall, or the high tension accompanying de Gaulle's expulsion order, it would also outlive the Arab-Israeli war of 1973. Neither détente nor the Nixon Doctrine had run its course.[47]

chapter 7

THE DUAL-TRACK DECISION: NEW ARMS AND ARMS CONTROL, 1974–1983

The Middle East crisis of 1973 was only one of many sharp blows against NATO's solidarity in the 1970s. It was followed a year later by a crisis of confidence over Portugal, particularly on the part of the United States, as the Salazar legacy was cast aside and Communists joined a new leftist government. There was another crisis over Cyprus involving the overthrow of Greece's "colonels," a Turkish occupation of two-fifths of the island, and the withdrawal of Greece from SHAPE from 1974 to 1980. The only apparent consistent pattern in the turmoil of the eastern Mediterranean was the anger of both Greeks and Turks against the United States. "Out-of-area" issues would continue to poison intra-alliance relations as Americans and Europeans took differing positions over the Soviet invasion of Afghanistan in 1979, the Argentine-British war over the Falkland Islands in 1982, and the Reagan administration's general Latin American policy throughout this period.

Even more unsettling were the European-American conflicts over the Soviet arms buildup in the 1970s: how to identify it, what steps to take, and whether détente could still be salvaged. No American president satisfied the NATO allies, although the American supreme allied commanders in Europe, Andrew Goodpaster, Alexander Haig, and Bernard Rogers, were well received by their European partners. Haig, like Norstad and Eisenhower before him, was considered a spokesman for European concerns. But the presidents were either too weak, as in the case of Gerald Ford, Nixon's successor after Watergate, or too volatile, as in the case of Jimmy Carter, who seemed to veer from extreme accommodation to the Soviets to extreme hostility, or too bellicose, as in the case of Ronald Reagan, whose rhetoric as much as his ideology seemed to promote a new cold war in which arms control and détente played little or no role.

Yet the alliance persevered. The dual-track decision of 1979 taken by the North Atlantic Council symbolized the compromise that kept NATO intact. The rising Soviet missile threat would be met with rising Western military budgets and, more dramatically, by the acceptance of 572 cruise and Pershing II missiles on the territory of five NATO nations. If this sounded like recurrence of the cold war at a heightened level of competition, it was to be modified by what the council called a "wide range of initiatives particularly in the fields of confidence-building and arms control designed to improve mutual security and cooperation in Europe."[1] This decision had consequences that reverberated into the mid-1980s. 1983 was itself a year of decision, as the Soviet Union walked out of arms talks in Geneva to protest the final implementation of the deployment of missiles in Germany, Italy, and the United Kingdom. The fate of the alliance once again seemed to be at stake.

CENTRIPETAL FORCES, 1973–1975

The unifying element in the "West-West" relationship was the wish on both sides of the Atlantic as well as on the other side of the Iron Curtain to maintain the momentum for détente. It would be an error to regard accommodation with the Soviet Union, the deescalation of tensions, and the drive for new economic links with the Warsaw bloc to be exclusively the preoccupation of the European partners in this period. The United States in 1974, increasingly under Kissinger's management of foreign affairs after Nixon wilted under Watergate's dominance over America's domestic scene, needed normalization of relations with the Soviet Union as urgently as the Europeans. So did the Soviet Union for its own reasons. Its expectations of the West's legitimizing Communist control of Eastern Europe and a full recognition of the German Democratic Republic, along with an increasing appetite for Western manufactures and American foodstuffs, yielded harmonies in East-West and West-West relations that had not been visible since the end of World War II.

For Kissinger, the mood fitted a major premise of the Nixon Doctrine: namely, that there were limits to American power. As Nixon faltered, these constraints were more evident. The nation had to face the fact that American invulnerability had ended, that the Soviet Union was a superpower with nuclear potential equal to that of the United States. This understanding underlay the behavior of the State Department's major Soviet specialist, Helmut Sonnenfeldt, who recognized the importance of tying the Soviet Union into a balance-of-power system rather than banishing it beyond a diplomatic pale. While the secretary of state never altered his perception of the Soviets as ideological adversaries, he was convinced that

"Soviet ideological hostility translated itself into geopolitical rivalry in the manner of a traditional great power." Differences between the past and present in the game of power politics stemmed from the power of nuclear weapons, which forced the Soviet Union to become "in a sense a partner in the avoidance of nuclear war—a moral political, and strategic imperative."[2]

Under these compelling circumstances the idea of "linkage" became an attractive alternative to confrontation. Its workings were subtle. No specific trade-offs were necessary. Building economic dependence that would flow from trading patterns could both tame the Soviet menace and render unnecessary an American or NATO arms buildup. Détente was the key to a new relationship that had its roots in presidential weakness stemming from the Vietnam War.

European distrust of Kissinger's motives in seeking détente persisted, particularly over a reduction in arms competition that might serve the superpowers at the expense of the Europeans. Yet the larger purposes were fully compatible: a world with a stability that the cold war could never provide. NATO partners could press in concert for the MBFR program that had been inspired by the Harmel Report of 1967. The North Atlantic Council meeting at Reykjavik in June 1968 formally adopted a declaration agreeing "that it was desirable that a process leading to mutual force reductions should be initiated" and called on "the Soviet Union and other countries of Eastern European . . . to join in this search for progress toward peace."[3] The MBFR offer was repeated at the North Atlantic Council meeting in Rome in 1970 with a new urgency; a mutual and balanced reduction of forces served as a device, according to Secretary-General Brosio, "to put a brake on a unilateral American decision" to reduce its troop force.[4] The pressure of the Vietnam War and Senator Mansfield's demands for U.S. troop withdrawals on the one side and the broad spirit of *Ostpolitik* on the other provided a centripetal force in the West.

The Soviets were less interested. Lip service was given to the principles in Leonid Brezhnev's address to the Congress of the Communist party in March 1971, but the emphasis in Rome on adequate verification and controls to ensure the observance of agreements on MBFR as well as the inclusion among the desired reductions of "stationed and indigenous forces and their weapons systems" were not welcome in Warsaw Pact councils.[5] It required President Nixon's personal diplomacy during his visit to Moscow in 1972 to extract an agreement to negotiate. The proceedings finally opened in Vienna on 30 October 1973.

Soviet reluctance to negotiate may have been based on its standing objective to have any reduction of NATO force levels equated with the removal of U.S. forces entirely from Europe. Ideally, the Russians preferred to deal with "Europeans" only, not as a NATO bloc but as individual nations sharing with them the European continent. By consenting to meet in Vienna in

1973, they temporarily gave up their intention to exclude the United States from the negotiations or to exclude NATO as a bargaining agent.

Opportunities to divide the allies, however, were still present. Alistair Buchan, an authoritative British analyst of NATO affairs in this period, remained suspicious that the MBFR would be a mask for American appeasement of Senator Mansfield, a cover for dangerous unilateral reductions of American troop strength in Europe.[6] The Soviets helped to foster this line of thought by removing whenever possible "balanced" from its publicity on the MBFR.

Although these concerns receded as the decade advanced, there was little progress in the Vienna talks until the cold war had come to an end. From the Western perspective a basic problem with the MBFR negotiations was the virtual impossibility of genuine parity. As with SALT, discussions began with an assumption of Warsaw Pact superiority in conventional capabilities in Europe. The problem of parity was further complicated by the geographical proximity of the Soviet Union to Central Europe compared with the distance of the American forces from their home base. The size of force reductions must be measured against the overall capability of each side when the cut is complete. As proposed by the Soviets in 1974, the initial reduction of 20,000 by each side would increase the relative superiority of the Warsaw Pact forces in the central sector. Even as this proposal was rejected out of hand, there remained the question of whether the initial NATO proposal of a 30,000 troop reduction for the United States versus a 70,000 for the Soviet Union would have achieved parity. Reduced numbers, even when substantially greater for the Eastern bloc, would be irrelevant if they did not touch the Soviet elite combat forces employed near the West German border. How to affect the Soviet capacity to initiate an attack with little or no warning was the problem disturbing NATO planners throughout the decade and was the substance of an influential report of Senators Sam Nunn and Dewey Bartlett to the Armed Services Committee in January 1977.[7]

Similar disillusionment followed the other major NATO initiatives that emerged from the Harmel Report: the Helsinki Final Agreement of 1975. It was the result of negotiations at the Conference on Security and Cooperation in Europe (CSCE) that were of much greater importance to the Soviets than the MBFR talks. It is worth noting that the talks in Helsinki began concurrently with those in Vienna, but the Helsinki negotiations ended with agreements ratified by both blocs in a relatively short time while the meetings in Vienna yielded one unproductive round after another. So anxious were the Soviets to convene the CSCE that the agreement to meet in Vienna appeared in retrospect to have been an exchange for Western agreement to a meeting of the CSCE.

The reason for such enthusiasm in the Warsaw bloc was the opportunity it found in the Helsinki accords to legitimize Soviet control of Eastern

Europe. In Helsinki 35 countries accepted the postwar boundaries, including East Germany's, as permanent. In exchange the Soviets allowed such issues as freedom of movement and freedom of information to be included in the Final Agreement. Such a happy event should have pushed aside memories of Soviet repression summoned by the Brezhnev Doctrine in Czechoslovakia in 1968 that hung over East-West relations or by burden-sharing quarrels highlighted in the Mansfield amendments that divided the NATO allies. Détente in Europe seemed to have been achieved.

DISILLUSIONMENT WITH DÉTENTE

No such state of balance or relief from tensions actually was realized in the mid-1970s. Instead, détente became an albatross around Kissinger's neck, as its effects appeared to benefit the East at the expense of the West. Less than a year after the Helsinki accords had been signed the idea of détente had become an obstacle to President Gerald Ford's campaign for Republican nomination in 1976. For Kissinger it became a symbol of how far he had fallen in popular esteem from his moments of national glamour. For a time, in the last months before Nixon fled from Washington in disgrace in the summer of 1974, one step ahead of impeachment, and in the first year of Ford's administration, the secretary of state was the most significant figure in government, speaking abroad with authority and holding off congressional assault on executive power by virtue of his popularity. This was the period when his shuttle diplomacy in the Middle East had extracted as much a victory for American influence as could be expected under adverse circumstances. President Ford, a lackluster Michigan congressman, earnest and honest, was catapulted into the vice presidency and presidency without benefit of electoral provenance. Untutored in foreign affairs, Ford placed the management of foreign relations entirely in the hands of his secretary of state and adviser for national security.

Kissinger's descent from Olympus was rapid. It was also probably inevitable. Vietnam damaged him as it damaged every other leader connected with that debacle. Nobel Peace Prize notwithstanding, Kissinger shared blame not only for the widening of that war but also for the deceptions that accompanied it and for the ultimate collapse of South Vietnam itself in 1975. But even without the Vietnam factor, lesions within NATO were spreading virulently, with immediate effect on the secretary of state. The Mediterranean sector was a proximate cause of difficulty both in the East and West. The long-standing struggle between Greece and Turkey over Cyprus erupted again in 1974, earning the United States the anger of both parties. The crisis was precipitated when the military regime in Athens conspired to oust the independent Makarios III from the presidency of Cyprus, presumably for his lack of concern for enosis (incorporation of Cyprus with Greece). Worldwide condemnation of the new outlaw regime in Cyprus induced Turkey to send troops in July 1974 to protect the Turkish minority. The result was Turkish occupation of 40 percent of the island, Greek over-throw of the "colonels," and the anger of both Greeks and Turks against Kissinger.

The new democratic regime of Constantine Karamanlis blamed Americans both for the sustenance to the overthrown dictatorship in the past and for its acceptance of Turkish military actions in Cyprus. The result was withdrawal of Greece in the manner of France from the NATO military command, which was to remain in effect until 1980. Kissinger's reputation suffered, particularly at the hands of an articulate and aroused Greek lobby in Washington. Even without this influential constituency, a study mission examining conditions in Greece delivered in February 1974 what historian S. Victor Papacosma has called a report with "an ominous title."[8] "Controlling the Damage: U.S. Policy Options for Greece" concluded that U.S. policy had been faulty for the past half dozen years.

Kissinger fared little better with the presumably favored Turks. Under congressional pressure the United States placed an embargo on transfers of military equipment to Turkey, effective February 1975. This in turn resulted in Turkey's decision to suspend U.S. operations at U.S. military installations in Turkey. As election year approached, Turks and Greeks struck out at NATO and particularly at the United States when they could not reach each other. NATO suffered damage, as did Kissinger's reputation.

From the other end of the Mediterranean NATO faced a new worry as well as a new opportunity. Just three months before the Turkish invasion of Cyprus, a military coup in Portugal ended the Salazar dictatorship then under the control of his successor, Marcello Caetano. While the NATO for-eign ministers praised the return of democracy to Portugal at the council meeting in Ottawa in June, and its new foreign minister, Mario Soares, recip-rocated with a profession of "full loyalty and good faith,"[9] a sharp turn to the left disturbed all the partners. Communist influence seemed to predominate, just as "Euro-communism" in France and Italy was presenting a new and moderate face in those countries. Kissinger feared for the future of the south-ern flank and for NATO itself if Communist parties moved into govern-ments of allied powers. In his memoirs President Ford asked what would happen if Communists dominated a Portuguese or other NATO govern-ment. "How could the West share military secrets with them? What would happen if the Soviets won access to Portuguese airfields or naval bases?"[10] At the very least Portugal would have been removed from access to military secrets.

These possibilities did not occur, but while the Soviet Union never won port privileges in Portugal, its influence was visible in such former Portuguese territories as Angola and Mozambique. There the linkages of coexistence broke down in 1976. Détente did not encompass Soviet activity in the Third World, and the Ford-Kissinger administration looked with concern but without effect on Cuban surrogates in southwest Africa and on massive Soviet intervention in northeast Africa, as Somalia seemed to fall into the Communist camp.

Other problems Kissinger blamed not on the activities of the Warsaw bloc but on the behavior of Americans. The authority acquired by Congress in the wake of Watergate and the Vietnam War interfered with the delicate task of diplomacy as the secretary of state saw it. If "linkage" was a generalized way of restraining Soviet conduct for the sake of a global equilibrium, it was never claimed that trade itself would moderate Soviet conduct. But in the hands of zealous ideologues, such as Senator Henry Jackson, the liberalization of trade with the Soviet Union was tied, in the Jackson-Vanik amendment of 1974, to the emigration of Russian Jews. The issue touched, of course, the provisions of the Helsinki Agreement and exposed the hollowness of Soviet promises. It also exposed the weakness of the administration in posing an act, which no matter how well intentioned, had the effect of raising the charge of U.S. interference in Soviet domestic affairs. Worse still, it resulted in undoing the economic package worked out by the superpowers, ending links that had been an important part of Kissinger's structure for peace. Nor did the Jackson-Vanik amendment, linking U.S. trade with freedom of emigration, serve the cause of human rights. Jewish emigration visas were drastically reduced by 1975, and the Soviets could excuse their suppression of liberties on the grounds that the United States had reneged on its commitments.

All these perceived failures undermined the credibility of détente as well as the ability of Kissinger himself to develop his policies. Bowing to the antimilitary mood of Congress, the Nixon and Ford administrations presided over annual cuts in defense requests from 1969 to 1976 on the average of $6.7 billion a year and a decrease in the defense-spending percentage of the gross government expenditures from 40.8 percent in fiscal year 1970 to 24.3 percent in fiscal year 1977. In this context arms controls agreements with the Soviet Union in SALT I and II were defensive measures that not only recognized the inevitability of Soviet military equality but also the impossibility of winning Congress over to reverse the trend.

Against this tide the warnings of Senator Sam Nunn, who had toured NATO facilities, had little chance of being heeded. The increase of Soviet forces by five divisions in central Europe and the modernization of their tanks and tactical air forces suggested the superiority the Warsaw Pact enjoyed in conventional strength. As Nunn observed in the report *NATO and the New Soviet Threat* in January 1977, "Soviet forces deployed in Eastern Europe now possess the ability to launch a potentially devastating conventional attack in Central Europe with little warning."[11]

Even though Nunn's reports had little effect in the mid-1970s, the overall disaffection with the Kissinger stewardship became a powerful theme in the election campaign of 1976. From the left came charges of the amorality of the Kissinger policies in Greece, Vietnam, and even Helsinki. George Ball, a veteran of the Kennedy-Johnson years, damned the CSCE agreements as "capitulation," submission to the logic of the Brezhnev Doctrine.[12] Eastern Europe was turned over to communism with the blessing of the West. This theme was taken up by the right and became part of Governor Ronald Reagan's campaign for the Republican nomination in 1976. To cope with its emotional appeal, Ford distanced himself from Kissinger's authority by removing the National Security Council from his jurisdiction; then he distanced himself from détente. The word in fact disappeared. As Ford put it in a press conference on 1 March 1976 (not included in the *Public Papers of the President*), "détente" would be discarded. The French word was too imprecise to transmit its proper meaning. Three English words, "peace through strength," best described American policy.[13] Détente had been removed from the American lexicon. Or so it seemed in 1976.

THE CARTER APPROACH TO NATO

The disappearance of détente, however, did not lead to an immediate revival of the cold war. The national mood and the NATO mood both required continued searching for modes of coexistence with the East. Even though Kissinger had set himself up for a fall by overselling détente, its allure carried over into the election of 1976 and beyond. And while the European allies were suspicious of superpower deals in SALT negotiations against their interests and were concerned with communist tactics in Portugal, France, and Italy, they had no desire to revive the cold war. *Ostpolitik* was too important for Germans to abandon, and normalization of cultural relations with East Germany and economic relations with all of Eastern Europe hung on the survival of détente.

Despite attacks against Ford and Kissinger on grounds that they had weakened American and NATO defenses against the East, the Republican administration's foreign policy was criticized primarily for its disregard for and manipulation of Third World nations, such as Chile and Angola, and for a Nixonian dissembling that had discredited the administration of foreign affairs in general. The Reagan right had been turned back, but the liberal forces were even more vehement in their use of the secretary of state as a scapegoat. They too ignored his remarkable accomplishments and centered on his flaws.

The Carter campaign had successfully labeled Kissinger as a dangerous "Don Juan of international diplomacy," as Leslie Gelb has characterized him, or as "the cowboy who rides all alone into town," a term he incautiously applied to himself.[14] Rather than condemn détente, the new administration saw itself as better able to effect the purposes of coexistence than had its opponents. Its commitment to NATO was just as great as Nixon's or Ford's, and its commitment toward peace, to disarmament, to cooperation with and understanding of communism was far greater—in its own judgment.

As with every president, Carter entered office determined to distinguish himself from his predecessors, and immediately did so, if only by virtue of his personality. An outsider in the Democratic party, Jimmy Carter had won a reputation for honesty and efficiency as governor of Georgia. A born-again Christian, he was concerned with applying moral principles to government and to foreign relations, in a manner that would contrast sharply and painfully with Nixon or Kissinger. Equally important was his conception of a seamless world in which every issue and problem are interconnected. By its own example the United States would abstain from the conventional manipulation of power. Said Carter, "Our power is derived from a larger view of global change. Our policy is rooted in moral values which never change. Our power is designed to serve mankind."[15] This sweeping vision not only assumed the relaxation of tensions with the East but a normality between East and West that would permit East and West together to concentrate on the more pressing issues of nuclear armament and the poverty of the Third World.

How to translate this grand design into reality was another matter. Carter was an unknown quantity in 1977 to Americans as well as to Europeans—East and West. A successful peanut farmer, an engineer with an Annapolis background, he fitted into no mold beyond a vague American populism, and he probably would never have made his way to the White House had not the Vietnam War turned the nation against the establishment—the "best and the brightest" of both parties, the insiders who had governed America since World War II. Hard-working and intelligent, he was also obsessive about detail to a fault. As Richard Barnet described him, "He turned out to be a man who abounded in good qualities he could neither discipline nor integrate."[16]

If this description was valid in general, it seemed even more appropriate when applied to his management of foreign relations. This was an area in which he had little experience, beyond his exposure to the work of the Trilateral Commission, a linkage between North America, Western Europe, and Japan under the sponsorship of David Rockefeller. Organized in 1973, it was intended to bring together leading members of the academic, business, and government communities. Their assignment was to help the developed nations coordinate management of their interdependent market economies and, even more important, to revive global thinking among elites who had become jaded by the events of Vietnam, Watergate, and the resurgence of nationalism. Jimmy Carter was present as a southern representative and was sufficiently impressed to bring many of its members with him to Washington when he was elected president. The trilateralists were as significant as his fellow Georgians in White House circles even if they were not quite as visible.

It was through this connection that the establishment, seemingly at bay in the mid-1970s, dominated foreign policymaking once again. Cyrus Vance, the secretary of state, was not a clone of Dean Acheson; he was sensitive to the diffusion of power in the world, to the relative decline of American dominance in the 1970s, and to the destructiveness of nuclear weaponry in ways that would not have affected Acheson or Dulles in the formative years of NATO's history. Yet Vance was a product of the same tradition—a Yale-educated Wall Street lawyer with a patrician's sense of noblesse oblige that had made public service as a diplomat or as a member of the Trilateral Commission a patriotic duty. For all his Georgian independence of Democratic party regulars, Carter turned to Vance for guidance much as Truman did to Acheson, Eisenhower to Dulles, or Johnson to Rusk.

A similar evocation of tradition was reflected in the choice of Zbigniew Brzezinski as adviser for National Security. A Harvard-educated intellectual and professor of government at Columbia, he was Carter's personal teacher on the Trilateral Commission. An inventive and prolific scholar, Brzezinski was knowledgeable and articulate about the problems of a multipolar world. As a Polish émigré, he was also deeply involved in Eastern European concerns and spoke of the language of *Machtpolitik* in dealing with the Soviet Union. With his Ivy League academic home, his European background, and his ambitions to translate scholarship into diplomatic action, Brzezinski could not help but be compared with Kissinger. While he disavowed any intention of emulating Kissinger's accumulation of power and deplored his predecessor's secretive habits and imperious behavior, his career as an academic and his conduct in office, not to mention the slight but impressive foreign accent, identified him with his predecessor. There is no evidence from his oral or written commentaries that his ambitions were any less exalted than Kissinger's. Where the difference lay was in part in his excessively flexible framework of ideas about foreign policy and in his difficulty in coping with the many constituencies that Kissinger's charm had won over. His historical reputation may be that of a Kissinger manqué.

Many of the difficulties Vance and Brzezinski encountered over the next four years emerged not from their weaknesses but from the character of the president. The buck indeed did stop at the desk in the Oval Office. Vance presented a program that emphasized the rule of law, the limitations of military power, and the centrality of arms reductions on the agenda of the Carter administration. The emphasis on the Third World as symbolized by Andrew Young's views as U.S. ambassador to the United Nations would be in sympathy with the emerging nationalism and not based on the assumption that there was a hidden Soviet hand in every contretemps in the world. While Brzezinski often seemed to share these positions, his figurative body language spoke of traditional power relationships and reflected a deep suspicion of the Soviet Union's objectives everywhere. The result was conflict—hardly surprising under any circumstance—between the national security adviser and the secretary of state. Given the personal interest of Presidents Kennedy and Nixon in foreign affairs, this conflict—structural or ideological—did not produce major problems. Nor did it in the administrations of Presidents Truman and Eisenhower, who clearly designated a single preeminent figure as their spokesmen for foreign affairs. In President Carter's case, his own disposition to be involved in all aspects of government, combined with an inability to make firm decisions in favor of one or the other of his advisers, made for confusion about America's stance on NATO and the world.

Given the annoyance and occasional anger that Kissinger's manipulative policies toward Europe aroused among the allies, there should have been widespread rejoicing over a president who spoke of normality in relations with the Soviet Union even if he did not use the term "détente." His concern for North-South problems and for moral postures in international relations seemed to evoke the finest of American traditions, particularly in their contrast with the cynicism of the Nixon period. Perhaps in another time and in other circumstances this would have been the case. Carter was burdened by partners such as Valéry Giscard d'Estaing of France and Helmut Schmidt of Germany, who saw not the ideals but the inconsistent positions of his advisers and the distance between the pronouncements from the White House and the new awareness of Soviet military buildup in Europe.

COPING WITH SOVIET POWER

There was actually little change in the Soviet advances. There had been steady increases in forces in almost all levels, nuclear and conventional, since the humiliation suffered by Khrushchev over the Cuban missile crisis in 1962. While there were relatively few increases in the numbers of NATO forces, the number of Warsaw Pact forces rose dramatically. Particularly in the years 1971 to 1976, the period of least NATO activity, Soviet military spending increased by 4 percent to 5 percent annually in real terms.[17]

Reasons for passivity in response to this recognized challenge ranged from the Vietnam syndrome, in which Americans soured on military expectations, to restructuring of the ground forces in the interest of cost efficiency. The Nixon Doctrine and the thrust for détente that dominated NATO councils obscured the growing disparity in force levels between the Warsaw and NATO organizations. Only occasionally was concern openly manifested in the mid-1970s, and then it would come primarily from such senatorial examinations as that of Senator Nunn, who warned in 1974 of the destabilizing effects of cuts in American troop strength in Europe and in 1977 added the doomsday note that the "the Soviets were moving toward a decisive conventional military superiority over NATO."[18] The latter warning appeared four days after an administration took office, promising to cut the U.S. military budget by $5 billion to $7 billion.

Yet the major response to the Soviet buildup came less from American alarm than from Europe's belated realization that the imbalance was not only in conventional forces—troop increases, new tanks, tactical aircraft—but in a new generation of missiles, particularly the SS-20, a triple-warhead mobile missile with a 1,500-mile range, targeted on Western European centers. The primary critic was Schmidt, chancellor of the Federal Republic, and arguably the most important European leader in NATO of the 1970s. Indeed, he may be identified as the most significant political figure in the alliance itself in this period. A defense expert as former defense minister in the Socialist government of Willy Brandt, he was aware of Europe's nuclear weakness. There was no European ability to carry out retaliation against the Soviet Union in the event of its use of intermediate nuclear weapons. The small British and French nuclear forces were inadequate, a European missile was not in operation, and the old American plan for an MLF failed to win acceptance or credibility.

The most immediate American answer to European anxieties was to ask, as President Carter did in May 1977, barely four months in office, to have each NATO partner agree to a 3 percent increase above inflation for national defense budgets. Secretary Vance reported that the European reaction to this call for specific changes, not generalizations, was encouraging. A long-term defense program to strengthen both conventional and nuclear theater forces was assigned to 10 working groups of experts, while the special problem of the intermediate-range nuclear weapons was assigned a High Level Group.[19] The council accepted this decision in London, despite the many difficulties inflation had imposed on all the allies.

The allies wanted something other than a 3 percent solution that would involve increasing sacrifices from them, particularly when even this rise would not match Soviet military power in this period. They could nourish some optimism from an awareness that the old adversary, at least of the United States, the People's Republic of China, was urging NATO to be steadfast in its opposition to Soviet power. As late as 1970 Communist China still spoke against all alliances, but by the middle of the decade it had found special virtues in European unity and in NATO. In 1977 China specifically urged Turkey not to abandon the alliance despite its grievances against Greece and the United States.[20] Even though China may have acted out of a concern that Soviet-Turkish rapprochement could free Soviet troops for movement from the Turkish to the Chinese border, the public stance of a leading Communist nation had a favorable impact on NATO spirits.

There were also periodic efforts at psychological self-help, such as the admonition of Robert Komer, under secretary of defense for policy in the Carter administration, who warned as early as 1974 of a "self-inflicted wound." While he urged some redistribution of NATO costs, he observed the internal strains within the Warsaw Pact group that limited its effectiveness. "The enemy," he asserted, "was not 10-feet tall."[21] How reliable were the Warsaw allies in light of the Romanian precedent in limiting its collaboration with the Soviet-led Warsaw forces? How far beneath the surface was domestic discontent with Soviet energy practices, consumer policies, or repressed nationalism against Soviet domination? Although the paucity of data required caution in interpreting the precise strength of the opposition, the Warsaw Pact's internal problems could ameliorate the apparently inferior NATO military posture.

A more empirically based response to the imbalance between East and West was presented by streamlining NATO's defenses. One of NATO's oldest aspirations was standardization of weapons and equipment, an aspiration never realized and probably unrealizable in view of each member's sense of both national interest and national economy. To mitigate rivalry the concept of "interoperability" was initiated as a more manageable version of standardization. It would permit communications and data systems as well as weapons of a particular country to employ such common elements as fuel, ammunition, and spare parts that might be manufactured or secured from one or more allied countries. The United States greeted the concept enthusiastically. Basing their action on a State Department report claiming that NATO had been wasting $10 billion a year in competitive research development and procurement of weapons, Senators Culver and Nunn introduced an amendment on NATO standardization to a Defense Department Appropriations Act in July 1975. It stated that future procurement of equipment for U.S. troops would be "interoperable with the equipment of other members of the North Atlantic Treaty Organization."[22]

But no matter how well intentioned American or other allied attempts at standardization may have been, national pressures inevitably stimulated controversies over tanks and aircraft of the 1980s, as the United States and Germany vied over the XM-1 versus the Leopard II tanks, or the United States and France over the F-llE and the F-16 planes. Still, there was a sense of progress abroad when the Department of the Army decided on 31 January 1978 that the United States would require the German-developed 120-mm gun for the new KM-1 battle tank. The decision was consciously intended as "an indication that the United States was sincere in its desire for a 'two-way' standardization."[23] Similarly, the principle of interoperability seemed to flourish when the first of 348 European-built F-16 aircraft was delivered to the Belgian Air Force on 26 January 1979. Four thousand suppliers and subcontractors in the United States and Europe were involved in the production of the new aircraft.

Streamlining production, with all its beneficial side effects, did not come to grips with the problems of meeting the challenge of Soviet modernization. A better hope for success seemed to come from the wonders of technology, the quick fix, whereby inferior numbers in the West could overcome with miracle weapons the tanks or planes or manpower of the East. New weaponry was a quicker and more effective solution, particularly the use of antitank weapons to neutralize the Soviets' superior tank forces. The October War in the Middle East seemed to dramatize their enormous potential sufficiently to induce one observer, Ian Smart of the Royal Institute of International Affairs, to claim that the introduction of highly mobile and simply operated antitank missiles "marks a transformation that recalls the way in which the longbow enabled the English footsoldier of the 14th century to overcome the mounted knight."[24] No matter how hyperbolic the linking of the Yom Kippur War of 1973 to the Battle of Crécy in 1346 may appear, there was little doubt that new air- or ground-delivered precision guided missiles and antitank guided missiles (PGMs and ATGMs) could reduce to some degree the advantages then enjoyed by the Warsaw Pact powers. It seemed to return the initiative to the West at a reasonable cost. Although there were technical limitations in the use of the ATGMs, the ability of the West to employ sophisticated technology helped to dissolve the bouts of pessimism that plagued the NATO allies periodically in the 1970s.

The ATGMs, if as effective as anticipated, would have breathed new life into MC 14/3, the "Overall Strategic Concepts for the Defense of the NATO Area," which had been the basis of NATO's military doctrine since its adoption by the Defense Planning Committee in March 1967. This doctrine had consolidated the principle of "flexible response" and presumably would enable NATO forces to meet a conventional attack with force equal to the occasion, deliberately escalating the means of resistance when necessary. The mode of expression was reminiscent of the Kennedy era, when a premium was placed on tactical reactions through nonnuclear arms. In this context the ATGM was an updated deterrence against Warsaw initiatives in the central region, as their superior numbers in tanks diminished in significance.

These expectations actually raised more difficulties than they solved. The expectations were excessive. A realistic interpretation of the Egyptian attack against Israeli forces in the Sinai revealed that the initial Egyptian successes were quickly checked by Israel's counterweapons. Within two weeks after the invasion Egypt had lost control of its troops east of the Suez Canal and much of the territory west of the canal. Moreover, the scenario centering on miracle weapons failed to take into account technological advances the Soviets could and did make since 1973. Tanks did not comprise the totality of Soviet power. Repeatedly, NATO commanders, including the SACEURs, sounded the alarm in the middle and late 1970s that the West's power of deterrence continued to decline in the face of the continuing modernization of Warsaw Pact forces, notably the introduction of the tactical SS-21 missile in 1979.

If conventional defenses did not solve NATO's troubles, the other two elements in the triad of flexible response—tactical and strategic nuclear weapons—raised even more concerns among the allies. While confidence in a U.S. strategic strike had been in question since *Sputnik*, the Soviet achievement of equality in strategic nuclear weapons exacerbated the sense of uncertainty in Europe. Even the most striking achievements of détente between the United States and Soviet Union, such as the first SALT agreement, created ambivalent feelings. Did agreements on limits to strategic arms imply a hidden agenda dangerous to European security? Would the United States in its negotiations with the Soviet Union not be tempted to trade off Europe's security for its own, as it worked its way through the SALT II negotiations? The essential illogic of the coexistence of over 300,000 American troops in Europe with the abandonment of the theater in which those troops were stationed was immaterial. The emotional dimension was by far more important than the common sense of the matter. And so when the question of limiting the range of missiles in Europe became part of Kissinger's bargaining with the Soviets, Schmidt articulated Europe's, and particularly Germany's, fear of abandonment.

The cruise missile, a pilotless aircraft armed with a warhead, and a product of German research in World War II, had been slighted by the United States in favor of ballistic missiles in the 1960s. But with the technological advances of the 1970s, a down-sized cruise missile could fly at low altitudes, avoid radar detection, and strike targets with pinpoint accuracy—and at low cost. But the cruise missile's usefulness was still in sufficient question in the mid-1970s for Kissinger to see the weapon simply as a bargaining chip, while Pentagon planners and European observers identified it as a "defense bargain."[25] When the United States accepted in mid-1977 the Soviet contention that the planned ceilings on strategic nuclear launch vehicles would include the cruise missile, it seemed to confirm the suspicions of Europeans. For the Soviets, anything that could strike their territory was considered strategic, wherever it was located. Europeans had no problem with the SALT I Treaty of May 1972, when the issue was ABMs or ICBMs. But when SALT II bound the United States "not to transfer strategic offensive arms to other states, and to assist in their development," the NATO partners recognized the potential effect of this noncircumvention clause on the use of a major counter to the SS-20, the cruise missile. This was made explicit in a protocol to the SALT II Treaty that would place constraints on cruise missile development and deployment through 1981.[26]

TOWARD THE DUAL-TRACK DECISION OF 1979

It was not surprising that Chancellor Schmidt, already skeptical of the Carter administration's abilities, would be the European to question also its intentions. At a highly visible forum, London's International Institute for Strategic Studies, he spoke out against the drift of U.S. policy. While the policy urged defense expenditures on Europeans, it seemed to turn its back on a major weapon that could deal with the SS-20 threat. Schmidt asserted that "strategic arms limitations confined to the United States and the Soviet Union will inevitably impair the security of Western European members of the alliance *vis-à-vis* Soviet military superiority in Europe if we do not succeed in removing the disparities of military power in Europe parallel to the SALT negotiations."[27] This speech carried a stinging rebuke to American policy and behavior, as it appeared to separate the balance of strategic nuclear forces in the world from a "Eurostrategic balance." It called the whole matter of U.S. strategic nuclear guarantee into question.

The message pushed Washington into a variety of responses. At the top level Brzezinski understandably responded that a "Eurostrategic balance" as such never existed. It was part of a larger deterrent effected through such uses as NATO-assigned submarines armed with nuclear missiles.[28] But the concerns had to be addressed, and Secretary Vance noted how carefully, and apparently successfully, he helped to convince Europeans that no "nontransfer provision" would be accepted in the SALT II Treaty under the rubric of the "noncircumvention clause." Existing patterns of defense cooperation and U.S. assistance in the modernization of the alliance's nuclear forces would continue intact.

Whatever reassurance Europeans may have accepted in the first year of the Carter administration was undercut by the neutron bomb debacle of 1978. Like the cruise missile, this enhanced radiation weapon, as it was pedantically identified, had been under consideration since the late 1950s. A "clean" rather than a "dirty" weapon, the neutron bomb was a low-yield device that could minimize blast and long-term radiation, releasing energy in the form of lethal neutrons almost at the point of detonation. Like the ATGM, it contained elements of a miracle weapon, since undermanned Western forces could destroy effectively tanks or troop concentrations without the radiation damage to the environment. Here was a theater nuclear weapon that could match the modernization and expansion of Soviet weaponry.

There appeared to be many features that made the new bomb so attractive, particularly its ability to destroy armored and mechanized troops while sparing civilian areas, especially buildings, from lethal damage. Its use would enable defenders to move into blast areas quickly; the space affected by the bomb could be occupied within several hours after its launching. If employed in Western Europe to halt an attack from the East, it would have none of the frightening aftereffects—fire and blast, or the destruction of civilian populations or properties—that any other tactical nuclear device would incur. By 1977 it seemed probable that all members of the alliance would endorse employment of enhanced radiation warheads that could be installed on the army Lance missiles, with a range of 75 miles. The NATO Defense Planning Committee gave its blessing at its December meeting in Brussels.[29]

Its development was accelerated in the Ford administration, which funded research and development of enhanced radiation weapons (ERWs) in 1976, but the debate over its use was left to the Carter administration to handle. It became a national issue when *Washington Post* writer Walter Pincus published an article entitled "Neutron Killer Warhead Buried in ERDA Budget" in June 1977. He referred to the neutron bomb as "the first battlefield weapon specially designed to kill people through the release of neutrons rather than to destroy military installations."

The exposure of the neutron issue immediately raised a furor in the United States that had immediate repercussions abroad. The objections derived from a variety of sources. Not least of the charges was that which accompanied the introduction of any innovative weapon: Would its promise be redeemed? Would the lethal effects of the bomb be limited to the battle-field? Moreover, the psychology of neutron warfare was untested. Conceivably, as scientist George Kistiakowsky suggested, tank operators exposed to radiation need not die immediately but, knowing "that they are walking dead," might fight all the harder in the hours or days left to them.[30] Beyond the technical limitations was the blurring of lines between conventional and nuclear warfare entailed in the use of enhanced radiation weapons, and with it the lowering of the thresholds of nuclear war itself. Obviously, this particular nuclear weapon undid the notion of an unwinnable nuclear conflict. The older tactical "dirty" bombs were so destructive to friend and enemy alike that their utility in a crisis was doubt-ful. It was the very practicality of the neutron bomb that distressed congressional critics like Mark Hatfield of Oregon, who called the effort to put the bomb into production, "Unconscionable."[31]

The deep emotions aroused by the particularly inhumane quality of this weapon doomed its production in 1977 as much as anything else. Inevitably, Soviet propaganda played on this theme, as it organized Western opposition to "the ultimate capitalist weapon"[32]—a bomb designed to kill people but spare property. The term was ironically coined by the Pentagon to celebrate the virtues of the neutron option. The weight of the world's moral disapproval affected President Carter, as it did Chancellor Schmidt. Schmidt, more than Carter, recognized the importance of the neutron bomb to the defense of Europe, however, and was willing to accept the bomb if other allies did so as well. But he too was concerned about public opinion in Germany. Consequently, Schmidt and other allied leaders sent out confusing signals to the United States. While demanding that the United States begin production of the bomb, they refused to take any initiative in offering their territories as sites for its deployment. Yet the bomb as a bargaining chip remained a valuable tool in dealing with the Soviet Union. Conceivably, the neutron weapon could be held in abeyance for 18 months or two years until the Soviet Union's reactions had been tested. A withdrawal of the SS-20 might be a worthwhile quid for a neutron quo.

Carter was buffeted from all sides. From the right came a drumbeat of advice, particularly from the new Committee on the Present Danger, many drawn from the ranks of hawkish Democrats such as Senator Henry Jackson of Washington and veterans of the Truman cold war days such as Paul H.

Nitze, chief architect of NSC-68. They pushed for speedy resolution in favor of the bomb. From the left came the cry of an immoral act, and this may have bothered Carter as much or more than any other issue, as he was uncomfortable with the role of "ogre"—as Brzezinski put it—that his support of the neutron bomb cast him. Under pressure he decided in late March 1978 against proceeding with its production, to the surprise and distress of his advisers. His basic reason was the "queasy" sense that "his administration would be stamped forever as the administration that kills people but leaves buildings intact," a conclusion similar to but not quite the same as the message Soviet propaganda was sending abroad.[33]

While Carter's conscience may have been relieved by the decision, Schmidt was outraged. Despite the German's own cautious management of the question, he saw in Carter's waffling an abandonment, even a betrayal of faith. It proved to the German leader that the president was unpredictable and willing to sell out the interests of the alliance for the sake of bilateral advantages with the Soviet Union. Schmidt's anger may have been excessive, particularly in light of Germany's own reservations; he might have been more sympathetic to the political problems that the neutron bomb posed for Carter, as they were not too different in kind from those raised by his Social Democratic party. In his memoirs the president claimed that "although some confusion was generated within the NATO alliance, under the existing circumstances my final decision not to produce neutron weapons was the proper one."[34]

Yet the consequences, no matter how unfair, further damaged Carter's image of leadership. Even his indecisive deferral of production of the neutron bomb did not end the controversy over its future. The Soviet improvements in their first-strike capabilities in Europe increasingly limited alternatives to ERWs. Or so it was perceived by the Nuclear Planning Group when it raised again the issue of the neutron option less than two weeks after the president had dismissed it. In January 1979 at a meeting of the leaders of the four major NATO powers at Guadeloupe, Chancellor Schmidt brought with him the continuing, but now more public, conviction that the neutron bomb was the only weapon that could balance Soviet superiority in tank numbers in the central sector of Europe.[35]

In the wake of the neutron debacle, the cruise missile assumed greater visibility as a counter to Soviet power. The SS-20 was being deployed at a rate of one a week. By the end of Carter's term, 180 had been deployed inside the USSR, with all but 23 targeted at Western Europe. So an answer to the imbalance was more imperative than ever in NATO councils. The Long-Range Theater Nuclear Force (LRTNF) seemed to hold the key to a solution. Deployment of cruise missiles and an improved Pershing missile would end all speculation about SALT II limiting options on those weapons. Second, LRTNF would provide a vital counter to the growing imbalance created by the SS-20 expansion; these weapons would be able to strike at the

Soviet Union from their European bases. Most important was the political dimension. The new missiles would show the world NATO's determination as well as ability to maintain a balance of forces in Europe, and they could do so without the drains in the economies that massive symmetrical conventional forces would require. With the support of the respected SACEUR Alexander Haig, the High Level Group, formed in 1977 under the Nuclear Planning Group, came up with recommendations for the deployment of 464 ground-launched missiles, with 160 in Britain, 112 in Italy, 96 in Germany, and 48 each in the Netherlands and Belgium. Additionally, the High Level Group, drawing on earlier Pentagon studies, replaced 108 Pershing missiles already in Germany with 108 new Pershing II missiles.

The numbers reflected political considerations above the military. Vital to the successful deployment of cruise missiles was the requirement that Germans had made with the neutron bomb: namely, that NATO powers share the responsibility for deploying the weapons on their own soil.

There was precedent enough in this plan. After all, the older generation of missiles had been placed in Europe in the 1960s and the early 1970s. But circumstances of the late 1970s had changed. Germany, the most vulnerable of the allies, was also the most powerful European partner. It needed not only assurances of defense but some hope of deescalation of the nuclear arms race. These were provided in a carefully written decision adopted at the December 1979 special meeting of the foreign and defense ministries in Brussels. Not only would there be withdrawal of 1,000 U.S. nuclear warheads from Europe as modernization proceeded, but the ministers agreed that accompanying deployment would be "a broad set of initiatives . . . to further the course of arms control and détente in the 1980s. Ministers regard arms control as an integral part of the Alliance's efforts to assure the undiminished security of its member States and to make the strategic situation between East and West more stable, more predictable, and more manageable at lower level of armament on both sides."[36] A SALT II was welcomed, and it was anticipated that in a SALT III framework limitations would be placed on long-range theater nuclear systems. But only through a credible response to Soviet theater nuclear force deployments—the 572 missiles—could there be a foundation for serious negotiations on the future of these weapons.

The dual-track decision was a milestone in NATO's history and presumably a potential boost to Carter's reputation in foreign relations. It was his administration that faced up to the rise in Soviet power and, despite setbacks, seemed to come to successful grips with it. In the short run of history, however, this initiative was a badge of failure. Carter's Camp David diplomacy resulting in peace between Egypt and Israel was forgotten; his reasonable settlement of the Panama Canal sovereignty, a sore point in Pan-American relations, was excoriated by the Republican opposition in 1980 as a sellout of U.S. interests. For all his reversal of defense expenditures he lost the hawkish Democrats who deserted the party for Ronald Reagan in 1980 as the executive to restore America's lost prestige. Carter's image as an indecisive bumbler in foreign affairs was a factor in Reagan's overwhelming victory in the election campaign.

But it was tragedy as much as ineptitude that may have hurt him most: the responsibility for the American hostages caught up in the Iranian revolution of 1979 was the president's; they were not to be released until Reagan assumed authority in 1981. The Shah's Iran, a keystone in the Nixon Doctrine, became a millstone for Carter. Not even his vigorous response to the Soviet invasion of Afghanistan in December 1979 erased the stain of humiliation. And yet the Carter administration's responses did have positive resonance in the alliance. Scenarios envisaging the loss of the Persian Gulf to a Soviet invasion via Afghanistan or to internal upheaval from Islamic fundamentalism or from Communist subversion were not confined to American planners. An "arc of crisis" was identified by Brzezinski involving the Horn of Africa, the Middle East, and the Persian Gulf. It needed protection, and the Carter Doctrine, with its creation of a joint task force—the Rapid Deployment Force (RDF)—in March 1980 was to raise four army divisions and the equivalent of two Marine divisions that year. NATO recognized its importance with the statement of the Defense Planning Committee meeting in Brussels in May 1981 urging allied coordination of "out-of-area deployment of forces" in support of the common NATO interest. Indeed, in September 1983 the director of the International Institute of Strategic Studies in London proclaimed that NATO and its relationship with the Third World was the most important single issue facing NATO in the 1980s.[37]

But if NATO was to take the RDF into serious account, the Carter administration, as in other parts of the world, would receive little credit for it. The strong American reaction to Afghanistan was unsettling to Europeans even if it was understandable. Carter seemed to move from one extreme to another. Revival of the cold war by embargoing agricultural exports from the United States or by boycotting the Olympic games to be held in Moscow in 1980 seemed a cosmetic reaction to Soviet behavior, with little likelihood of accomplishing anything beyond stiffening its positions. Schmidt was sufficiently exercised over U.S. pressures for a common stance to urge Carter to fire his national security adviser.[38]

Schmidt's attitude may have been a knee-jerk reaction to another Washington initiative, but it contained two elements that in one way or another were endemic in the European-American differences over East-West conflict. First was the continuing importance of détente for economic as well as political reasons; the Afghanistan invasion should not be a reason to jeopardize the delicate negotiations of Western Europe for multibillion-dollar plans for building a natural-gas pipeline from Siberia to the West. Second was the recognition that Afghanistan had long been a Soviet preserve. The invasion had followed a second leftist coup. The government that triggered the incursion was itself a Communist regime. Was Carter focusing on Afghanistan to ward off his own right-wing critics as the United States moved toward the presidential election?

Yet Europe's, if not Schmidt's, emotions on the Carter foreign policy reflected sorrow more than anger over the disarray in the administration, as it ended its term with a sense of failure. Secretary of State Vance resigned in the spring over the ill-fated rescue attempts of American hostages in Iran. In Congress the growing opposition to SALT II, after six long years in germination, prevented the administration from submitting the treaty to ratification. Reagan entered office not only with the treaty in abeyance but with his own promise to overturn it.

THE REAGAN INITIATIVES, 1981

Reagan rode to victory on a tidal wave of public support. His personality held none of the dark and brooding features of his predecessor. Carter's doubts about himself and his country were replaced by a man of little depth but with a sunny optimism about his ability to turn the country around. Reagan's career seemed itself to be a triumph of luck and charm over brains and skills. A Hollywood actor of the 1930s and 1940s he moved easily from a superficial support of the New Deal to a more emotionally satisfying embrace of the Republican right wing. His path to the governorship of California had been smoothed by his service as a radio spokesman of the General Electric Company in the 1950s. It was in this role that he honed his talents as a superb communicator on behalf of the principles of free enterprise and of a strong defense. His record on foreign policy should have been one to raise fears about American isolationism in the 1980s: from unregenerate support of Vietnam to hostility to the Panama Canal concessions to a fire-eating enmity of the Soviet Union at every level. He promised a speedy end to what was left of détente.

If his affable manner and simple solutions to problems of government—domestic and foreign—won the hearts of Americans in 1980, they frightened and antagonized his European partners. It was not that he turned his back on Europe. Indeed, he promised his allies the leadership that presumably had been so lacking in his predecessor, and some of the European leaders at least hoped that any change would be an improvement over the Carter years. But it soon appeared that King Stork had replaced King Log. Aside from Reagan's cancellation of the grain embargo—a move done to appease American farmers—his behavior seemed to follow his rhetoric. The Soviet Union was literally a diabolical enemy led by sinister figures who reserved "the right to commit any crime, to lie, to cheat, to achieve their immoral ends." He made particular mention of these Soviet qualities at his first White House press conference on 29 January 1981 and repeated them six weeks later in an interview with Walter Cronkite.[39]

The Reagan administration acted accordingly. A massive defense buildup marked his first term, although little recognition was given to the Carter administration for establishing the infrastructure for the modernization of American defenses. In 1980 the United States had spent approximately 5.5 percent of its gross domestic product on defense; four years later that figure had risen more than 7 percent. Concurrently SALT II was frozen in time, its provisions honored informally but its name anathema to the ideologues of the new Republican administration. It symbolized weakness and inferiority in American defenses at a time that the Soviet Union was seen as able to exploit what was called "a window of vulnerability." In this mood the buildup of theater nuclear forces in Europe was a natural concomitant to the expansion of the American defense structure.

For the other half of the dual-track commitment, arms control, formal obeisance was offered, and little more. The spirit was reminiscent of Dean Acheson's "situation of strength" a generation before. The deployment of cruise missiles in 1983 was the key to any serious negotiations with the Soviets. Until then, according to Strobe Talbott, "nuclear arms control would be a matter of keeping up appearances, of limiting damage, of buying time, and of laying the groundwork for agreement later."[40]

Europeans were taken aback by the apparent atavism of the American posture in the early 1980s. It was not that they were nostalgic for the Carter years. It was more a problem of Reagan's simplicity or even innocence about the subtleties of foreign relations that they feared would harden relations with the Soviet Union and possibly precipitate conflict. The president's bloodcurdling language did not seem to fit his pleasing personality. More than ever, Europeans recognized that they had to share a continent with the Soviet Union, whatever was done in Afghanistan or in Poland. Reagan's advisers appeared to be true believers in the efficacy of military superiority as an end in itself. Conceivably, even a nuclear war was survivable if they could believe the advice of T. K. Jones, deputy under secretary of defense for strategic nuclear forces, who envisaged salvation for Americans if only they would "dig a hole, cover it with a couple of doors, and then throw three feet of dirt on top." With enough shovels to go around "everyone's going to make it."[41]

But it was at the level of the National Security Council and the cabinet that ideology, rigidity, and simplicity seemed to dominate. From Secretary of Defense Caspar Weinberger came the message that quantity of weapons would close the gap. The president's advisers were either Republican ideologues such as Richard Allen, the national security adviser, or youthful zealots such as Richard Perle, a Henry Jackson Democrat and assistant secretary of defense for international affairs. Weinberger, known as "Cap the Knife" as the budget-cutting head of the Office of Management and Budget under Nixon, became the most articulate and influential booster of the military buildup, and Perle the most effective figure in separating arms control from rearmament.

In this new administration only Alexander Haig, former SACEUR, appeared to be a friendly familiar figure to Europeans, sympathetic to their concerns and knowledgeable about world affairs from his experience as Kissinger's aide as well as military leader. And unlike the way things were run in the Carter period, he intended to gather foreign policy authority under his wing as secretary of state, avoiding the Vance-Brzezinski standoff, and permitting the administration to speak with one voice. Haig's imperious personality, his position as outsider in the Reagan circle, and his perceived drive for power forced his removal from office after the Falklands War and the Lebanon bombing of 1982. Although his successor, George Shultz, a respected economist and former secretary of labor under Nixon, provided somewhat smoother relations within the Reagan administration, his inexperience in foreign affairs and mild manner left room for more hawkish figures to direct the administration's foreign policy.

The result was confrontation with allies as well as with the Soviets. Europeans were distressed by America's excessive deference to Taiwan, reflecting both ideology and old loyalties, which slowed the warming relations with China; its excessive support for the Israelis, which led to the Lebanon debacle of 1982; its excessive zeal in Latin America—in aid of repressive forces in El Salvador in opposition to leftist forces in Nicaragua, in invading Grenada for less than clear cause—and its excessive hostility to the Warsaw bloc, in apparent intransigent positions on arms control. Even their putative ally Haig rattled them with his talk of a Communist takeover in Central America.

But the harshest area of confrontation was over trade relations. Again the Acheson era may be summoned from the past. The strong Reagan hostility to a natural-gas pipeline supplying the West with fuel from Siberia was a major point of friction among the allies in 1981 and 1982. It underscored differences among allies over the significance of the economic factor in the cold war that went back to the Korean War. In the American view, underscored in the Battle Act of 1951, the Communist empire was vulnerable to restrictions in trade, particularly in strategic matériel. Encouraging trade would only enhance the empire's war potential. The Europeans, however, looked on commercial relations as vital to the health of their own economies, with trade relations serving as a means of moving Eastern nations westward.

Embargoes, successful or not, were employed periodically as symbolic punishment of Communist crimes as well as outlets for popular frustrations in the United States. When the Polish government declared martial law in 1981, American retaliation took the form of ending scientific and technological exchanges and forbidding the European allies from shipping any machinery containing American parts for the pipeline carrying Soviet natural gas to Western Europe. European governments—West German, French, British, and Italian—along with Canada, refused to cooperate. For them the putative dangerous dependence on Soviet natural gas and the Soviet gains in Western currency were reasonable trade-offs for a $10 billion pipeline deal that would energize their economies at a time of recession. The Reagan position was weakened by the cry of a double standard; one of his administration's first acts was to lift a grain embargo imposed by Carter after the Afghanistan invasion because of the damage it had done to American agriculture. It did not go unnoticed by the allies that the Reagan administration did not have International Harvester cancel a contract for heavy construction vehicles at the same time that it pressed for abandonment of the pipeline. The alliance was damaged.

What lay beneath the surface in all economic conflicts was the rising power of nationalism that was manifested in a variety of conflicts with the European Community, from steel to butter. The alliance could have come apart over U.S. resentment against European dumping of subsidized products in America or over the European allies' anger at the excessively high interest rates resulting in an overvalued dollar and diminution of European economic growth rates, all from an American economic policy over which Europe had little control.

Yet the alliance held fast in the mid-1980s, as it did in the crises of the mid-1970s. One explanation may be in the palliatives, such as the soporific statements of the North Atlantic Council as it attempted to smooth over differences. Sometimes prudent actions at the right moment defused tension, as in the quiet diplomacy of George Schultz, who backed away from threats over the Soviet pipeline. Europe went ahead, and the United States looked the other way.

A more persuasive explanation may be found in the continuing sense of common interests served by NATO. The divisive issue of missile deployment led in 1983 to massive demonstrations in Britain, Germany, and the Low Countries and to Soviet threats against their governments as they voted on implementing the decision of 1979. The Soviet leadership further signaled that if deployment should take place it would end hope of arms negotiations. The result was a test of solidarity in which Soviet intimidation united rather than divided the alliance.

The United States attempted to place the burden of intransigency on the Soviet Union. Most of the efforts appeared to be semantic. Theater Nuclear Force (TNF), a term that appeared to dissociate European nuclear defense from the American, was replaced with Intermediate-Range Nuclear Force (INF) as a more acceptable rubric for the new missiles. A "zero option" was put forth in negotiations whereby the United States would agree not to deploy its missiles if the Soviet Union would withdraw its SS-20s. And as Richard Burt defined it, the president unveiled in a speech at Eureka College on 9 May 1982 a substitute for SALT with the acronym START (Strategic Arms Reduction Talks): "Rather than seeking an agreement that would do no more than codify and marginally influence the growth of strategic forces, the U.S. would make a proposal for substantial, equitable and verifiable reductions."[42]

It is probable, however, that these cosmetic measures were less effective in winning over the allies than the Soviet Union's heavy-handed attempts to intimidate the European members of the alliance. Once again, Soviet behavior proved to be a centripetal force. Elections in the United Kingdom and in the Federal Republic in 1983 confirmed the Conservative party's power in the former and brought back the Christian Democrats to power in the latter. By the end of that year the peace demonstrations had peaked, and the deployments in Germany had begun. The subsequent termination of the Geneva negotiations by the Soviet Union did not bring the alliance to its knees. A little more than a year later, under different labels, the Soviet Union returned to the negotiating table in Geneva.

On balance, this was a modest success at best. Nothing really had been solved. The argument over the utility of the missiles themselves continued, arms control remained as contentious an issue between East and West as before, suspicions about the direction of Reagan leadership in his second administration were as powerful as in the first, hostility to U.S. actions in the Third World increased rather than decreased, and the economic competition within the alliance abated little or not at all. Equally significant, the vitality of the defense triad—conventional weapons, tactical nuclear weapons, and strategic nuclear weapons—continued to be in question. How reliable was the U.S. commitment? How serious was the European part of the bargain? On both sides of the Atlantic the question found no definitive answers.

But in the mid-1980s there was consensus that the alliance and the organization acting for it continued to be important to the stability of the West. There was no viable alternative in place, or even in prospect.

NATO Civil and Military Structure

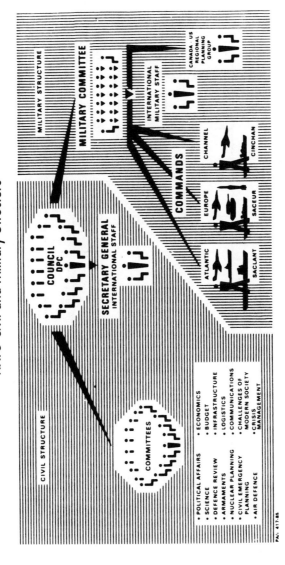

Source: *NATO Handbook*, 1986, 32.

Principal Committees of the North Atlantic Council

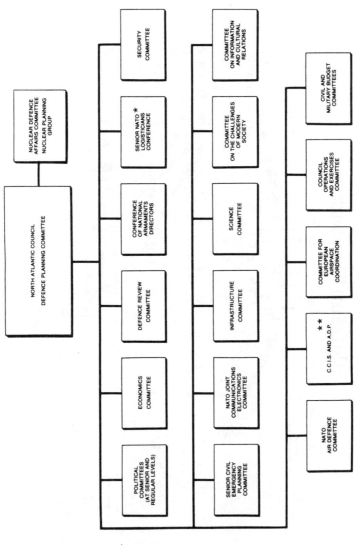

* The SNCL is a joint Civil/Military Committee which reports both to the Council or
  Defence Planning Committee and to the Military Committee.

** Command, Control and Information Systems and Automatic Data Processing Committee.

Source: *North Atlantic Treaty Organization: Facts and Figures, 1984, 94.*

NATO International Staff

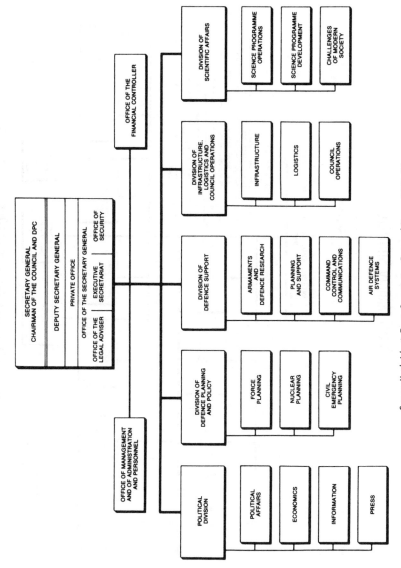

SECRETARY GENERAL
CHAIRMAN OF THE COUNCIL AND DPC

DEPUTY SECRETARY GENERAL

PRIVATE OFFICE

OFFICE OF THE SECRETARY GENERAL

OFFICE OF THE
LEGAL ADVISER | EXECUTIVE
SECRETARIAT | OFFICE OF
SECURITY

OFFICE OF THE
FINANCIAL CONTROLLER

OFFICE OF MANAGEMENT
AND OF ADMINISTRATION
AND PERSONNEL

POLITICAL DIVISION
- POLITICAL AFFAIRS
- ECONOMICS
- INFORMATION
- PRESS

DIVISION OF DEFENCE PLANNING AND POLICY
- FORCE PLANNING
- NUCLEAR PLANNING
- CIVIL EMERGENCY PLANNING

DIVISION OF DEFENCE SUPPORT
- ARMAMENTS AND DEFENCE RESEARCH
- PLANNING AND SUPPORT
- COMMAND CONTROL AND COMMUNICATIONS
- AIR DEFENCE SYSTEMS

DIVISION OF INFRASTRUCTURE, LOGISTICS AND COUNCIL OPERATIONS
- INFRASTRUCTURE
- LOGISTICS
- COUNCIL OPERATIONS

DIVISION OF SCIENTIFIC AFFAIRS
- SCIENCE PROGRAMME OPERATIONS
- SCIENCE PROGRAMME DEVELOPMENT
- CHALLENGES OF MODERN SOCIETY

Source: *North Atlantic Treaty Organization: Facts and Figures,* 1985, 95.

NATO Military Structure

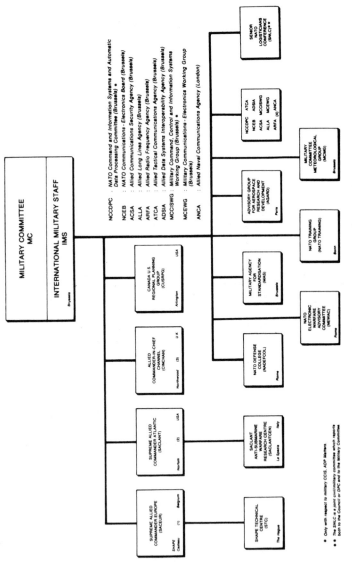

Source: *North Atlantic Treaty Organization: Facts and Figures*, 1985, 101.

Major NATO Commanders

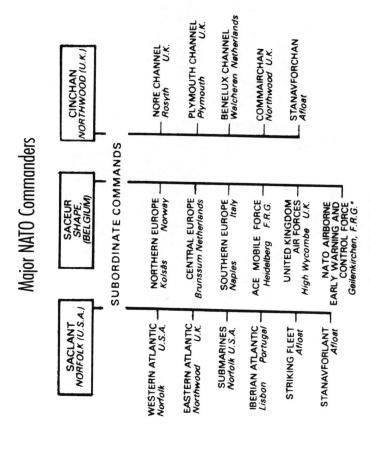

SACLANT *NORFOLK (U.S.A.)*	**SACEUR** *SHAPE, (BELGIUM)*	**CINCHAN** *NORTHWOOD (U.K.)*

SUBORDINATE COMMANDS

WESTERN ATLANTIC *Norfolk U.S.A.*

EASTERN ATLANTIC *Northwood U.K.*

SUBMARINES *Norfolk U.S.A.*

IBERIAN ATLANTIC *Lisbon Portugal*

STRIKING FLEET *Afloat*

STANAVFORLANT *Afloat*

NORTHERN EUROPE *Kolsås Norway*

CENTRAL EUROPE *Brunssum Netherlands*

SOUTHERN EUROPE *Naples Italy*

ACE MOBILE FORCE *Heidelberg F.R.G.*

UNITED KINGDOM AIR FORCES *High Wycombe U.K.*

NATO AIRBORNE EARLY WARNING AND CONTROL FORCE *Geilenkirchen, F.R.G.*

NORE CHANNEL *Rosyth U.K.*

PLYMOUTH CHANNEL *Plymouth U.K.*

BENELUX CHANNEL *Walcheren Netherlands*

COMMAIRCHAN *Northwood U.K.*

STANAVFORCHAN *Afloat*

Source: NATO Handbook, 1986, 56.

NATO and the Warsaw Pact

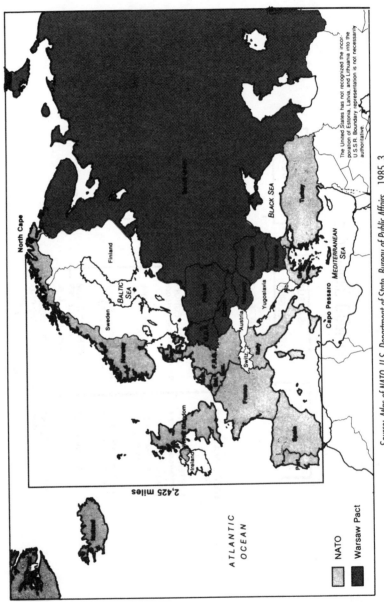

Source: *Atlas of NATO, U.S. Department of State, Bureau of Public Affairs,*, 1985, 3.

Defense of Northern and Central Regions

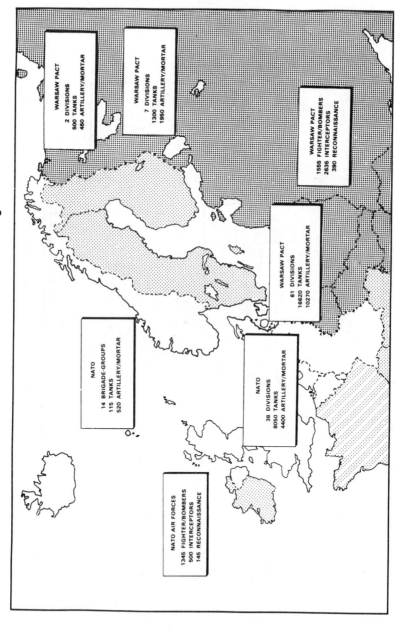

WARSAW PACT
2 DIVISIONS
500 TANKS
450 ARTILLERY/MORTAR

WARSAW PACT
7 DIVISIONS
1300 TANKS
1950 ARTILLERY/MORTAR

WARSAW PACT
1555 FIGHTER/BOMBERS
2635 INTERCEPTORS
390 RECONNAISSANCE

WARSAW PACT
61 DIVISIONS
16620 TANKS
10270 ARTILLERY/MORTAR

NATO
14 BRIGADE-GROUPS
115 TANKS
520 ARTILLERY/MORTAR

NATO
38 DIVISIONS
8050 TANKS
4400 ARTILLERY/MORTAR

NATO AIR FORCES
1345 FIGHTER/BOMBERS
500 INTERCEPTORS
145 RECONNAISSANCE

Depicts Forces in place in Europe reinforced by rapidly deployable forces.

Source: *NATO and the Warsaw Pact: Force Comparisons,* 1984.

Defense of Southern Region

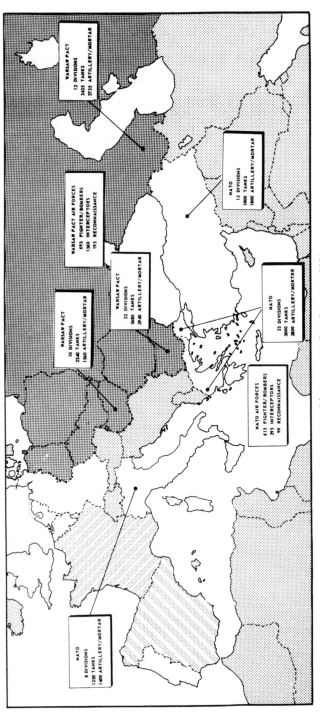

Source: *NATO and the Warsaw Pact: Force Comparisons,* 1984.

chapter 8

THE GORBACHEV CHALLENGE, 1984–1989

THE BALANCE OF TERROR IN THE 1980S

By the mid-1980s the uneasy balance of terror between the United States and the Soviet Union, between NATO and the Warsaw Pact, seemed immutable. The two sides appeared to be evenly balanced. When one side made an effort to upset the balance, the other responded either by uniting to confront the threat or by trying to divide the opposing bloc. The results lessened the impact of change. This precarious equilibrium became visible in the implementation of the dual objectives of defense and détente contained in the dual-track decision of the North Atlantic Council in 1979.

The Soviets' move to accelerate the development of SS-20s solidified NATO's stance rather than divided it. The bellicose pronouncements from the Reagan White House led not to an outbreak of hostilities between the Soviets and the West but to deployment of cruise and Pershing II missiles in 1983 and the electoral victories of governments in Britain and Germany that supported deployment. This outcome was not immediately apparent. The self-imposed deadline announced in 1979 for the deployment of a specific number of missiles on the territory of five allies by 1983 invited trouble from friends and enemies. Internal political opponents of the parties in power in Belgium and the Netherlands—as well as in Britain, Germany, and, to a lesser extent, Italy—made the deployment of weapons a political issue. Peace demonstrators, orchestrated by the Soviets, exploited fears of a nuclear holocaust and blamed the United States for creating new perils in Europe. The Soviet Union did its utmost to stimulate dissent by walking out of arms talks in Geneva in 1983.

But the opponents of deployment failed. The perceived need to counter Soviet IRBMs targeted at European members of NATO overcame misgivings. Not only did the governing parties in Britain and Germany survive the elections, but their victories affected the Low Countries acceptance of missiles. These victories also affected the Soviet Union. Instead of initiating a new round of threats, the only riposte made under the geriatric leadership of Konstantin Chernenko was a walkout from the START negotiations in Geneva without a date for their resumption.

On the other side, when the United States raised prospects of a new weapon in the West's arsenal against Communist domination—the Strategic Defense Initiative (SDI)—its implied threat to the Soviets was diluted by opposition within the alliance. The SDI—also referred to as "Star Wars"—was announced in 1983 and circulated over the next few years; it called not for a strike against the Soviets but a plan to make nuclear war obsolete. In distant space, technology could find a way of crumpling any Soviet ICBM with 50-foot-long bolts of high-energy electrons at nearly the speed of light. Ultimate impregnability of America's defense system was the objective, to be achieved within the foreseeable future. If successful, the SDI would nullify any Soviet threat against the Western Hemisphere and force the Soviets into a potentially ruinous revamping of its military machine to cope with the American weapon. For President Reagan, Star Wars represented both a vision of a world free from nuclear nightmares and a thrust that would render obsolete the Soviet's ICBMs.

There was no way of telling the full impact of Star Wars on Soviet leaders; their initial response was visceral and yet pro forma, as might be expected of their reaction to any new U.S. plan. What served to calm Soviet concerns, at least in the short run, were the reactions of America's NATO partners, who saw three dangerous elements within the amorphous frame of the project. First, it would advance technology in the United States at the expense of Europe; second, it would escalate the arms race by challenging the Soviets to find means of countering a new nuclear defense system; and, third, it represented a startling reversal of American strategy. The older idea of mutual assured destruction was based on the vulnerability of all defense systems, and this vulnerability had given meaning to deterrence. A Soviet thrust would be parried by counterforce at different levels, but the ultimate offensive level was a nuclear strike that would destroy the aggressor's society.

Successful achievement of the SDI would have undermined the credibility of NATO's strategy. The ICBM was at the apex of the doctrine of flexible response.

Still, the uneasiness of America's NATO partners with American policies was not wholly focused on the SDI; its realization, after all, would be in the future. It was the difficulty of balancing defense with arms control measures that agitated NATO in the mid-1980s. At the same time that the North

Atlantic Council pushed aside the SDI in 1985, it continued to invite, as it had in the past, American initiatives for the defense of Europe at all levels. While demanding continuation of arms control talks, the council rejected, just as the Reagan administration had, the call for a "no first use" of nuclear weapons, which had been widely publicized when distinguished American former policymakers—McGeorge Bundy, George Kennan, Robert McNamara, Gerard Smith, and Charles Schulze—proposed them in 1982. Deterrence remained dependent on a nuclear response to Soviet measures, as NATO solidarity against the SS-20s attested.[1]

But periodic relaxation of tension led to temptation among Western nations to consider one-sided force reductions. SHAPE planners met this temptation by offering a variety of options that drew attention to both the continuing dangers from the East and the means available for the defense of Europe. In a forceful 1984 article SACEUR Bernard Rogers pointed out the various ways in which the emerging technologies were more than prohibitively "'Buck Rogers' style weapons" designed for the future; they were a current part of NATO's defense structure. Conventional forces, according to Rogers, through such measures as "follow-on forces attack"—striking out at Warsaw Pact forces behind front lines in the event of war—continued to be a means of raising the nuclear threshold as well as reinforcing détente.[2]

The underlying reality of a balance of forces in Europe did not conceal mutual distrust among the allies. While the American partner was gratified and relieved over Europe's consensus on nuclear weapons, it was disturbed by Europe's reluctance to share more of the burden in conventional arms. The Nunn amendment of 1984—a proposal to mandate troop reductions in Europe by almost a third unless the European allies met the target commitment of 3 percent per annum real increase in defense expenditures—reflected widespread American discontent. Despite evidence that Europe's contribution to the common cause in the 1970s was more than equal to that of the United States, there was no countering the fact that since 1980 the United States was more than doubling the minimum requirement while most European nations were failing to meet it.

This amendment was a one-day phenomenon in the United States. It was designed to be a signal to Europeans that was made all the stronger because its main author, Senator Sam Nunn of Georgia, was known as one of NATO's strongest American supporters. Actually, the amendment was replaced by a toothless resolution on the same day. Although it attracted no special attention in the United States, the Nunn initiative shocked European allies. It did not create a change in European contributions to NATO's defenses, but it did emphasize allied recognition that NATO's conventional military arm was still vital and that the American component was indispensable. Arguably, the American troop presence was even more important for another reason. As Ted Galen Carpenter observed, "The symbolic importance of those ground forces increased rather than diminished; they reassured Europeans that the transatlantic protector would never abandon Europe during an hour of military need."[3]

AMERICA, EUROPE, AND "OUT-OF-AREA"

The existential condition of dependence was a constant irritation to Europeans and Americans alike. Nowhere was mutual ambivalence more pervasive than in NATO's relations with the Third World. From an American standpoint, European colonialism in the early years of the alliance was a gratuitous gift to the Soviets, a relic of the past that was an embarrassment in the 1950s. Until 1960 the United States continued to see itself as an anticolonial nation and feared that the European allies, even as they were liquidating their empires, would compromise NATO's ability to compete with communism for the allegiance of new African and Asian nations. This superior stance antagonized the Dutch in Indonesia, the French in Indochina, and the British throughout their far-flung but rapidly diminishing empire. It led to the United States' replacing France in Indochina in 1954 and to the spectacle of the American ally of Britain and France standing alongside their common Soviet antagonist in condemning the Anglo-French-Israeli invasion of the Suez Canal in 1956.

The intra-NATO relationship was reversed after 1960. America's appeal to a common "revolutionary tradition" had been eroded by its hostility to the left-leaning Jacobo Arbenz regime in Guatemala in 1954 and by its reaction to Fidel Castro's Cuba moving into the Communist sphere in 1960. Concurrently, the emerging nations, organized into an Asia-Africa bloc in the United Nations, began to transfer their enmity to colonialism from Western Europe to the United States. It did not matter that the Eisenhower administration had risked the fate of NATO over its support of Egypt in the Suez crisis or that the Kennedy administration had demonstrated its good faith by its support of the United Nations in the Belgian Congo in 1961. Freed from their colonial responsibilities, the European allies seemed almost as critical as their former colonies of America's approach to "out-of-area" problems. The Yom Kippur War in 1973 dramatized the differences between the allies and the United States more sharply than ever before, but points of contention were to be found in Latin America as well. The refusal of many Europeans to see a Communist menace in the Sandinistas taking control of Nicaragua in the mid-1980s was as vital an element in unifying Europeans as the Arab cause had been in the mid-1970s. When the United States invaded Grenada in 1983, it evoked a U.N. Security Council resolution "deeply deploring" the intervention as a "flagrant violation of international law." In that instance the vote was 11 in favor of the resolution—including the permanent members. Britain abstained, while France and the Netherlands voted in favor of the resolution. Only a veto by the United States prevented adoption of the resolution.[4]

Yet America's out-of-area problems presented opportunities for coopera-tion as well as occasions for conflict among the NATO allies. During the brief British-Argentine war over the Falkland Islands in 1982 the United States had to choose between a neutrality over a colonial relic in the south Atlantic—with all the implications it had for relations with Latin America—and NATO solidarity. It chose the latter. NATO not only stood together—although Italy probably would have defected had the war lasted longer—but it recognized clearly the alliance's stake in the problem. Even though the Soviet Union was not involved, the very fact that the British navy was a major actor in the recovery of the islands meant that British ships had to be diverted from their NATO assignments in the North Atlantic. While the organization could not act in this crisis, its voice could be heard—and it was—when the North Atlantic Council gave its blessing to the British cause in 1982.[5]

The uneasy cooperation with the British in this crisis could conceivably have cleared a path to similar solutions in the future. Just as the United States in the 1950s recognized limits to its traditional anticolonial postures, so the European partners increasingly shared interests in out-of-area prob-lems in the mid-1980s. The allies approach was usually through an informal distribution of responsibilities—witness French activity in Francophone Africa to counter Soviet or Libyan initiatives or Malta's military preference for Italy over the United States and Great Britain—or NATO itself—as pro-tector against an aggressive and erratic Libya. The very diversity of interests among the allies seemed to have provided opportunities for the United States and NATO to move unfriendly or Marxist nations in the Third World away from the Soviet orbit more effectively than a show of NATO solidarity might have managed.

Still, there were distinct limits even to informal collaboration within the alliance. Even though political stability and economic progress had been common threads of NATO's aspirations in the out-of-area world, there was no realistic expectation that the Soviets could be excluded from areas where tensions existed. Furthermore, nationalist, ideological, or religious passions have a momentum of their own that no amount of military or economic aid or political support from NATO nations could control. And reactions to these passions will vary according to the national sensibilities of the allies.

NATO AND EUROPEAN UNIFICATION

Troubles within the alliance over Europe's efforts at unification were more fundamental than differences over relations with the Third World. The United States could take pride in its sponsorship of these efforts. As I suggested in the Introduction to this volume, a United States of Europe firmly in the Western camp was one of the inspirations for the Atlantic alliance. Forty years later the form (and even the definition of integration) was still incomplete, but the institutions that the concept had spawned and the behavioral patterns that developed alongside them had created a European entity considerably different from the Europe of 1949. The European community was strong enough to be restive under American leadership but not free enough to dissolve the relationship.

Of all the direction toward European unity, the path of Jean Monnet—through the Coal and Steel Community to the European Community—seemed to Americans to be the most practical and most functional. Linked in 1957 by the Treaty of Rome, six nations, including France and Germany, became nine when Britain, Ireland, and Denmark joined in 1973, and then 12 within the next dozen years when Greece, Spain, and Portugal joined the community. By this time the initially narrow-based coal and steel union of France and Germany had assumed a political dimension, with aspirations for a federated Europe fed by a European Parliament directly elected by citizens of the member states. Since 1979 the Parliament's headquarters has been in Strasbourg, while the European executive commission and the Court of Justice have their centers in Brussels and Luxembourg, respectively.

What meaning did all this activity have? Lindsay Armstrong, editor of the Common Market's monthly publication, claimed that in 1985 the European Community remained basically an agricultural customs union built on a network of highly complicated farm subsidies. Given the wrangling within the community over economic issues, given the unwillingness of the sovereign nations to allow Parliament or the executive commission powers over political and military issues, the vision of Monnet appeared lost in the scramble. Gloomily, Armstrong pronounced that "the European Revolution never took place. . . . Thirty years later we are trying to start all over again."[6]

Yet a Europe had emerged in the 1980s that did not exist a generation ago, with a population and resources larger than those of either the Soviet Union or the United States. Europeans have repeatedly shared common positions that differed from those of its American partner—on issues ranging from Latin America to the Middle East, from détente to the Strategic Defense Initiative, from steel marketing prices to the Siberian natural-gas pipeline. Forty years after the signing of NATO Europe had not found a credible spokesman to articulate these differences. The first advocate for Europe vis-à-vis America—and the Soviet Union—was Charles de Gaulle. His words were not acceptable even if they were emotionally satisfactory. The trouble, however, had not been the absence of voices or forums to express a sense of European interests. Indeed, it was the opposite: there were too many voices and too many forums.

With the removal of France from NATO military planning, room was made for discussion of possibilities for European influence on NATO's direction along the lines of the two pillars envisaged in the earliest days of the alliance. Abandoning both the confrontational tactics of de Gaulle and the cosmetic devices of the American-inspired MLF, European members organized the EUROGROUP in 1968. It began with British Defense Minister Denis Healey's proposal for informal discussions in the wake of congressional pressures for unilateral reductions of U.S. troops in Europe. Initially, EUROGROUP was an informal association of 10 members that intended to show the world, and most particularly the United States, just how much the Europeans were doing to serve the alliance.

This function was as important in the 1980s as in the 1960s, as the issue of burden sharing was raised regularly in the United States. EUROGROUP members, individually or in concert, reminded the United States frequently that the European allies during the 1970s increased their total real defense by over 2 percent each year, while the United States' real defense spending during the same period declined by slightly more than 1 percent. Europe's active forces provided approximately 75 percent of NATO's readily available ground forces in Europe, 75 percent of the tanks, 65 percent of the air forces, and 60 percent of the naval vessels. EUROGROUP also provided glossy brochures, with charts and graphs, along with a film, to advertise the European contribution to NATO.[7]

EUROGROUP claimed in the 1980s that it had gone beyond its propaganda function. From an informal forum in which defense ministers exchanged views on major political and strategic questions, it has created subgroups for greater defense cooperation at practical levels. Staffed by senior experts from national defense ministries, these groups dealt with such areas as the interoperability of tactical communications systems (EUROCOM), cooperation in logistics systems (EUROLOG), and procurement of defense equipment (EURONAD). Outside the EUROGROUP ministers was the Independent European Programme Group (IEPG), a new unit that included France. It focused on seeking the most efficient use of funds for research, development, and procurement and on promoting a European defense industrial and technological base that would increase the interoperability of equipment and provide a better balance in armaments cooperation between Europe and the United States.

But none of these intra-NATO devices equalized Europe and America in the alliance. EUROGROUP seemed more show than substance and lacked the important presence of France. The IEPG represented all the European allies and had the potential of becoming the fulcrum around which Europe could compete with the United States in the transatlantic armaments trade. But the IEPG lacked an institutional framework. Nor had it found a way to settle on a "European" weapons system as opposed to national products.

As a consequence of a continuing inability to bury their sovereignties under a federated entity, inside or outside NATO, European frustrations with their impotence remained in the 1980s more divisive than any other issue in the alliance. The allies knew what they wanted: (1) a role within NATO commensurate with their potential, (2) progressive détente with the Soviet Union, and (3) increased and improved arms control, particularly in nuclear weaponry. They looked with apprehension at the American claims of global responsibility as masking insensitivity toward Europe's sharing a continent with the Soviet Union.

But Europeans were equally concerned with the power of their eastern neighbor, and they continued to rely on the guarantee of American involvement to maintain the balance. So despite the impressive strides made in integrating the resources of a united Europe, the sense of dependence that had characterized the European partners in the 1940s did not evaporate in the second generation. The result of these conflicting drives seemed to ensure the survival of the alliance, no matter how unhappy its members may have been about its conditions.

THE GORBACHEV INITIATIVES

Such was the state of the alliance as Chernenko passed from the Soviet scene. His successor, Mikhail Gorbachev, might have been merely a younger version of his mentor, Yuri Andropov. Gorbachev had moved up the ranks of the Soviet hierarchy and could have been expected to maintain the harsh posture his three successors—Brezhnev, Andropov, and Chernenko—had maintained. The only initial hint of change in the wind was that the ailing Andropov himself wanted to reform the Soviet system and his youthful disciple could breathe life into a process that the dying Andropov was unable to initiate.

Gorbachev formally became general secretary of the Communist party of the Soviet Union on 11 March 1985, and a new era of Soviet-American relations, if not Warsaw-NATO relations, had begun. But even before the formal announcement of succession had been made, the February issue of the *NATO Review* featured a photograph of a broadly smiling Secretary of State George Schultz shaking hands with a painfully smiling Soviet Foreign Minister Andrei Gromyko. The caption above read that new negotiations were to begin. The Soviet walkout following U.S. deployment of missiles in 1983 ended without fanfare.[7] The day after Gorbachev's installation as Soviet leader the two superpowers began new arms control negotiations in Geneva that encompassed defense and space systems, strategic nuclear forces, and intermediate-range nuclear forces.

Such was the outcome of the preliminary meeting between Schultz and Gromyko in early January 1985. Skeptics could identify this renewal as a Soviet maneuver to cover up its misjudgment of Western Europe's solidarity on INF issues. The announcement on 26 April that the Warsaw Pact was extended for 20 years did not augur a retreat from the building of SS-20s.

But the old suspicions and intransigence on both sides had begun to dissolve. Gorbachev was responding to President Reagan's stated wish in January 1984 that "we must and will engage the Soviets in a dialogue as serious and constructive as possible, a dialogue that will serve to promote peace in the troubled regimes of the world, reduce the level of arms, and build a constructive working relationship."[8] Gorbachev showed by the end of 1985 that he was more than willing to take up Reagan's initiative and, indeed, to assume leadership himself in reducing the levels of nuclear weaponry. For the first time in six years there was a U.S.-Soviet summit meeting (in Geneva, in November 1985), where Gorbachev asserted his interest in achieving the goal of a 50 percent reduction in nuclear arms. There was no specific common understanding, however, about this reduction's application to strategic arms, to intermediate-range weapons, or to space systems. Nor was there appreciable advances in the long-standing negotiations on MBFR negotiations in Vienna toward a verifiable agreement for Warsaw Pact–NATO reduction of ground forces.

Yet a momentum had been building toward constructive relations in 1985 that accelerated in 1986. It was symbolized by the agreement of the two leaders to visit their respective countries in the immediate future. It was further advanced by perceived advances in the conclusion of the Stockholm Conference on Confidence- and Security-Building Measures and Disarmament in Europe (CDE) in September 1986. The CDE included mandatory notification and observation of military activities throughout Europe, from the Atlantic to the Urals. These measures would apply to all of Soviet Europe, not just the 250-kilometer-wide strip along the USSR's western border (as under the Helsinki Final Agreement of 1975). There would be no right of refusal of on-the-spot verification inspections.[9]

This was the psychological infrastructure for the meeting of Reagan and Gorbachev in Reykjavik, Iceland, in October 1986. There the contrast between the two leaders was sharply displayed, as American diplomats uneasily anticipated. The week before the meeting Rozanne Ridgway, assistant secretary of state in charge of European and Canadian affairs, tried to discourage excessive expectations as she told Congress that it was essentially a preparatory meeting, "an occasion for private and informal talks between the President and the General Secretary" in anticipation of Gorbachev's visit to the United States.[10]

The State Department was justified in its uneasiness over the meeting. An aging American president, buffeted by the Iran-contra affair and pressed by a dynamic younger Soviet leader, stirred the alliance with hope and dread at their meeting in Iceland on 11 and 12 October 1986. The initiative behind closed doors appeared to have been with Gorbachev when he pressed Reagan to honor the Anti-Ballistic Missile Treaty of 1972 and to adhere to an interpretation of the treaty that would prohibit work on the SDI outside of laboratory research. European partners could accept this outcome, even if Reagan refused to accept restrictions on testing the SDI technology. The meeting ended on this sour note.

Secretary of State George Schultz disagreed with this negative judgment. He felt that the Reykjavik meeting revealed a flexibility in Soviet thinking that could break the stalemate between East and West, even if the Soviets ultimately withdrew their concessions on such matters as counting rules for bombs and the acceptance of British and French nuclear systems. Rather than writing off the president's behavior at Reykjavik as a blunder, Schultz implied that it exposed the weaknesses of the Soviet system and opened the way to the INF agreement in the following year.[11]

What disturbed Europeans, however, was less the president's intransigence over the SDI than his apparently impulsive counterproposal to eliminate within 10 years not just MRBMs but, as Senator Nunn quoted him, "everything else, including bombs."[12] This statement, quickly rephrased by the White House, evoked an image of a Soviet-American deal that would decouple America from Europe by removing a basic element in flexible response. Secretary Schultz's briefing for the North Atlantic Council a day later did little to soothe apprehensions. NATO's gloss on the Reykjavik meeting officially ignored the allies' misgivings, as its communiqué emphasized, along with "warm appreciation to President Reagan for his efforts," the need to work toward balanced agreements, particularly with respect to reduction in conventional forces.[13]

Despite the uncertainties that followed the Reykjavik meeting, Gorbachev expressly linked his IRBM initiative to Soviet acceptance of a broad range of understanding on reduction of both strategic and medium-range weapons. This opening with respect to the SS-20s and deployment of cruise missiles paved the way in the following year for what appeared to be fulfillment of the dual-track initiative of NATO of 1979: the removal of a major element in the nuclear threat. In the short run this was a more pressing issue than progress on START. Reagan's zero-zero proposal in 1982 would have had NATO cancel its plans to deploy cruise and Pershing II missiles if the Soviets gave up their SS-4s, and SS-20s. American officials feared that Gorbachev would seize on a ploy carelessly made in 1982 to reduce strategic arms, which Reagan's arms control advisers thought would never be accepted, and carry it forward. But the Reykjavik meeting did raise an issue that would be picked up later: namely, a 50 percent reduction of strategic nuclear missiles over a 10-year period.

Attention in 1987, however, focused on IRBMs. Reagan and Gorbachev signed the INF treaty in Washington on 8 December 1987. It involved removal of 470 long-range INF missiles (SS-20s and SS-4s) on the part of the Soviet Union. For the United States, 429 Pershing IIs and GLCMs would be removed. The INF treaty marked the first disarmament agreement ever to reduce rather than merely limit nuclear weapons. And the machinery to make it work was put into place. The intermediate-range missile systems would be eliminated in two phases over two years, with the shorter-range missiles going within a single 18-month period. The key element lay in verification of the treaty: five types of inspections by a force of 200 inspectors, 200 monitors, and 200 aircrew members from each side were included in the agreement. Secretary of State Schultz, was hopeful that "historians may come to see the INF experience as one of NATO's finest hours."[14]

The zero-zero level generated problems as well as solutions. Former SACEUR General Bernard Rogers thought in 1981 that the idea of zero-level "was a magnificent political gesture, but it gave me military gas pains because it returned us to where we were in 1979 which we had found to be unsatisfactory." What Rogers feared—even granting the success that the INF treaty achieved in forcing the Soviets into serious negotiations—was the undermining of flexible response by moving toward removal of a nuclear option. "It puts," he felt, "Western Europe on the slippery slope of de-nuclearization."[15]

This reaction was widely shared in Europe. If intermediate-range weapons were given up, the next subject would be strategic weapons, already on the table in START talks. Would this mean the abandonment of Europe as the two superpowers worked out a détente at the expense of the NATO allies? The byproduct of such an arrangement could be a normalization of relations between the Soviet Union and the United States that would permit American troops to leave Europe. If so, the alliance itself would be meaning-less. Moreover, if the new agreement should be a prelude to the denucleariza-tion of Europe, it would leave the allies vulnerable to the Warsaw bloc's superiority in conventional arms. In this circumstance the treaty would pro-duce less rather than more stability in Europe.

In this volatile scene Gorbachev was a one-man centrifugal force. His behavior toward the West as NATO moved into its fortieth anniversary might have been enough to put the finishing touches on an alliance he was helping to make obsolete. NATO was assaulted on three psychological fronts. First, the general secretary, strongly supported by his able foreign min-ister, Eduard Shevardnadze, braved the wrath of the Soviet military estab-lishment by beginning Soviet troop withdrawals from Afghanistan, thereby bringing to a close the war that provoked the Carter Doctrine in 1979. Begun in May 1988, the withdrawal was completed in February 1989 in accordance with a schedule announced by the then-President Gorbachev. While the continuing drain of a guerrilla war was probably a larger factor in Gorbachev's reasoning than the need to appease the United States, the results seemed to confirm a belief in the West that the Soviet Union was no longer supporting wars of national liberation.

At the same time that he was phasing out Soviet involvement in the Afghanistan war, Gorbachev impressed the world with his determination to reduce not only nuclear weaponry but armaments on every level. It was more than the 50 percent reduction in strategic weapons that the Soviets were seeking. This was clear in the Soviet leader's comments at the Moscow sum-mit of May 1988. It was even clearer when Gorbachev announced unilateral conventional force reductions in an address to the U.N. General Assembly in December 1988. The CFE agreements that seemed so distant in the recent past, considering the 15 years of lingering negotiations at Vienna on MBFR, now seemed realizable. Two days after Gorbachev's address the North Atlantic Council formally welcomed the Soviet announcements and went on to propose correcting "the large asymmetries that will still remain and to secure a balance at lower level of forces."[16] The council asked as well for a wide-ranging and comprehensive annual exchange of information with reliable measures for monitoring and verification. In brief, the verification principles worked out in the INF agreement would be a model for conventional forces as well.

Yet the caveats noted by the council also reflected some concerns about the seriousness of Soviet behavior. Was there a trap? At his farewell address in Brussels, before turning over the secretary-general's post to Germany's Manfred Wörner, Lord Carrington worried that "our interest in concluding binding agreements with the Soviet Union must not degenerate into allowing ourselves to be led by the siren songs of unilateral disarmers, misplaced fears, or Soviet peace rhetoric into failing to distinguish between good and bad negotiations." What worried him more than any NATO policy on formal arms control was what he called "involuntary of structural disarmament," which might be increasingly harder for the allied governments to avoid. There could be a point where the West would not have adequate resources to maintain an adequate defense.[17]

It was uncertain that Europe, about to be seized with "Gorby fever" would listen to these cautionary notes. The West was too stunned by a third step toward deescalation of East-West relations that was even more spectacular than Gorbachev's confidence-building measures on arms control and his actions in Afghanistan: namely, the dissolution of the Warsaw Pact.

RAISING THE IRON CURTAIN

The Soviet efforts to end the cold war were both internal and external. The most dramatic transformations were inside the Iron Curtain. At the conclusion of the CSCE meeting in Vienna on 19 January 1989, Soviet Foreign Minister Eduard Shevardnadze claimed that "the Vienna meeting has shaken up the Iron Curtain, weakened its rusty supports, made new breaches in it and sped up its corrosion."[18] This meeting adopted a concluding document that mandated new negotiations on conventional armed forces in Europe. But its immediate impact was a new confidence that resulted not from negotiations between the blocs but from measures adopted by the Soviet Union itself. They were far-reaching and revolutionary (or perhaps better identified as counterrevolutionary from a Soviet perspective). They involved nothing less than the disbanding of the Warsaw Pact and the disentangling of the member states from the Soviet grip.

As NATO began celebrating the fortieth anniversary of the signing of the treaty, the first multicandidate elections in an open contest on 27 March

1989 rebuffed official Communist party candidates for the Congress of People's Deputies. The former satellites followed suit. Nine days later Gorbachev gave tacit approval to agreements on political reforms in Poland between the government and the opposition, which included free elections and recognition of the proscribed Solidarity movement. The success of Solidarity in winning 35 percent of the seats in the Polish Parliament in June fulfilled the promises of April and was a prelude to the rapid disintegration of the Communist regime in that country. In August 1989 Tadeusz Mazowiecki became prime minister of the first non-Communist government in Poland in 40 years, even though the Communist party retained control of four ministries.

If ever there was a domino effect, it occurred in 1989. In September Hungary opened its western border, permitting thousands of East Germans to cross freely to the West. And in October the Hungarian Parliament adopted a new constitution that cleared the way for multiparty elections. The urge to throw off the Communist regimes in the Warsaw bloc now seemed to be irresistible as well as contagious. Czechoslovakia was rent by violent demonstrations that helped give power to the Civic Forum, led by the playwright Vaclav Havel. Gustav Husák resigned on 7 December and Havel was elected president six days later. Even the more devoted regime of Bulgaria experienced change as the Communist party leader since 1954, Todor Zhivkov, was removed from office on 16 November. In Romania a month later the Communist dictator Nicolai Ceausescu was arrested by the military. A National Salvation Front promised free elections.

Glasnost had reached the Warsaw bloc, and the consequences were not necessarily perestroika as much as the loosening of bonds in each of those nations, leading to the overthrow of their Communist regimes. Gorbachev's voice was the instrument in effecting changes, opening a Pandora's box to let out the repressed passions of nationalism and anticommunism. The breakdown of long-established Communist regimes in Czechoslovakia, Bulgaria, Hungary, and Romania in the fall of 1989 was not coincidental. Gorbachev's conversation with President George Bush in Malta on 2–3 December, followed by the Warsaw Pact leaders' denunciation in Moscow of the invasion of Czechoslovakia in 1968, were unmistakable signals of Gorbachev's intention to terminate the Warsaw Pact and with it the cold war.

The most dramatic of all the changes in this period was the opening the gates of—and then the tearing down of—the Berlin Wall on 9–10 November 1989. This event took place two months after Hungary opened its borders to permit East Germans to move to the West and only a month after Gorbachev, speaking in Berlin, urged reforms on the German Democratic Republic. The popular demonstrations that followed contributed not only to the continued exodus of East Germans but to the replacement of Erich Honecker, a symbol of the Brezhnev era. Small wonder that the celebrations in the West over the removal of the Wall were accompanied by an outburst of "Gorbymania," in honor of the Soviet leader who started it all. The road to German unification was cleared of its major obstacle. The cold war was in its final days.

NATO'S RESPONSE TO GORBACHEV

As these events rapidly unfolded NATO watched from the sidelines. It was not that the Western allies were unresponsive to the lifting of the Iron Curtain. Some of the hesitations that had accompanied the INF agreement dissolved. President Bush made an effort to accelerate the pace of negotiations on conventional forces by laying down a precise timetable for reaching an initial agreement. He could not have done much less in light of the propaganda advantages Gorbachev's dramatic unilateral reductions had given the Soviet Union. The EUROGROUP and the Defense Planning Committee communiqués in June 1989 paid tribute to developments in the Warsaw bloc. But while applauding change as "welcome in themselves and as a clear endorsement of the policy of the Alliance,"[19] the ministers were wary of continuing imbalances in military capabilities and saw no evidence of arms reductions in Soviet modernization programs.

The allies remained a step or more behind the Soviets, without a clear sense of the major convulsions taking place in the East. In effect, the United States and its allies held positions that did not move from the special report of the North Atlantic Assembly on "NATO in the 1990s," written in 1988, which acknowledged Gorbachev's efforts in favor of reducing the military confrontation and recognizing "asymmetries" in the European military balance. But this important document also expressed skepticism over Gorbachev's sincerity and concern over the gullibility of some Western Europeans.[20]

NATO leaders were forced to concede that the threat from the Soviet Union and its allies had diminished drastically and with increasing momentum over the past year. A Brookings Institution study claimed that the Soviet proposal for cutting conventional arms in Europe would benefit the West more than it would the Warsaw bloc. If the military units affected by the Moscow proposals were disbanded rather than relocated, NATO's reinforcement capabilities would be superior to those of the Soviet Union. The study assumed that NATO had sufficient stockpiles of munitions to wage a conventional war over a long period of time. The loss of the Soviets' quantitative superiority in tanks and artillery and armored troop carriers would give the West an advantage even if limits were placed on fighter bombers.[21]

The view from SHAPE was not as comforting as it was from Washington think tanks. There was some concern that the public might be lulled into complacency by Gorbachev's style. Reductions in conventional armament might be acceptable if carefully managed, but the nuclear issue was more sensitive. SACEUR John Galvin presented to the NPG a report on the nuclear weapons requirements for the 1990s that projected large cuts in nuclear artillery over the 1990s—a decrease from 7,200 warheads and bombs in the late 1960s to approximately 3,000 projected for the near future. But the key to these reductions, according to NATO military leadership, was the deployment of a modernized short-range nuclear missile.[22]

Instead of concentrating on—and welcoming—the prospects of extensive cuts in the nuclear arsenal, the European allies, particularly Germany, directed their attention to Galvin's plans for modernizing the reduced tactical nuclear weaponry in Europe. They balked at support of new and improved short-range missiles. While the Lance missile might be more efficient as a battlefield weapon, it reminded Europeans that its deployment would strike only forces in Western Europe. At another time, when the Soviet bloc was more threatening, this concern would be muted. But proposing new weaponries at a time when Gorbachev was promising a new relationship with the West seemed needlessly provocative. Chancellor Helmut Kohl urged postponement of the issue at least until after the next German elections. Here was the dilemma. NATO leaders recognized the importance of maintaining the organization's defensive posture, but at the same time they did not want to be outplayed in the Soviet game of détente.

Public opposition to the Lance missile did not diminish. Neither did the military demand for action on what was called "modernization" of nuclear defenses. The Soviet peace "offensive," demonstrated by the falling away of Communist regimes in the Warsaw bloc, seemed to undermine the deterrent strength of the allies. As late as September 1989 a NATO conference in Brussels was held to instruct the youth of the member nations about the importance of the alliance. The key problem facing the alliance, according to NATO officials, was not how to match the deescalation of the Soviets but how to win approval of a new Lance missile. When a German general from SHAPE spoke to the group, one member of the conference asked, with mischievous intent, what other issues were central to NATO planners. For example, how much thought was given to the possibility of German unification and its impact on NATO? With a smile, the general responded that he and his colleagues were giving as little thought as possible to such an outlandish prospect. Less than two months later the Berlin Wall was torn down.

What was so apparent to NATO leaders in 1989 was not the putative sincerity of Gorbachev's passion for nuclear and conventional disarmament but its impact on the moral fiber of the alliance. The demands on the part of British, German, and even French publics for a quick response to Soviet initiatives on short-range nuclear weapons raised suspicions in the United States that a new Soviet face was a variation of old peace drives designed to lull the West into inaction and drive the United States out of Europe. The alliance could be in greater danger from Soviet goodwill than from overt but familiar signs of malevolence. The increasing opposition of Germans in particular to what NATO leaders considered a vital need for new short-range missiles was added to more strident opposition to NATO maneuvers—tanks that chewed up arable land, planes that generated unbearable noise pollution. Sacrifices that could be borne in times of peril were unacceptable in times of détente. It was even more unacceptable at a time when the Warsaw bloc appeared to be coming apart at the seams.

From SHAPE's vantage point, the Soviet Union was as dangerous as ever. SACEUR Galvin noted that since March 1985, when Gorbachev took power, the Soviets continued to build up their conventional forces, particularly tanks and artillery. Such reductions as Gorbachev announced on 7 December at the United Nations would make at best only a modest dent in Soviet capabilities. In examining the state of East-West relations in May 1989, the North Atlantic Council acknowledged brighter prospects in qualitative improvements in East-West relations. But also warned that "although the WTO [Warsaw Treaty Organization] had recently announced and begun unilateral reductions in some of its forces, the Soviet Union continued to deploy military forces and to maintain a pace of military production in excess of legitimate defense requirements."[23] The language of negotiation for Americans throughout the period reflected President Bush's concern with his predecessor's maxim: "Trust but verify." Verification was the key element in the commentary of Ambassador Richard Burt, the chief U.S. negotiator in Round XL of START, which ended on 7 August 1989, three months before the wall fell.[24]

It was the dismantling of the wall that became the most impressive confidence builder in the Soviet empire. What was apparent to much of Europe was finally communicated to American leaders as well: namely, that the cold war was indeed in the process of dissolution and that the wall's dismantling was the end product of changes taking place throughout the Warsaw Pact bloc and in the Soviet Union. There was a glimmer of recognition that the Soviet Union under its charismatic leader was trying to extricate itself from an economic system that had failed, and that reducing friction between East and West was a vital step in the Soviet Union's regeneration.

This realization was dramatically reflected on the cover of the December 1989 issue of the NATO Review, where Soviet Foreign Minister Shevardnadze was shown shaking hands with NATO Secretary-General Manfred Wörner on the occasion of the former's visit to NATO headquarters. This photo opportunity had followed a summit meeting between Bush and Gorbachev in Malta on 2–3 December. The warmth of the sentiments exchanged compensated for the unusually stormy weather that greeted the two leaders on that Mediterranean island. When the North Atlantic Council met the following day, the language of the communiqués was different from those of the past. Tribute was paid to the remarkable changes in the East, as the council took credit for its own contribution to these "unprecedented changes by the maintenance of a credible and effective defense."[25] Only minor mention was made of the risks involved in these changes. The council's December meeting was an occasion for self-congratulation in contrast to its suspicion expressed in meetings earlier that year. The modernization of short-range tactical nuclear missiles in Europe was suddenly less relevant, and in the next year it disappeared from the agenda altogether. In May 1990 President Bush announced cancellation of a "follow-on" to the Lance missiles.[26] The termination of the cold war presumably rendered modernization of tactical missiles, or any other kind, unnecessary.

As NATO completed its fourth decade its leaders could take satisfaction in unanticipated successes. The antagonist was not only defeated but seemingly converted to the goals of the West. And the instrument of this conversation was the enigmatic figure of Mikhail Gorbachev. Was his introduction of glasnost and perestroika a response to the failure of the Afghanistan invasion? Was it a recognition of the excessive burden that the Soviet military machine inflicted on Soviet society? Did Reagan's insistence on the Strategic Defense Initiative awaken the Soviet leader to new costs counterweapons would impose? It is likely that these were all factors in the changes Gorbachev initiated in order to restructure a failing economic system. And it is equally likely that in attempting to achieve these ends by removing the burden of the cold war he unwittingly brought down the system he was trying to revive. In any event, his actions appeared to open a new era of cooperation between East and West in the last decade of the century.

chapter 9

NATO IN THE 1990S

If the events of 1989 were dramatic, those of the following years were revolutionary. Germany was reunited. The Warsaw Pact was disbanded, along with the Soviet Union itself. The Baltic republics regained their independence, and the Commonwealth of Independent States (CIS) replaced the Soviet Union. The United States was left as the sole superpower, and NATO the sole alliance. In brief, the domino that Gorbachev set in motion in 1985 finally stopped with the end of the cold war in 1990.

The euphoria accompanying these drastic changes induced State Department official Francis Fukuyama to suggest that "what we may be witnessing is not just the end of the Cold War, or the passing of a particular period of Cold War history, but the end of history as such: that is, the end point of man's ideological evolution and the universalization of Western liberal democracy as the final form of human government."[1]

The auguries for a new world order seemed to have been in place in that annus mirabilis, at least in three vital areas that had been at the center of NATO's concerns since its inception: (1) the deescalation of military confrontation between East and West, (2) the achievement of German unification, and (3) the development of a European community, with political and military as well as economic functions. What was only barely visible at this juncture was the rise of ethnic particularism in the former Warsaw Pact countries, the revival of fears of German domination in the united Germany, and the challenge of disorder in the Third World.

ARMS REDUCTIONS: CFE

The breakdown of the Soviet Union was accompanied by breakthroughs in arms agreements that would have been impossible a decade earlier.

In February 1990—the same month Gorbachev announced political plural-ism in the Soviet Union—NATO and the Warsaw Pact's foreign ministries agreed to steps leading to the Conventional Forces in Europe (CFE) agree-ment before the end of the year. Nine months later, in the framework of the CSCE summit meeting in Paris, NATO and Warsaw Pact members signed a major treaty on conventional armed forces in Europe. The CFE agreement limited the total deployment of equipment in the two alliances to 40,000 battle tanks, 40,000 artillery, 60,000 armored combat vehicles, 13,600 com-bat aircraft, and 4,000 attack helicopters. One analyst claimed that "the CFE Treaty closes the book on the military confrontation in Europe that has defined East-West relations during the past 40 years."[2] Two days later the CSCE heads of government, also meeting in Paris, endorsed the adoption of the Vienna Document on Confidence and Security-Building Measures. All the frictions of the past 15 years over the reduction of conventional forces appeared on the verge of being swept away. While there was no immediate dissolution of armed forces, the way was now cleared for just such drastic changes.

Advocates of CFE were aided by the concurrent collapse of the Warsaw bloc and the Soviet empire. The CFE treaty entered into force provisionally on 17 July 1992 with the arrangement of verification procedures. A battered Russia looked to major troop reductions as one method of relief from its eco-nomic plight. Acceptance of Western initiatives would not only reduce the cost of the military establishment in the long run but would win the kind of approval in the West needed to reconstruct the Russian economy.

American attitudes toward the CFE were mixed. The military worried about a future troop level that would be unable to function effectively in an emergency. On 21 May 1991 the U.S. House of Representatives called for a reduction of troop strength in Europe from 250,000 to 100,000 by 1995. This was not a figure that the administration could easily accept. There was con-cern among NATO partners that such a severe cut would be a prelude to the removal of all forces in Europe—the goal that the Soviet Union in better days had hoped for and the European partners had long feared.

These concerns notwithstanding, the CFE treaty and its possibilities minimized the dangers of an excessive reduction of forces. As Stanley Resor, former head of the U.S. delegation for MBFR negotiations noted, the treaty enjoyed the support of the secretaries of state and defense as well as SACEUR John Galvin and the chairman of the Joint Chiefs of Staff, Colin Powell.[3] The momentum for troop reduction took on a life of its own, ranging far beyond the cuts President Bush had announced on 29 May 1989. There followed a 20 percent reduction in army and air force personnel—from 305,000 to 270,000. This seemed at the time to be as far as NATO was ready to go in response to Gorbachev's unilateral troop and weapons reductions. General Galvin observed that when he took office in 1987 U.S. forces in NATO numbered 326,414. If he could accept a reduction to 150,000 by 1995, it was because of the disproportionate reductions the Soviets would take to give NATO a genuine parity; Soviet forces would be reduced by 500,000. While he noted that the Soviet forces would still be able to generate 60 divisions west of the Urals, NATO's 30 divisions would put the West in better shape than any time in the past four decades when NATO was outnumbered 3 to 1 instead of 2 to 1.[4] Conceivably, General Galvin's cautions, particularly over a potential buildup of men and arms east of the Urals, were pro forma in light of the disbanding of the Warsaw Pact three weeks before he testified at the Senate hearings on the CFE. In September 1991 the Soviet Union itself was dissolved. The new Russian state competed with the new republics created out of the Soviet Union for the largesse of the West. The Soviet military capabilities seemed almost irrelevant, at least for the immediate future.

ARMS REDUCTIONS: STRATEGIC NUCLEAR WEAPONS

It was hardly surprising that progress in nuclear arms control proceeded more rapidly than in conventional forces. The record of Soviet-American cooperation, if uneven, provided an infrastructure for further reductions. The INF agreements facilitated more ambitious plans to reduce the nuclear armories of both powers. Unlike in the past, when NATO allies expressed their worry over Soviet-American deals that would weaken their security, Europeans welcomed the reductions. The United States completed its withdrawal of intermediate-range missiles in March 1991. The Soviets in turn announced the elimination of the remaining SS-20 missiles two months later. Europeans welcomed even more warmly President Bush's cancellation on 3 May 1990 of the modernization programs for Lance nuclear missiles—a sore point that had agitated many of the allies, particularly the Germans.

In this new climate the Strategic Arms Reduction Talks (START), which had been initiated in 1982 as a tactical device to quiet domestic and foreign critics of the Reagan administration's nuclear program, became a launching pad for serious negotiations. The talks were resumed in Geneva on 19 June 1989. East-West relationships had changed sufficiently to give meaning to the North Atlantic Assembly's report on "NATO in the 1990s," "in the hope that new agreements would make it possible to reduce the overall numbers of nuclear weapons in Europe."[5]

On 31 July 1991 Presidents Bush and Gorbachev signed the START agreement in Moscow, which not only planned major reductions in U.S. and Soviet strategic nuclear arms but, in the words of Secretary-General Manfred Wörner, would "expand bilateral military transparency in that area as well as provide a framework for strategic stability into the next century."[6] The number of Soviet long-range nuclear warheads would be cut from over 11,000 to 6,100, while the United States would reduce its warheads from over 12,600 to under 8,900.

In the last days of the Bush administration the president concluded with Russia's President Boris Yeltsin a START II treaty, which called for a two-thirds reduction of their respective nuclear arsenals by the year 2003.

Although the European partners of the United States welcomed the treaty as a confidence-building measure rather than a threat to the deterrent capacity of the alliance as they might have seen it a few years earlier, Soviet opponents of Gorbachev saw the agreement as a confession of weakness. An attempted coup on 19 August 1991 temporarily removed Gorbachev from power while he was vacationing at a Black Sea resort. With the aid of Russian President Yeltsin, an old political rival of Gorbachev, the coup was defeated and Gorbachev was restored to office, at least temporarily. A general strike with its centers in Moscow and Leningrad not only frustrated the coup leaders but deterred the West from terminating its assistance to the tottering Soviet Union.

The North Atlantic Council endorsed the Bush initiatives, considering them to be a historic step toward enhanced security and stability at lower levels of nuclear weaponry. To encourage Gorbachev, President Bush announced on 27 September 1991 sweeping unilateral reductions in American nuclear arms, including destruction of all GLCMs and the removal of nuclear cruise missiles from submarines and surface ships. Nine days later Gorbachev responded with an equivalent action. NATO's reaction to these Alphonse-Gaston announcements was delivered at the Defense Committee meeting in Taormina, Italy, where they promised reductions of 80 percent of the NATO stockpile of substrategic nuclear weapons.

These activities took place as the Soviet Union dissolved. After the failed coup Gorbachev no longer stood in the way of the secession of the Baltic states. The Soviet Congress of People's Deputies suspended all operations of the Communist party on 29 September 1991 and a week later turned over the powers of the Soviet Union to the new republics, organized as the Commonwealth of Independent States, initially composed of Russia, Belorussia, and Ukraine, with headquarters in Minsk. The CIS vowed to continue the process of strategic nuclear deescalation, although the rise of nationalist sentiments in Ukraine slowed negotiations in 1992 and 1993.

THE NEW ARCHITECTURE OF EUROPE

As important as the deescalation of nuclear and conventional confrontation was in the history of NATO, its significance in 1991 had shrunk with the demise of the cold war. The challenge ahead for NATO and the United States was to promote the perestroika in the East that Gorbachev had initiated through glasnost. The danger was that the new freedom from communism, together with the enthusiasm for a market economy, could lead to disillusionment both with democracy and capitalism if the economic troubles of former Warsaw Pact countries were not addressed. Moreover, the breakup of the Soviet empire ignited ethnic conflicts throughout the area between Armenia and Azerbaijan, between Georgia and a host of minorities, and, not least, between Russia and the Baltic republics over treatment of the Russian minority. While the agreements for Russian troop withdrawal had been made with all the former allies and with the Baltic areas, they had not been fully implemented.

The United States and its allies recognized its stake in the survival of the new states and made plans for extending economic aid to tide them over the difficult transition. But the aid was never sufficient—or wisely used. Although Western economic aid to date has never come close to meeting needs, the West's efforts to provide political support of the CIS and eastern European states were serious. If the newly liberated satellites could have their way, NATO would be opened to their membership. Visits of political and military leaders to Brussels or Casteau were not sufficient; such encounters had been under way in the Gorbachev years. The East wanted something more material, and NATO complied by establishing the North Atlantic Coordinating Council on 20 December 1991. Asserting that security in the 1990s was based on a broad concept that "encompasses more than ever political, economic, social and environmental subjects as well as defense," the alliance's foreign ministers met with their counterparts of Bulgaria, the Czech and Slovak Republic, Hungary, Latvia, Lithuania and what was still the Soviet was still the Soviet Union (eight former Warsaw Pact and Baltic countries) to create an "interlocking network" that would meet regularly as "liaison partners" to deal with all aspects of defense issues as well as with civil-military relations, management of conversion of defense production to civilian purposes, and development of scientific and environmental programs.[7] Although Eastern Europe could not join NATO formally, its countries would be informal members whereby the smaller nations would feel the warmth of NATO's protection and the larger the benefits of NATO's political and economic support.

When the Warsaw Pact disintegrated into competing states, it was hardly surprising that the Atlantic alliance would itself undergo dramatic change. When the antagonist that had given birth to the alliance disappeared, NATO could follow the path of the Warsaw Pact into oblivion or it could find new missions for the future. The embrace that it was willing to extend to its former adversaries suggested that the route to NATO's future was to preserve order in a rapidly evolving new world.

One means of achieving this goal was to proceed quietly in the creation of the North Atlantic Coordinating Council. If the new democracies of Eastern Europe could not become part of NATO, then NATO itself could become a key partner in a larger organization that would embrace East and West: namely, the CSCE. NATO could be the engine that would set the CSCE in motion.

Such was the hope formally expressed in the London Declaration of a Transformed North Atlantic Alliance that emerged from the council meeting on 5–6 July 1990. The declaration proposed that NATO "work together not only for common defence, but to build new partnership with all nations of Europe."[8] It was at this meeting in London that the alliance looked ahead to a future beyond the cold war, when the concept of "defense" would be irrelevant as nuclear and conventional weaponry alike would be removed from the scene. In place of confrontation the CSCE would set standards for cooperation on every level—a secretariat would coordinate meetings, a mechanism would be created to monitor elections in all CSCE countries, a parliament body building on the Council of Europe would set up a Center for Prevention of Conflict. NATO would be its guide.

The momentum propelling the CSCE to the center of a new Europe received firm NATO endorsement when, a few months later at a summit meeting in Paris on 19–21 November 1990, the CSCE not only signed the CFE treaty but pledged in a joint declaration of 22 nations that they were "no longer adversaries." Thus the Council of Europe took up the recommendations of the NATO Council in London and expanded on the roles that the ministers of foreign affairs would play in providing a central forum for political consensus "within the CSCE process."[9] A secretariat in Prague would supply administrative support for the consultations. The Center for Conflict Prevention would meet in Vienna and an Office for Free Elections would be established in Warsaw. Recognizing that there were still obstacles to peace even as the threat of conflict in Europe waned, the CSCE planned to meet again in Valetta, Malta, in early 1991 to fashion new ways to settle disputes peacefully. All 34 members of the CSCE enshrined these principles in a charter for a new Europe.

NATO AND "OUT-OF-AREA"

There was euphoria in Paris in November 1990, particularly as German reunification had taken place peacefully only a month before. But even as these ceremonies were celebrated, the crisis in the Persian Gulf raised questions about European security that could not be answered by the CSCE. There was no machinery in place to bring about the admirable goals sought by the CSCE. Such changes would have to come about through established organizations like NATO. Of all the challenges of the 1990s, NATO's "out-of-area" involvement could well offer the greatest potential for justifying its survival. The current civil war in the former Yugoslavia and potential future civil wars in the former Soviet Union are arenas the alliance may enter. Conversely, out-of-area involvement might also expose vulnerabilities that could terminate the life of the alliance. NATO's first 40 years demonstrated that West-West tensions often had been more intense than

East-West confrontations. The history of the alliance has been punctuated by a succession of out-of-area crises that have generated bitterness among the allies, almost to the point, on more than one occasion, of dissolving the alliance. Grievances were nourished on both sides of the Atlantic.

As for the legality of NATO acting within the limits of its treaty obligations, a barrier exists only in the most literal sense. Although Article 6 specifically defines areas in which an armed attack on one or more of the parties would activate Article 5, there is room in Article 4 for the allies to act whether or not a direct assault is involved. Civil war spilling over the borders of one of the NATO members might not meet the definition of an armed attack, nor would damage from loss of a vital resource in an out-of-area nation fit the criterion of Article 5. Yet the consequence to one or more allies might be as severe as an armed attack from outside the organization's boundaries. In these circumstances Article 4, providing consultation whenever the security of any one of the parties was threatened, could provide a rubric for collective action.

Nonetheless, it was only after lengthy debates in the DPC and the North Atlantic Council that the alliance agreed to a formula in 1982 to respond to conflict in Southeast Asia, based not only on consultation on out-of-area deployments but also on Europe's agreement to facilitate the transport of U.S. troops and compensate for the diversion of U.S. assets. Charles Kupchan claimed that this formula, framed at the Bonn summit meeting in 1982, "has served as the basis of NATO's out-of-area policy since 1982."[10]

The formula was put to a severe test in the 1990s when the Middle East was the scene once again of the tensions "out-of-area" crises could generate within the alliance between Americans and Europeans. NATO appeared to be paralyzed by Saddam Hussein's sudden assault on Kuwait in August 1990. It stood aside, unable to take common action as it witnessed the United States mobilizing a coalition to liberate Kuwait and destroy the enormous military complex assembled by Saddam Hussein. In the face of NATO's inaction, President Bush introduced a series of measures, including the use of armed force, in the United Nations. Despite some reluctance on the part of the Soviet Union to accept drastic actions without more diplomatic efforts to influence its former client, Gorbachev's support was vital for the solidarity needed in the Security Council to sanction an invasion of Iraq.

Although NATO stood on the sidelines, it did, as Secretary General Wörner noted, "pledge [its] continued full support and endorsement for implementation and full compliance with its sanctions." Moreover, he observed that some of the allies had sent naval and air forces to the Gulf region as well as lending logistic support to this enterprise.[11] He might also have noted that without the NATO allies on the U.N. Security Council, Iraq's aggression might not have been challenged by the United Nations.

But the main point of this affirmation was that the allies had acted as individual nations, not as members of the Western alliance. In a formal statement on the Gulf crisis the council, meeting in Brussels on 17–18 December, repeated its support of Security Council Resolution 678, requiring Iraq to comply fully with mandatory U.N. decisions. Still, NATO's position on the use of force was equivocal: "Each of us, to the best of our ability, undertakes to provide further support for this continuing effort, in line with evolving requirements." The only specific application of force was the reaffirmation of Article 5 of the North Atlantic Treaty, which would go into effect if "one of our Allies having common borders with Iraq" were attacked.[12] That country was Turkey.

When the U.S.-led coalition, which included Saudi Arabia, Egypt, and Syria as well as France, Britain, and Italy, engaged Iraq in a brief but overwhelming assault, NATO was still on the sidelines. Indeed, at one point Germany raised doubts whether it would honor its NATO commitment to Turkey. But the triumph of the coalition over Saddam Hussein's forces seemed to energize the allies. The Defense Planning Committee and the Nuclear Planning Group, meeting in Brussels on 28 and 29 May 1991, not only welcomed the success of the coalition forces in the Gulf War but noted "with satisfaction the effectiveness of prompt action taken by the Alliance in deploying naval and air forces to the Southern region to deter any possible attacks on its members."[13] It is worth noting, however, that this action did not change the reality of a war in which NATO members functioned individually, not collectively.

If NATO failed to act as an organization in the war against Iraq, it could, however, take appropriate satisfaction from its indirect role in the conflict. Its large infrastructure in Germany, with troops and equipment freed from a Soviet threat that had disappeared in the previous year, was drawn on for the emergency in the Persian Gulf. Men and equipment from U.S. forces in Germany were the source of much of the impressive buildup in Saudi Arabia in the fall of 1990.

This factor also gave NATO an incentive to seek new functions for the alliance. At their meeting in May the defense ministers unveiled a new three-layered plan for dealing with future military crises with smaller forces. Working with half the number of forces currently in Europe, the allies would create a multinational rapid-reaction corps of 50,000 to 70,000 troops based in Germany under British command. Personnel would be contributed from Germany, the Low Countries, Italy, Greece, Spain, and possibly Turkey, as well as from Britain and the United States. The United States would provide tactical airlift and sealift transportation for the corps, which would be composed of two British and two multinational divisions. In the initial stage of a crisis, a mobile unit of 5,000 troops would respond within 72 hours. The corps' rapid mobility was expected to compensate for reduced numbers. There was also a third stage, "Augmentational Forces," drawn from all member nations and composed of U.S. Reserve and national Guard units that could be dispatched over a period of weeks. The target date for full operation was 1995.[14]

The war in the Persian Gulf, with its quick and successful strikes, inspired most of the allies in the spring of 1991 to expand their vision of NATO's functions. Presumably future crisis points would be on the periphery of the alliance, Norway and Turkey, bordering on the Soviet Union. While there was no specific statement identifying crises beyond NATO's borders as legitimate raisons d'être for the new force, this was the message implied in these actions.

THE NEW STRATEGIC CONCEPT

The war also provided a stimulus for completing NATO's new strategic concept, which had been in progress since the London meeting of the council. When the new concept was unveiled in Rome in November 1991, it should have laid to rest questions about NATO's future as a military organization. It was built on the assumption that the "CSCE process" was almost complete, as the unification of Germany presaged the end of a divided Europe. The heads of state and government agreed that the "threat of a simultaneous, full-scale attack on all of NATO's European fronts has effectively been removed and [is] thus no longer a focus for Allied strategy." The allies did take into account, however, potential dangers arising from the wreckage of the Soviet empire—ethnic strife in the new republics, a counter-revolutionary coup in the former Soviet Union, territorial disputes between former members of the Warsaw Pact. NATO would be the crisis manager in the event of new threats of disorder, which might emanate not from "calculated aggression against the territory of the Allies, but rather from the adverse consequences of instabilities."[15]

Parts of the concept had a ring of familiarity. The call for consultation under Article 4 of the North Atlantic Treaty when vital interests of the allies were affected or a reminder about the indivisibility of Allied security under Article 5 hardly broke new ground. What appeared to be new was acceptance of significant reductions in the overall size of allied forces and a recognition that emphasis on a rapid reaction force would replace the old linear defensive posture in Germany. The guidelines went on to anticipate benefits from "integrated and multinational European structures as they are further developed in the context of an emerging European Defence Identity." In sum, the new strategic concept looked ahead to a minimal force, nuclear and conventional to cope with problems stemming from instability and disorder rather than from the single powerful entity that NATO had confronted for more than a generation. Buttressed by dialogue with the East and cooperation with the CSCE, the EC, and the WEU, security would be won "at the lowest possible level of forces consistent with requirements of defence."[16]

How meaningful was the new strategic concept was a question asked by NATO's friends and foes alike. For its enemies, the Rome declarations were simply a last desperate effort to keep alive an alliance whose missions had been fulfilled. The issue was not implementation but conception. For NATO's supporters there were questions to which the brave words in Rome provided no clear answers. Among the most troublesome was the direction the reduced size of NATO forces would take the alliance. The Bush administration had fought a losing battle with Congress to keep the number of troops in Europe at 250,000. The administration of President Bill Clinton lowered the number to 100,000, to be achieved by 1995. What might be the consequence of the American military presence diminishing to the point where it would lose all military value? Was it not conceivable that the United States might remove all its forces from Europe, to be returned, if necessary, under the auspices of the Reforger airlift plan of the 1960s.

As domestic concerns dominated the nation, the old Soviet objective of driving American troops out of Europe could be realized. Before the end of the Bush administration the Congressional Research Service projected military effectiveness at different levels of troop strength and the likely consequences at each level. At 100,000, a "medium" army corps could be formed in place of a "large" corps, with consequent reduced combat power in battle. This number could still meet NATO expectations by relying on contingency units from the United States. At 50,000, however, the most that could be expected would be an army division, similar to the force currently maintained in South Korea.[17] Below that figure the Joint Chiefs anticipated that the American military could make noncombat contributions through peacekeeping and humanitarian aid, but not much more. Given the limited functions the American presence would have in these circumstances, the report concluded that the United States might as well leave the European continent to the Europeans.

The Canadian precedent was a model that alarmed European partners. Canada's announcement in February 1992 that it would close all its bases and pull its combat forces out of Europe by the end of 1994 inspired bitter criticism from its NATO allies at the Lisbon meeting of the North Atlantic Council in April. When Canada justified the move not only because the cold war had ended but because its troops were serving peace missions elsewhere under the auspices of the United Nations, the allies were not mollified. Secretary-General Wörner expressed "considerable regret, given the political and military importance of Canadian forces in Europe." Alex Morrison, executive director of the Canadian Institute of Strategic Studies, criticized the decisions as "a withdrawal of Canada into itself." The underlying reason for the emotional storm that this announcement evoked, according to Simon Serfarty of the Johns Hopkins School of Advanced International Studies, was its confirmation of "the perception that all of the New World is going home, and it might increase European interest in developing an autonomous defense entity that would be distinct from NATO."[18] Such was the message unwittingly sent from Ottawa.

As the Bush administration prepared to leave office in January 1993, Secretary of Defense Dick Cheney was less pessimistic over the reduction of American forces in Europe. Down-sizing the military force did not mean abandoning Europe or the alliance; it simply reflected, he claimed, the realities behind the transition from containment of a superpower to a regional defense strategy capable of handling new but smaller-scale challenges. It was based on Russian-American cooperation, as reflected in the Washington charter, signed by Presidents Bush and Yeltsin in June 1992. The bonds between the two former adversaries begun under Gorbachev were expected to continue and expand under Bush's successor. Similarly, NATO and the United States were expected to play a prominent role in the "emerging security architecture of Europe"—a term used frequently as the Soviet Union turned to perestroika. That architecture, according to Cheney, would include the many entities already in place in Europe—CSCE, NACC, EC, and WEU.[19]

THE UNITED STATES VERSUS EUROPE

A second assumption that followed from the Rome summit of 1991 was that NATO would coexist in harmony with what could be competitive rather than complementary European organizations. A successful evolution of the EC into a genuine United States of Europe, as envisioned by its leaders in Brussels, would threaten NATO at its most elemental level. There would be no need for the Atlantic alliance, with or without the Americans, if Europe developed defense capabilities to assure its own security. In this circumstance pressures for the removal of American troops would become irresistible from both sides of the Atlantic.

While "1992" became a metaphor for a single European economy, "Maastricht"—the Netherlands site where the important treaty was drafted—was the metaphor for the evolution of the EC into a political community with a military arm in the form of the WEU. For years some Europeans, particularly the French, had wistful ambitions for the WEU to lessen dependence on the American-dominated NATO. In Maastricht in December 1991 the EC negotiated a treaty that would transform the relationship among its members—all NATO partners with the exception of Ireland—into a tight economic union. Most internal border controls in a barrier-free market would be eliminated by the end of 1992, and, most important, the

Maastricht treaty would bring 12 members into "ever closer union among the peoples of Europe."

At long last the vision of a United States of Europe seemed to be close to realization. The political expectations were as exciting as the economic opportunities when the EC determined to expand the process of political cooperation into the area of defense. The EC at Maastricht determined that the WEU would become the EC's defense arm. WEU headquarters would be moved from London to Brussels to strengthen the links between the two institutions. In looking ahead to the end of the decade, the EC acted on the assumption that it had found a consensus among its members. And in a broad sense it had. All agreed to the desirability of the WEU serving a larger community, and all recognized the importance of completing the economic integration that had begun a generation before.

But schisms within the community quickly surfaced on the question of monetary union, a key element in the Maastricht treaty. Germany, the most powerful member of the community, asserted its dominance too quickly and too strongly. Its tight control over interest rates out of fear of inflation damaged the economies of many of its partners. The German mark would in effect become the currency of Europe in the future. Doubts about loss of national sovereignty accounted for Denmark's rejection of the treaty in 1992, a bare majority in its favor in France, and Britain's holding off from final judgment until Denmark reviewed its decision. It was likely that if the treaty's provisions did go into effect, they would be watered down by limiting the authority of the EC bureaucracy in Brussels and allowing more national deviations from common policy than had been anticipated when the treaty was framed.

Implicit in all the activities relating to the EC in the 1990s was the lowering of the NATO profile in Europe's future. This was an inevitable consequence of the end of the cold war. In effect, references to NATO were increasingly a euphemism for the United States. In a revealing commentary on the WEU relationship to NATO, the WEU assembly treated the organization as the equivalent of NATO and articulated a concern shared by all Europeans: namely, that the Canadian decision to withdraw its troops from Europe foreshadowed an American departure as well. Canadian action in the past and American action in the future would be done without consultation with its partners beforehand. The rapporteur of the WEU assembly made a point of noting a Pentagon paper, floated in the winter of 1992 and subsequently modified, that asserted America's interest on preventing "the emergence of a European-only arrangement which would undermine NATO." It did not escape European attention that the Pentagon document asserted that it was America's political and military mission to ensure that no rival superpower be allowed to challenge the preeminence of the United States in the post–cold war era. European resentment took the form of wondering why the United States and Canada would even be allowed to participate in the

CSCE, which had been "hitherto justified by their military presence in Europe."[20]

The EC at Maastricht was ambiguous in its references to NATO, using such elusive terms as "transparency" and "complementary" to define the WEU connection with NATO. Of the two terms, "complementary" was the more lucid. In the American view it would simply mean that if NATO would not, or could not, take a specific action, as in the Persian Gulf in 1990 or in Yugoslavia the following year, the WEU could be called on to act for NATO. The WEU's conception of complementarity would give Europe more initiative, with tasks defined by the WEU council rather than by the NATO council. There was obviously room for further development of the meaning of "complementary." The notion of "transparency" was even more opaque. For once, as the WEU rapporteur noted, transparency meant only that the chairman of the WEU council would report its discussion to the North Atlantic Council. By contrast, the American perspective would have no initiative undertaken by the WEU without prior agreement with NATO, particularly the United States.

What emerged, however, in European-American relations in the 1990s was a bloc, led by France and Germany, that would give lip service to its NATO provenance but operate independently. This development suggested Franco-German abandonment of the WEU as the military arm of the EC. It was obvious in 1993 that the United States would prefer that European defense efforts, which it had fostered in the past, would function in the framework of the WEU rather than in a separate Continental form, with an anti-American bias. Britain, after all, was a member of the WEU, and if there was no replication of a "special relationship" such as Britain had hoped for in the 1950s and 1960s, at least there was a harmony of views on France and Germany between the Anglo-American powers.

The British-led Rapid Reaction Corps, in which France was conspicuous by its absence, provoked French opposition from the beginning and indirectly challenged American as well as British roles in Europe. Periodically over the years France had encouraged the conversion of the WEU into the military arm of the EC, and its negative reaction to the Rapid Reaction Corps reflected this sentiment. At the meeting of EC's heads of state in May 1991 France recommended bringing the Rapid Reaction Corps under WEU auspices, where it would have a major voice. France's Foreign Minister Roland Dumas claimed that the Rapid Reaction Corps lacked both political and strategic reasoning. "Logic would require," he asserted, "that one first define the political objectives, then that one work out the strategy, before deciding on force structures. NATO has chosen the opposite path."[21]

There was no question that Dumas had a case to be made. How the corps would be meshed with other NATO forces and just how it would be used was not clarified in 1991. But Dumas's argument could also be turned against the French alternative program that was adopted when French views were not accepted. The prospect of a Franco-German led corps of 35,000 that would become operational by October 1995 was even murkier than the Rapid Reaction Corps. Just what relation it would have with NATO, considering France's continued self-exclusion for the SHAPE command, has not been resolved.

The Franco-German corps could evolve into a genuine European corps that would serve NATO defense in a crisis. But both Britain and the United States saw it as another French challenge to the integrity of NATO. The best gloss that Secretary of Defense Dick Cheney could put on the force in 1992 was that a crisis would bring French forces under SACEUR's command via the WEU.[22] The SACEUR himself judged that the new corps would not be able to act without cooperation from NATO. As General Galvin noted in regard to the placing of the Europe corps within a WEU context, "If the Western European Union has to have an infrastructure and the only one that is available is NATO's, then it seems to me that the first opportunity for a decision about acting in a crisis should be NATO's."[23]

The conflict over how Europe would be protected after the end of the cold war highlighted the confusion about roles and missions of the alliance. Given the strains already present in the alliance it was difficult not to judge the Mitterand-Kohl plan of May 1992 as another means of removing Europe from American domination. Predictably, Americans reacted as if they had a sovereign right to maintain the same controls they had held in Europe since the darkest days of the cold war. They had trouble taking seriously the Mitterand-Kohl statement that the corps "will contribute to strengthening the alliance" and was a response to Washington's persistent demand for burden sharing.[24] Former Secretary of Defense Caspar Weinberger thought it was absurd for the German defense minister to say that NATO should not worry since no German troops would be taken out of NATO and that the new army would consist of the same German troops now assigned to NATO. "This is cold comfort," he wrote in his biweekly "Commentary" for *Forbes* magazine in November 1991, "and reveal[s] the plan for what it is—an attempt to undermine NATO."[25]

France's initiative in sponsoring a Franco-German military force may have as much to do with its wariness of Germany as with its resentment of American domination. It was reasonable to assume that resurgent power would be more firmly anchored in a joint Franco-German army corps than in the more loosely knit NATO context. As a respected German newspaper recognized, François Mitterand's concern about a threat from a reunited Germany was reflected in his call in 1990 for Gorbachev to slow down the Soviet abandonment of the German Democratic Republic.[26]

YUGOSLAVIA AS A TEST CASE

If there was a more positive aspect to the confusion implicit in the abundance of arrangements for the protection of Central Europe from a disintegrating Eastern threat, it was the impetus it gave to NATO's effort to restructure its military organization. The new strategic concepts celebrated in London in 1990 and Rome in 1991 were still too vague: they had to be translated into specific actions. At the London summit the allies agreed to move away from the concept of forward defense and to modify the principle of flexible response by reducing reliance on nuclear weapons. In Rome they agreed that the "maintenance of a comprehensive in place linear defensive posture in the central region will no longer be required."[27] But just what would be the new "appropriate force" structures and procedures were not spelled out in that document.

Progress was made in implementing the strategic concept in 1992. In May the Defense Planning Committee announced a number of command changes. They included making the Standing Naval Forces the core of the Maritime Reaction Forces and the amalgamation of the five senior headquarters of Allied Forces Central Europe (AFCENT), particularly the merger of the Northern Army Group's headquarters with the Central Army Group's to form Land Force Central Region.[28] This reorganization reflected a shift of emphasis from Central Europe to the Mediterranean, where future conflicts were more likely to be found than on the North European plain. From Libya to the Balkans to the Middle East, NATO's military presence could be a vital factor in providing stability in the 1990s.

Arguably, the most significant statement in the DPC's communiqué concerned the establishment of the Standing Naval Force in the Mediterranean, which would be placed alongside the U.S. Sixth Fleet. This force consisted of eight frigates and destroyers, provided by eight NATO members, including the United States.[29]

To dramatize NATO's new focus the alliance conducted a major exercise, Operation Dragon Hammer, involving land as well as amphibious operations in and around Sardinia, the Italian mainland, and the Tyrrhenian Sea. As General Galvin told reporters, the new strategy emphasized "that we do not have adversaries, that what we do have is a situation of instability and unpredictability."[30]

NATO in 1992 had no enemy comparable to the Soviet Union in the organization's first 40 years, but in the Mediterranean area the instability and unpredictability that Galvin identified were present in abundance. Mu'ammar al-Qaddafi remained in power in Libya, while Islamic fundamentalists threatened the stability of Algeria and Egypt. But the disintegrating Yugoslavia was the major focus of attention, and might have been the venue for the kind of Rapid Reaction Corps that a restructured NATO was developing. Conceivably, a mobile, well-equipped force, under NATO or the WEU or the new Franco-German auspices, might have intervened to keep the peace just as the United States and its allies did in the Persian Gulf in 1990. The EC itself was partly responsible for the wars in the Balkans by prematurely recognizing the independence of Croatia before arrangements were made to protect the Serbian minority. A limited war between Croatia and the rump Yugoslavia (now just Serbia and Montenegro) gave an opportunity for Serbia to occupy parts of Croatia and indulge in the "ethnic cleansing" of areas to be resettled by Serbians.

Arguably, the distinctions between aggressor and victim in Croatia were blurred, excusing NATO from intervening. Such was not the case in Bosnia in 1992, where a powerful Serbian minority, armed and supported by the Yugoslavian army, seized all the territory it could manage from a country with a Muslim plurality. The Serbian aim was to create a Greater Serbia from territory formerly occupied by Muslims. The Croats, too, were victims of this new drive, but the Croats-Muslim coalition was outmanned and out-gunned by the Serbs. Moreover, the Croat contribution was suspect. To a lesser degree, Croatia had plans for annexing territory of Bosnia-Herzegovina. In Bosnia there was a clear opportunity for NATO to display its new mission with its reorganized forces.

The United States hesitated; NATO hesitated for understandable reasons. Unlike the Persian Gulf, there were no natural resources on which the West was dependent; the national interest of the United States and the collective interest of the NATO allies did not seem to be at stake. Conditions for a surgical strike that could win a victory at minimal cost were not present; the heavily armed Yugoslav army fighting in mountainous territory could wreak havoc on an invader, just as the Chetniks and Partisans were able to do in World War II. As in the Persian Gulf, NATO as an alliance could not bring itself to intervene. Germany continued to provide a strict construction to its constitutional bars against military action outside the bounds of the alliance; Britain and France, with peacekeeping forces in Bosnia, were fearful of Serbian retaliation; and the United States, in the throes of an election year, not only concentrated on domestic issues but remembered the ill-fated Lebanon expedition 10 years before. The result was, as Neal Ascherson wrote in August 1992, NATO staying "in its bunk with its polished boots on."[31]

There was no lack of attention, however, given to the suffering of Bosnian Muslims. The allies looked to the United Nations for assistance. The Security Council denounced Serbian aggression. The secretary-general dispatched peacekeeping teams and made valiant efforts to bring food and supplies to the besieged victims. Unlike the actions against Saddam Hussein, however, the United Nations was not a rubric under which the United States could mobilize a coalition against Serbian president Slobodan Milosevič The NATO allies hoped the good offices of U.N. representative Cyrus Vance, joined by the EC representative, David Owen, could bring the warring parties to the peace table. The council itself was not prepared in 1992 to conduct a war against the Serbs to enforce U.N. resolutions.

Still, after a year of observing the destruction of Bosnia, NATO was inching its way toward greater involvement. Meeting separately in Helsinki at the time of the CSCE summit in July 1992, NATO and the WEU agreed to conduct a coordinated maritime operation in the Adriatic to monitor compliance with Security Council resolutions 713 and 757 concerning the embargo against Yugoslavia.[32] Had Operation Dragon Hammer in June been placed in the Adriatic off the eastern shores of Italy instead of in the Tyrrhenian Sea off the western shores, NATO's message might have been stronger. As it was, the statement of 15 July was more symbolic than substantive. Whatever surveillance activities might be undertaken would have of itself limited effect. The sea approach was not the key to a successful embargo of Yugoslavia.

By the end of the year NATO's language was more explicit as the council warned Serbia and Bosnian Serbs of NATO's concern. But the message was still that of a distant well-wisher to U.N. actions. The foreign ministers rejected unilateral change in borders, territory, or populations; demanded restoration of the sovereignty and territorial integrity of Bosnia-Herzegovina; and agreed that strict enforcement of U.N. embargoes was essential. But the specific actions of NATO itself remained primarily the contribution of data from NATO Airborne Early Warning Aircraft to help monitor the Bosnia no-fly zone. The NATO communiqué of December 1992 mentioned vaguely further steps and "appropriate measures" without specifying what those steps and measures would be.[33]

In 1993 the agony of the Bosnian Muslims and the embarrassment of NATO, the EC, and the United States grew exponentially. Serbia colluded with Bosnian compatriots to continue its campaign to drive Muslims out of the unitary state that Bosnian Serbs had demanded. The face-saving Vance-Owen plan to keep Bosnia together in a loose confederation of semi-autonomous provinces was the subject of negotiations in Geneva and New York. But while negotiations were proceeding Bosnian Serbs stepped up their efforts at ethnic cleansing of the region even as they intended to negotiate short-lived cease-fires. As the war raged in the Balkans, President Clinton, who had made a more active support of the Muslims a campaign pledge in the presidential race, looked for ways to increase American involvement without placing American lives at risk.

The initial response was to employ U.S. planes flying at high altitudes to drop food and supplies to starving Muslims in isolated villages. These air drops, however, were not only too modest and frequently wide of their mark, but they also sent the wrong signal to the Serbs. The action suggested timidity rather than boldness and at best only postponed the day when the victims would either starve to death or be forced into exile. Collaboration between NATO and the United Nations appeared to offer a way out of this dilemma. As Jamie Shea, senior planning officer in the Political Directorate pointed out, a precedent was established in January 1993 when the United Nations requested NATO to draw up a detailed plan for the implementing of the no-fly zone over Bosnia. This was in response to NATO's offer to employ NATO aircraft to enforce the no-fly zone. The plan went into effect in April 1993 and represented "the first time that NATO forces have been engaged out-of-area and directly in a war zone."[34]

Such a role for NATO in the Balkans would fit a pattern that had been developing since the Gulf War two years before. The peace-keeping function of both NATO and the United Nations would benefit from the synergy between the two organizations. The United Nations would have the benefit of the infrastructure NATO had built over a generation in Europe and at the same time legitimize a new mission for NATO—the maintenance of stability in Europe. General John Shalikashvili, General Galvin's successor as SACEUR, pointed out that the precedent for full NATO implementation had already made NATO involved: "NATO is already involved. It has ships in the Atlantic enforcing sanctions; it has early warning aircraft; it has elements of a headquarters corps sitting outside Sarajevo. All these things were unheard of when we were debating whether NATO should have an out-of-area role. Today, they are taken for granted."[35] Among other objectives this function could serve to show the primacy of NATO over competing European structures that had failed to make a mark in Yugoslavia.

But would the operation take place? And if it did, would it be in time to preserve Bosnia from being absorbed into a Greater Serbia? In mid-1993, as NATO entered its forty-fifth year, there was no clear answer. As for NATO allies France and Britain, the former was uncomfortable with being part of a NATO force unless it was clearly under U.N. command. Britain, with its peacekeeping contingent in Bosnia, was vulnerable to Serbian retaliation from the beginning and was from the first a reluctant partner of United States' efforts to resolve the Balkan crisis. Outside the Security Council was Germany, which paid more attention to its growing internal problems than to the ongoing crisis it helped to ignite. As long as there is uncertainty about German military forces participating in a conflict outside NATO borders, NATO capabilities will be severely limited. But the key player is the United States, where the military leaders remain fearful of being pulled into a quagmire. The preferred position would be to participate in a NATO force only after all the parties had agreed to a peaceful resolution of their differences.

What the Balkan crisis highlighted was not simply that NATO has a function that it has not yet been able to fulfill in the 1990s but that other potential peacekeeping forces have been unable to fill this need. If any crisis outside the borders of NATO deserved an appropriate arena for an all-European action, it is in Croatia and Bosnia. The Franco-German corps or the British-led Rapid Reaction Corps might have been the spearheads of Europe's response to a European crisis. They were not. While the WEU made its presence known in participating in the naval blockade of

Yugoslavia, it was a minor role that complicated matters with overlapping lines of authority. As British analyst Christopher Coker pointed out, "The somewhat unconvincing WEU patrols in the Gulf [1987] and the Adriatic [1992] reveal demonstrably that the union has neither the political will nor the military resources to conduct a policy independent of NATO. It has no reconnaissance capability, no space satellites, and no data collection facilities in space."[36] In short, it made little sense for the WEU to duplicate what the United States through NATO already provided for its allies.

In the background lies the CSCE, the European version of a United Nations, where hopes were placed in the beginning of the decade for a Europe in which the United States and former Soviet Union would be engaged. But the CSCE lacks an infrastructure even if it could muster unanimity. As for the EC evolving into a United States of Europe, the immediate fate of the Maastricht treaty emphasized the long road ahead before a political federation of Europe was likely. As Conor Cruise O'Brien claimed flatly, "there is not going to be a United States of Europe."[37]

THE FUTURE OF NATO: THE GERMAN QUESTION

On the surface the Danish vote against the new community, along with France's tepid affirmative, began the downward spiral after the signing of the Treaty of Union in January 1992. Denmark's subsequent acceptance of the treaty in May 1993 did little to reverse the trend. But behind the slide was the recognition of German dominance of the community and the memories this reality invoked. Edith Cresson, the sharp-tongued though short-lived prime minister of France, in 1991 recalled that only twice in her 57 years had she feared for the very existence of her country—during German occupation in World War II and during the night when the Berlin Wall came down. She warned that if you "don't force the Germans to their knees, they'll be at your throats."[38] This was an extreme statement, but in one form or another it characterized sotto voce Europe's concern about a future Europe without America.

From the moment a united Germany was inevitable qualms were expressed in the United States, the Soviet Union, and France. None of the victorious allies of World War II was comfortable with the rapid transformation of the Two-Plus-Four agreement on unification into an intra-German arrangement that left out the "four." Within a year after the fall of the Berlin Wall, Germany was reunited by its own actions on a timetable different from those of the Soviets, the Americans, the British, and the French. Despite the enormous economic burden unification imposed on Germany, there was a new assertiveness that left Germany's allies wary of its future direction. This discomfort was aggravated over the next two years by

Germany's insistence on recognition of Croatia without guarantees to minorities in the newly independent nation. And the Bundesbank's insistence on maintaining high interest rates was blamed for the recession afflicting EC countries. In this context the European corps, with the nominal equality accorded to the French, was a thin cover for a German Europe. Europeans looking at the shape of things to come looked at the American component of NATO as a necessary counterbalance.

In April 1993 the creation of an American-German corps appeared to offer a way to resolve both the cognate problem of American reduction of forces in Europe and concurrent German domination of the shrunken forces. Claiming that the two new multinational corps "heralds a new era," General Shalikashvili saw the military merger as a means of preserving the dwindling financial resources of the alliance while maintaining a level of military readiness sufficient to maintain stability in Europe. The agreement on a corps called for 17,000 soldiers of the American First Armored Division to report under the German II Corps in the event of a NATO crisis. At the same time, the German 5th Panzer Division would report to the commander of the U.S. V Corps. Although in peacetime the two divisions would remain under control of their own countries, they would train together in military exercises.[39]

THE FUTURE OF NATO: EAST EUROPEAN PROBLEMS

If the containment of Germany is an unspoken but nonetheless genuine factor in the maintenance of Europe's links to America, the uncertainties in the East reinforce the need for the alliance to continue. The end of the cold war has opened the way for a new world disorder in the form of ethnic conflicts ranging from the former Yugoslavia to the nationalities bordering the former Soviet Union—and for that matter to ethnic groups within Russia itself. Presumably most of these conflicts, all the more bitter for having been repressed by Communist dictatorships in the past, would not have international implications. But there is no certainty that a war between Armenia and Azerbaijan or between the Romanian and Russian populations of Moldavia would not expand to war between Russia and Romania—and beyond. One of the nightmares about Yugoslavia centered on a triumphant Serbia having absorbed most of Bosnia, moving on to expel Albanian ethnics from Kosovo. Such an event might involve the two NATO allies Greece and Turkey. The state of the Balkans in the 1990s dramatizes the need for a stabilizing presence in Europe for the time being.

But of all the challenges to the stability of Europe, the danger of civil war in Russia between the former Communists and the new democrats looms the largest. Not least of the dangers that would follow would be the temptation for one party or another to use nuclear weaponry in such an internal conflict. When asked what worried him most about the future of Europe's security,

SACEUR Shalikashvili immediately drew attention to the potential of political chaos in Europe. "Bosnia and Iraq may be important," he noted, "but the real security of the Atlantic alliance will be determined by what happens in Moscow."[40]

The future of a democratic Russia in 1993 was by no means secure. Despite his personal victory over nationalists and ex-Communists in Parliament in an April 1993 national referendum concerning his presidency and the reform movement, Boris Yeltsin and his supporters could not relax their vigilance. Six months later Yeltsin barely survived a showdown with an array of enemies centered in Parliament but joined by an alliance of former Communists and ardent nationalists. It is not beyond possibility that a new right-wing coup exploiting economic discontent and Yeltsin's dependence on American support would have better success. The role of the Russian military was crucial in Yeltsin's suppression of Parliament in October. That support may not be present in the next crisis. If so, what impact would these changes have on NATO's mission in its relations with a Russia weaker than the Soviet Union but armed with nuclear weapons and intent on a foreign policy hostile to the interests of the alliance? The immediate result could be to energize the alliance in a fashion that the importance of financial aid to Eastern Europe could never do. NATO had to anticipate the significance of a Russian nationalist regime that could emerge from disillusionment with Western capitalism.

THE FUTURE OF NATO: AMERICA'S ROLE

It is worth noting that pressures for removal of American forces have not come from Europeans. Nor for that matter has there been any action on the part of any member to withdraw from the alliance in conformity with the provisions under Article 13 of the North Atlantic Treaty. Nor have there been any perceptible efforts on the part of any party to push American troops out of Europe. In fact, the primary pressures in Europe have come from Eastern Europeans anxious to join the alliance to assure security against potential Russian intimidation.

If there are pressures for dissolution they may be found in the United States more than in Europe. It is hardly surprising that voices have been raised seeking a peace dividend through withdrawal of American troops from Europe. Pressures to reduce troop level below the 250,000 level of the Bush administration, and even below the 100,000 figure cited in the Clinton administration, are inevitable by-products of the end of the cold war. Unlike the Vietnam era, however, the animus toward Europeans who refused to follow American leadership in Southeast Asia is missing. There is no crisis such as the Mansfield resolution created in 1971, when the future of the alliance appeared to have been at stake. In fact, a case may be made that NATO in the 1990s is accepted as a part of American foreign policy in the way that abstention from alliances had been in the 1930s.

The major opponents of the alliance in the 1990s have not been politicians reacting to popular demands but pundits claiming that the alliance no longer has meaning. Ronald Steel's *End of the Alliance* made this argument in the 1970s; Irving Kristol's 1980 question, "Does NATO Still Exist?" was recalled by Melvin Krauss in 1986, with some embellishments. Kristol claimed that NATO was as irrelevant to American interests as SEATO was at the time it was dissolved a decade before.[41] With the dissolution of the Soviet Union itself, Ted Galen Carpenter in 1992 concluded that "there is simply no longer a credible superpower threat to the security of Western Europe. Under vastly changed conditions, a U.S.-dominated NATO protectorate is an anachronism, and the time has come to devolve full responsibility for the security of Europe to the Europeans."[42] These analysts have logic on their side. In light of all the obstacles confronting NATO after the cold war, its chances for survival should be dim in the mid-1990s. As NATO plans (as of this writing) for its summit meeting in January 1994, it has been weakened by the inability of the allies to reach a consensus on dealing with civil war in Yugoslavia. The Clinton administration was split at the end of 1993 between a wish to punish Serbia for its aggression and a fear of being entangled in a conflict the nation would not support. Given the uncertainties in American leadership, it is a tribute to NATO's reputation that former Warsaw Pact nations planned to lobby at the NATO meeting for admission to the alliance.

Such an expansion of members, however, is unlikely, not only because of opposition by the Russian military establishment but because NATO has enough problems without taking on those of countries unprepared for an equal partnership in the alliance. The most hopeful prospect would be a re-affirmation of the NACC and a promise of membership in the distant future, as well as an offering of a security blanket across Eastern Europe. Despite the strong if unofficial recommendations of Rand analysts and the clear statement of Senator Richard Lugar,[43] former chair of the Senate Foreign Relations Committee, NATO will do little more than offer its moral support for stability. It is doubtful that Poles, Czechs, and Hungarians will consider this offer to be a satisfactory translation of Secretary of State Warren Christopher's "partnership for peace."

If the alliance surmounts the many crises facing it in 1994 it will not be because of any new military strategy NATO is fashioning. It will be because Europe has failed to come up with any viable alternative. Lack of security in the face of ethnic conflicts in the Balkans and elsewhere, the potential upsurge of Russian nationalism, the fears engendered by a powerful Germany all leave NATO, flawed as it is, as the only stabilizing multinational instrument in the world.

While the United States remains a player on the European world scene, NATO will remain in place. It is the only vehicle legitimizing the American presence in Europe, and it is one that no ally wishes to remove. It is also the only organization with the means, if not the will, to act in a crisis. As long as NATO contains the potential for action, the organization has a future, even when the will to act is missing.

APPENDIX A

THE BRUSSELS PACT

Treaty of Economic, Social and Cultural Collaboration and Collective Self-Defense between the Governments of the United Kingdom and Northern Ireland, Belgium, France, Luxembourg, and the Netherlands, signed at Brussels, March 17, 1948.

Article I

Convinced of the close community of their interests and of the necessity of uniting in order to promote the economic recovery of Europe, the High Contracting Parties will so organize and coordinate their economic activities as to produce the best possible results, by the elimination of conflict in their economic policies, the coordination of production and the development of commercial exchanges.

The co-operation provided for in the preceding paragraph, which will be effected through the Consultative Council referred to in Article VII as well as through other bodies, shall not involve any duplication of, or prejudice to, the work of other economic organizations in which the High Contracting Parties are or may be represented but shall on the contrary assist the work of those organizations.

Article II

The High Contracting Parties will make every effort in common, both by direct consultation and in specialized agencies, to promote the attainment of a higher standard of living by their peoples and to develop on corresponding lines the social and other related services of their countries.

The High Contracting Parties will consult with the object of achieving the earliest possible application of recommendations of immediate practical interest, relating to social matters, adopted with their approval in the specialized agencies.

They will endeavor to conclude as soon as possible conventions with each other in the sphere of social security.

Article III

The High Contracting Parties will make every effort in common to lead their peoples towards a better understanding of the principles which form the basis of their common civilization and to promote cultural exchanges by conventions between themselves or by other means.

Article IV

If any of the High Contracting Parties should be the object of an armed attack in Europe, the other High Contracting Parties will, in accordance with the provisions of Article 51 of the Charter of the United Nations, afford the party so attacked all the military and other aid and assistance in their power.

Article V

All measures taken as a result of the preceding Article shall be immediately reported to the Security Council. They shall be terminated as soon as the Security Council has taken the measures necessary to maintain or restore international peace and security.

The present Treaty does not prejudice in any way the obligations of the High Contracting Parties under the provisions of the Charter of the United Nations. It shall not be interpreted as affecting in any way the authority and responsibility of the Security Council under the Charter to take at any time such action as it deems necessary in order to maintain or restore international peace and security.

Article VI

The High Contracting Parties declare, each so far as he is concerned, that none of the international engagements now in force between him and any other of the High Contracting Parties or any third State is in conflict with the provisions of the present Treaty.

None of the High Contracting Parties will conclude any alliance or participate in any coalition directed against any other of the High Contracting Parties.

Article VII

For the purpose of consulting together on all the questions dealt with in the present Treaty, the High Contracting Parties will create a Consultative Council, which shall be so organized as to be able to exercise its functions continuously. The Council shall meet at such times as it shall deem fit.

At the request of any of the High Contracting Parties, the Council shall be immediately convened in order to permit the High Contracting Parties to consult with regard to any situation which may constitute a threat to peace, in whatever area this threat should arise; with regard to the attitude to be adopted and the steps to be taken in case of a renewal by Germany of an aggressive policy; or with regard to any situation constituting a danger to economic stability.

Article VIII

In pursuance of their determination to settle disputes only by peaceful means, the High Contracting Parties will apply to disputes between themselves the following provisions:

The High Contracting Parties will, while the present Treaty remains in force, settle all disputes falling within the scope of Article 36, paragraph 2, of the Statute of the International Court of Justice by referring them to the Court, subject only, in the case of each of them, to any reservation already made by that Party when accepting this clause for compulsory jurisdiction to the extent that that Party may maintain the reservation.

In addition, the High Contracting Parties will submit to conciliation all disputes outside the scope of Article 36, paragraph 2, of the Statute of the International Court of Justice.

In the case of mixed dispute involving both questions for which conciliation is appropriate and other questions for which judicial settlement is appropriate, any Party to the dispute shall have the right to insist that the judicial settlement of the legal questions shall precede conciliation.

The preceding provisions of this Article in no way affect the application of relevant provisions or agreements prescribing some other method of pacific settlement.

Article IX

The High Contracting Parties may, by agreement, invite any other State to accede to the present Treaty on conditions to be agreed between them and the State so invited.

Any State so invited may become a Party to the Treaty by depositing an instrument of accession with the Belgian Government.

The Belgian Government will inform each of the High Contracting Parties of the deposit of each instrument of accession.

Article X

The present Treaty shall be ratified and the instrument of ratification shall be deposited as soon as possible with the Belgian Government.

It shall enter into force on the date of the deposit of the last instrument of ratification and shall thereafter remain in force for fifty years.

After the expiry of the period of fifty years, each of the High Contracting Parties shall have the right to cease to be a party thereto provided that he shall have previously given one year's notice of denunciation to the Belgian Government.

The Belgian Government shall inform the Governments of the other High Contracting Parties of the deposit of each instrument of ratification and of each notice of denunciation.

In witness whereof, the above-mentioned Plenipotentiaries have signed the present Treaty and have affixed thereto their seals.

Done at Brussels, this seventeenth day of March 1948, in English and French, each text being equally authentic, in a single copy which shall remain deposited in the archives of the Belgian Government and of which certified copies shall be transmitted by the Government to each of the other signatories.

APPENDIX B

THE NORTH ATLANTIC TREATY,

WASHINGTON, D.C., APRIL 4, 1949

The Parties to this Treaty reaffirm their faith in the purposes and principles of the Charter of the United Nations and their desire to live in peace with all peoples and all governments.

They are determined to safeguard the freedom, common heritage and civilisation of their peoples, founded on the principles of democracy, individual liberty and the rule of law.

They seek to promote stability and well-being in the North Atlantic area.

They are resolved to unite their efforts for collective defence and for the preservation of peace and security.

They therefore agree to this North Atlantic Treaty:

Article 1

The Parties undertake, as set forth in the Charter of the United Nations, to settle any international dispute in which they may be involved by peaceful means in such a manner that international peace and security and justice are not endangered, and to refrain in their international relations from the threat or use of force in any manner inconsistent with the purpose of the United Nations.

Article 2

The Parties will contribute toward the further development of peaceful and friendly international relations by strengthening their free institutions, by bringing about a better understanding of the principles upon which these institutions are founded, and by promoting conditions of stability and well-being. They will seek to eliminate conflict in their international economic policies and will encourage economic collaboration between any or all of them.

Article 3

In order more effectively to achieve the objectives of this Treaty, the Parties, separately and jointly, by means of continuous and effective self-help and mutual aid, will maintain and develop their individual and collective capacity to resist armed attack.

Article 4

The Parties will consult together whenever, in the opinion of any of them, the territorial integrity, political independence or security of any of the Parties is threatened.

Article 5

The Parties agree that an armed attack against one or more of them in Europe or North America shall be considered an attack against them all and consequently they agree that, if such an armed attack occurs, each of them, in exercise of the right of individual or collective self-defence recognised by Article 51 of the Charter of the United Nations, will assist the Party or Parties so attacked by taking forthwith, individually and in concert with the other Parties, such action as it deems necessary, including the use of armed force, to restore and maintain the security of the North Atlantic area.

Any such armed attack and all measures taken as a result thereof shall immediately be reported to the Security Council. Such measures shall be terminated when the Security Council has taken the measures necessary to restore and maintain international peace and security.

From *The North Atlantic Treaty Organisation* (Brussels: NATO Information Service, 1984), 264–66, 289–91, 295–97; and from Hastings Lord Ismay, *NATO: The First Five Years, 1949–1954* (Paris: NATO, 1955), 266.

Article 6[1]

For the purpose of Article 5 an armed attack on one or more of the Parties is deemed to include an armed attack on the territory of any of the Parties in Europe or North America, on the Algerian Departments of France,[2] on the occupation forces of any Party in Europe, on the islands under the jurisdiction of any Party in the North Atlantic area north of the Tropic of Cancer or on the vessels or aircraft in this area of any of the Parties.

Following this statement the Council noted that insofar as the former Algerian Departments of France were concerned, the relevant clauses of this Treaty had become inapplicable as from July 3, 1962.

Article 7

This Treaty does not affect, and shall not be interpreted as affecting in any way the rights and obligations under the Charter of the Parties which are members of the United Nations, or the primary responsibility of the Security Council for the maintenance of international peace and security.

Article 8

Each Party declares that none of the international engagements now in force between it and any other of the Parties or any third State is in conflict with the provisions of this Treaty, and undertakes not to enter into any international engagement in conflict with this Treaty.

Article 9

The Parties hereby establish a Council, on which each of them shall be represented, to consider matters concerning the implementation of this Treaty. The Council shall be so organised as to be able to meet promptly at

---

[1]The definition of the territories to which Article 5 applies has been revised by Article 2 of the Protocol to the North Atlantic Treaty on the accession of Greece and Turkey (see Part 10, Section 3).

[2]On January 16, 1963, the North Atlantic Council has heard a declaration by the French Representative who recalled that by the vote on self-determination on July 1, 1962, the Algerian people had pronounced itself in favour of the independence of Algeria in cooperation with France. In consequence, the President of the French Republic had on July 3, 1962, formally recognised the independence of Algeria. The result was that the Algerian departments of France no longer existed as such, and that at the same time the fact that they were mentioned in the North Atlantic Treaty had no longer any bearing.

any time. The Council shall set up such subsidiary bodies as may be necessary; in particular it shall establish immediately a defense committee which shall recommend measures for the implementation of Articles 3 and 4.

Article 10

The Parties may, by unanimous agreement, invite any other European State in a position to further the principles of this Treaty and to contribute to the security of the North Atlantic area to accede to this Treaty. Any State so invited may become a Party to the Treaty by depositing its instrument of accession with the Government of the United States of America. The Government of the United States of America will inform each of the Parties of the deposit of each such instrument of accession.

Article 11

This Treaty shall be ratified and its provisions carried out by the Parties in accordance with their respective constitutional processes. The instruments of ratification shall be deposited as soon as possible with the Government of the United States of America, which will notify all the other signatories of each deposit. The Treaty shall enter into force between the States which have ratified it as soon as the ratifications of the majority of the signatories, including the ratifications of Belgium, Canada, France, Luxembourg, the Netherlands, the United Kingdom and the United States, have been deposited and shall come into effect with respect to other States on the date of the deposit of their ratifications.

Article 12

After the Treaty has been in force for ten years, or at any time thereafter, the Parties shall, if any of them so requests, consult together for the purpose of reviewing the Treaty, having regard for the factors then affecting peace and security in the North Atlantic area, including the development of universal as well as regional arrangements under the Charter of the United Nations for the maintenance of international peace and security.

Article 13

After the Treaty has been in force for twenty years, any Party may cease to be a Party one year after its notice of denunciation has been given to the Government of the United States of America, which will inform the Governments of the other Parties of the deposit of each notice of denunciation.

Article 14

This Treaty, of which the English and French texts are equally authentic, shall be deposited in the archives of the Government of the United States of America. Duly certified copies will be transmitted by that Government to the Governments of other signatories.

APPENDIX C

RESOLUTION ON RESULTS OF THE FOUR AND NINE POWER MEETINGS

(ADOPTED BY THE NORTH ATLANTIC COUNCIL ON 22ND OCTOBER 1954)

For Portugal:	Paulo Cunha
For Turkey:	F. Köprülü
For the United Kingdom:	Anthony Eden
For the United States:	John Foster Dulles

The North Atlantic Council:

Recognising that all the arrangements of arising out of the London Conference form part of one general settlement which is directly or indirectly of concern to all the NATO Powers and has therefore been submitted to the Council for information or decision;

Have learnt with satisfaction of the arrangements agreed between the Governments of France, the United Kingdom and the United States of America and of the Federal Republic of Germany for the termination of the occupation regime in the Federal Republic as set forth in the Protocol communicated to the Council;

Welcome the decision of the Brussels Treaty Powers to invite the Federal Republic of Germany and Italy to accede to the Brussels Treaty as modified and completed by the Protocols and other documents communicated to the Council, and hereby record their agreement with the provisions of those protocols and documents insofar as they concern action by the North Atlantic Treaty Organization;

Welcome the extension of the Brussels Treaty as an important step toward the achievement of European unity; and express confidence that there will be the closest co-operation between the Western European Union and the North Atlantic Treaty Organization which remains the foundation of the security and progress of the Atlantic Community.

Take note with satisfaction of the statements made on 29th September 1954 in London by the United States Secretary of State and the Canadian Secretary of State for External Affairs, and of the declaration by the Foreign Secretary of the United Kingdom concerning the maintenance of United Kingdom forces on the continent of Europe;

Finally,

Record their deep satisfaction at the happy conclusion of all the above arrangements which together constitute a decisive step in fortifying the North Atlantic Alliance and uniting the Free World.

APPENDIX D

THE FUTURE TASKS OF THE ALLIANCE (HARMEL REPORT)

REPORT OF THE COUNCIL
ANNEX TO THE FINAL COMMUNIQUÉ OF THE MINISTERIAL MEETING

DECEMBER 1967

1. A year ago, on the initiative of the Foreign Minister of Belgium, the governments of the fifteen nations of the Alliance resolved to 'study the future tasks which face the Alliance, and its procedures for fulfilling them in order to strengthen the Alliance as a factor for durable peace'. The present report sets forth the general tenor and main principles emerging from this examination of the future tasks of the Alliance.

2. Studies were undertaken by Messrs. Schütz, Watson, Spaak, Kohler and Patijn. The Council wishes to express its appreciation and thanks to these eminent personalities for their efforts and for the analyses they produced.

3. The exercise has shown that the Alliance is a dynamic and vigorous organisation which is constantly adapting itself to changing conditions. It also has shown that its future tasks can be handled within the terms of the Treaty by building on the methods and procedures which have proved their value over many years.

4. Since the North Atlantic Treaty was signed in 1949 the international situation has changed significantly and the political tasks of the Alliance have assumed a new dimension. Amongst other developments, the Alliance has played a major part in stopping Communist expansion in Europe; the USSR has become one of the two world super powers but the Communist world is no longer monolithic; the Soviet doctrine of 'peaceful co-existence' has changed the nature of the confrontation with the West but not the basic problems. Although the disparity between the power of the United States and that of the European states remains, Europe has recovered and is on its way towards unity. The process of decolonization has transformed European relations with the rest of the world; at the same time, major problems have arisen in the relations between developed and developing countries.

5. The Atlantic Alliance has two main functions. Its first function is to maintain adequate military strength and political solidarity to deter aggression and other forms of pressure and to defend the territory of member countries if aggression should occur. Since its inception, the Alliance has successfully fulfilled this task. But the possibility of a crisis cannot be excluded as long as the central political issues in Europe, first and foremost the German Question, remain unsolved. Moreover, the situation of instability and uncertainty still precludes a balanced reduction of military forces. Under these conditions, the Allies will maintain as necessary a suitable military capability to assure the balance of forces, thereby creating a climate of stability, security and confidence.

In this climate the Alliance can carry out its second function, to pursue the search for progress towards a more stable relationship in which the underlying political issues can be solved. Military security and a policy of détente are not contradictory but complementary. Collective defence is a stabilising factor in world politics. It is the necessary condition for effective policies directed towards a greater relaxation of tensions. The way to peace and stability in Europe rests in particular on the use of the Alliance constructively in the interest of détente. The participation of the USSR and the USA will be necessary to achieve a settlement of the political problems of Europe.

6. From the beginning the Atlantic Alliance has been a cooperative grouping of states sharing the same ideals and with a high degree of common interest. Their cohesion and solidarity provide an element of stability within the Atlantic area.

7. As sovereign states the Allies are not obliged to subordinate their policies to collective decision. The Alliance affords an effective forum and clearing house for the exchange of information and views; thus, each Ally can decide its policy in the light of close knowledge of the problems and objectives of the others. To this end the practice of frank and timely consultations needs to be deepened and improved. Each Ally should play its full part in promoting an improvement in relations with the Soviet Union and the countries of Eastern Europe, bearing in mind that the pursuit of détente must not be allowed to split the Alliance. The chances of success will clearly be greater if the Allies remain on parallel courses, especially in matters of close concern to them all; their actions will thus be all the more effective.

8. No peaceful order in Europe is possible without a major effort by all concerned. The evolution of Soviet and East European policies gives ground for hope that those governments may eventually come to recognise the advantages to them of collaborating in working towards a peaceful settlement. But no final and stable settlement in Europe is possible without a solution of the German question which lies at the heart of present tensions in Europe. Any such settlement must end the unnatural barriers between Eastern and Western Europe, which are most clearly and cruelly manifested in the division of Germany.

9. Accordingly the Allies are resolved to direct their energies to this purpose by realistic measures designed to further a détente in East-West relations. The relaxation of tensions is not the final goal but is part of a long-term process to promote better relations and to foster a European settlement. The ultimate political purpose of the Alliance is to achieve a just and lasting peaceful order in Europe accompanied by appropriate security guarantees.

10. Currently, the development of contacts between the countries of Western and Eastern Europe is mainly on a bilateral basis. Certain subjects, of course, require by their very nature a multilateral solution.

11. The problem of German reunification and its relationship to a European settlement has normally been dealt with in exchanges between the Soviet Union and the three Western powers having special responsibilities in this field. In the preparation of such exchanges the Federal Republic of Germany has regularly joined the three Western powers in order to reach a common position. The other Allies will continue to have their views considered in timely discussions among the Allies about Western policy on this subject, without in any way impairing the special responsibilities in question.

12. The Allies will examine and review suitable policies designed to achieve a just and stable order in Europe, to overcome the division of Germany and to foster European security. This will be part of a process of active and constant preparation for the time when fruitful discussions of these complex questions may be possible bilaterally or multilaterally between Eastern and Western nations.

13. The Allies are studying disarmament and practical arms control measures, including the possibility of balanced force reductions. These studies will be intensified. Their active pursuit reflects the will of the Allies to work for an effective détente with the East.

14. The Allies will examine with particular attention the defense problems of the exposed areas, e.g. the south-eastern flank. In this respect the present situation in the Mediterranean presents special problems, bearing in mind that the current crisis in the Middle East falls within the responsibilities of the United Nations.

15. The North Atlantic Treaty area cannot be treated in isolation from the rest of the world. Crises and conflicts arising outside the area may impair its security either directly or by affecting the global balance. Allied countries contribute individually within the United Nations and other international organisations to the maintenance of international peace and security and to the solution of important international problems. In accordance with established usage the Allies, or such of them as wish to do so, will also continue to consult on such problems without commitment and as the case may demand.

16. In the light of these findings, the Ministers directed the Council in permanent session to carry out, in the years ahead, the detailed follow-up resulting from this study. This will be done either by intensifying work already in hand or by activating highly specialised studies by more systematic use of experts and officials sent from capitals.

17. Ministers found that the study by the Special Group confirmed the importance of the role which the Alliance is called upon to play during the coming years in the promotion of détente and the strengthening of peace. Since significant problems have not yet been examined in all their aspects, and other problems of no less significance which have arisen from the latest political and strategic developments have still to be examined, the Ministers have directed the Permanent Representatives to put in hand the study of these problems without delay, following such procedures as shall be deemed most appropriate by the Council in permanent session, in order to enable further reports to be subsequently submitted to the Council in Ministerial Session.

APPENDIX E

LONG-RANGE THEATER NUCLEAR FORCE MODERNIZATION AND RELATED ARMS CONTROL

Communiqué Issued Following the Special Meeting of Foreign and Defense Ministers in Brussels on December 12, 1979[1]

1. At a special meeting of Foreign and Defense Ministers in Brussels on 12th December 1979:

2. Ministers recalled the May 1978 Summit where governments expressed the political resolve to meet the challenges to their security posed by the continuing momentum of the Warsaw Pact military build-up.

3. The Warsaw Pact has over the years developed a large and growing capability in nuclear systems that directly threaten Western Europe and have a strategic significance for the Alliance in Europe. This situation has been especially aggravated over the last few years by Soviet decisions to implement programmes modernising and expanding their long-range nuclear capability substantially. In particular, they have developed the SS-20 missile, which offers significant improvements over previous systems in providing greater accuracy, more mobility, and greater range, as well as having multiple warheads, and the Backfire bomber, which has a much better performance than other Soviet aircraft deployed hitherto in a theatre role. During this period, while the Soviet Union has been reinforcing its superiority in Long Range Theatre Nuclear Forces (LRTNF) both quantitatively and qualitatively, Western LRTNF capabilities have remained static. Indeed these

---

[1]France did not participate in the Special Meeting of Foreign and Defense Ministers.

forces are increasing in age and vulnerability and do not include land-based, long-range theatre nuclear missile systems.

4. At the same time, the Soviets have also undertaken a modernization and expansion of their shorter-range TNF and greatly improved the overall quality of their conventional forces. These developments took place against the background of increasing Soviet inter-continental capabilities and achievements of parity in inter-continental capability with the United States.

5. These trends have prompted serious concern within the Alliance, because, if they were to continue, Soviet superiority in theatre nuclear systems could undermine the stability achieved in inter-continental systems and cast doubt on the credibility of the Alliance's deterrent strategy by highlighting the gap in the spectrum of NATO's available nuclear response to aggression.

6. Ministers noted that these recent developments require concrete actions on the part of the Alliance if NATO's strategy of flexible response is to remain credible. After intensive consideration, including the merits of alternative approaches, and after taking note of the positions of certain members, Ministers concluded that the overall interest of the Alliance would best be served by pursuing two parallel and complementary approaches of TNF modernization and arms control.

7. Accordingly Ministers have decided to modernize NATO's LRTNF by the deployment in Europe of US ground-launched systems comprising 108 Pershing II launchers, which would replace existing US Pershing I-A, and 464 Ground-Launched Cruise Missiles (GLCM), all with single warheads. All the nations currently participating in the integrated defense structure will participate in the program: the missiles will be stationed in selected countries and certain support costs will be met through NATO's existing common funding arrangements. The program will not increase NATO's reliance upon nuclear weapons. In this connection, Ministers agreed that as an integral part of TNF modernization, 1,000 US nuclear warheads will be withdrawn from Europe as soon as feasible. Further, Ministers decided that the 572 LRTNF warheads should be accommodated within that reduced level, which necessarily implies a numerical shift of emphasis away from warheads for delivery systems of other types and shorter ranges. In addition they noted with satisfaction that the Nuclear Planning Group is undertaking an examination of the precise nature, scope and basis of the adjustments resulting from the LRTNF deployment and their possible implications for the balance of roles and systems in NATO's nuclear armory as a whole. This examination will form the basis of a substantive report to NPG Ministers in the autumn of 1980.

8. Ministers attach great importance to the role of arms control in contributing to a more stable military relationship between East and West and in advancing the process of détente. This is reflected in a broad set of initiatives being examined within the Alliance to further the course of arms control and détente in the 1980s. Ministers regard arms control as an integral part of the Alliance's efforts to assure the undiminished security of its member States and to make the strategic situation between East and West more stable, more predictable, and more manageable at lower levels of armaments on both sides. In this regard they welcome the contribution which the SALT II Treaty makes toward achieving these objectives.

9. Ministers consider that, building on this accomplishment and taking account of the expansion of Soviet LRTNF capabilities of concern to NATO, arms control efforts to achieve a more stable overall nuclear balance at lower levels of nuclear weapons on both sides should therefore now include certain US and Soviet long-range theater nuclear systems. This would reflect previous Western suggestions to include such Soviet and US systems in arms control negotiations and more recent expressions by Soviet President Brezhnev of willingness to do so. Ministers fully support the decision taken by the United States following consultations within the Alliance to negotiate arms limitations on LRTNF and to propose to the USSR to begin negotiations as soon as possible along the following lines which have been elaborated in intensive consultations within the Alliance:

A. Any future limitations on US systems principally designed for theatre missions should be accompanied by appropriate limitations on Soviet theater systems.

B. Limitations on US and Soviet long-range theater nuclear systems should be negotiated bilaterally in the SALT III framework in a step-by-step approach.

C. The immediate objective of these negotiations should be the establishment of agreed limitations on US and Soviet land-based long-range theater nuclear missile systems.

D. Any agreed limitations on these systems must be consistent with the principle of equality between the sides. Therefore, the limitations should take the form of de jure equality both in ceilings and in rights.

E. Any agreed limitations must be adequately verifiable.

10. Given the special importance of these negotiations for the overall security of the Alliance, a special consultative body at a high level will be constituted within the Alliance to support the US negotiating effort. This body will follow the negotiations on a continuous basis and report to the Foreign and Defense Ministers who will examine developments in these negotiations as well as in other arms control negotiations at their semiannual meetings.

11. The Ministers have decided to pursue these two parallel and complementary approaches in order to avert an arms race in Europe caused by the

Soviet TNF build-up, yet preserve the viability of NATO's strategy of deterrence and defence and thus maintain the security of its member States.

A. A modernisation decision, including a commitment to deployments, is necessary to meet NATO's deterrence and defence needs, to provide a credible response to unilateral Soviet TNF deployments, and to provide the foundation for the pursuit of serious negotiations on TNF.

B. Success of arms control in constraining the Soviet build-up can enhance Alliance security, modify the scale of NATO's TNF requirements, and promote stability and détente in Europe in consonance with NATO's basic policy of deterrence, defence and détente as enunciated in the Harmel Report. NATO's TNF requirements will be examined in the light of concrete results reached through negotiations.

APPENDIX F

THE ALLIANCE'S NEW STRATEGIC CONCEPT

AGREED BY THE HEADS OF STATE AND GOVERNMENT PARTICIPATING IN THE MEETING OF THE NORTH ATLANTIC COUNCIL IN ROME ON 7–8 NOVEMBER 1991

1. At their meeting in London in July 1990, NATO's Heads of State and Government agreed on the need to transform the Atlantic Alliance to reflect the new, more promising, era in Europe. While reaffirming the basic principles on which the Alliance has rested since its inception, they recognized that the developments taking place in Europe would have a far-reaching impact on the way in which its aims would be met in the future. In particular, they set in hand a fundamental strategic review. The resulting new Strategic Concept is set out below.

Part 1—The Strategic Context

The new strategic environment

2. Since 1989, profound political changes have taken place in Central and Eastern Europe which have radically improved the security environment in which the North Atlantic Alliance seeks to achieve its objectives. The USSR's former satellites have fully recovered their sovereignty. The Soviet Union and its Republics are undergoing radical change. The three Baltic Republics have regained their independence. Soviet forces have left Hungary and Czechoslovakia and are due to complete their withdrawal from Poland and Germany by 1994. All the countries that were formerly adversaries of NATO have dismantled the Warsaw Pact and rejected ideological hostility to the West. They have, in varying degrees, embraced and begun to implement policies aimed at achieving pluralistic democracy, the rule of law, respect for human rights and a market economy. The political division of Europe that was the source of the military confrontation of the Cold War period has thus been overcome.

3. In the West, there have also been significant changes. Germany has been united and remains a full member of the Alliance and of European institutions. The fact that the countries of the European Community are working towards the goal of political union, including the development of a European security identity; and the enhancement of the role of the WEU, are important factors for European security. The strengthening of the security dimension in the process of European integration, and the enhancement of the role and responsibilities of European members of the Alliance are positive and mutually reinforcing. The development of a European security identity and defence role, reflected in the strengthening of the European pillar within the Alliance, will not only serve the interests of the European states but also reinforce the integrity and effectiveness of the Alliance as a whole.

4. Substantial progress in arms control has already enhanced stability and security by lowering arms levels and increasing military transparency and mutual confidence (including through the Stockholm CDE agreement of 1986, the INF Treaty of 1987 and the CSCE agreements and confidence and security-building measures of 1990). Implementation of the 1991 START Treaty will lead to increased stability through substantial and balanced reductions in the field of strategic nuclear arms. Further far-reaching changes and reductions in the nuclear forces of the United States and the Soviet Union will be pursued following President Bush's September 1991 initiative. Also of great importance is the Treaty on Conventional Armed Forces in Europe (CFE), signed at the 1990 Paris Summit; its implementation will remove the Alliance's numerical inferiority in key conventional weapon systems and provide for effective verification procedures. All these developments will also result in an unprecedented degree of military transparency in Europe, thus increasing predictability and mutual confidence. Such transparency would be further enhanced by the achievement of an Open Skies regime. There are welcome prospects for further advances in arms control in conventional and nuclear forces, and for the achievement of a global ban on chemical weapons, as well as restricting establishing arms exports and the proliferation of certain weapons technologies.

5. The CSCE process, which began in Helsinki in 1975, has already contributed significantly to overcoming the division of Europe. As a result of the Paris Summit, it now includes new institutional arrangements and provides a contractual framework for consultation and co-operation that can play a constructive role, complementary to that of NATO and the process of European integration, in preserving peace.

6. The historic changes that have occurred in Europe, which have led to the fulfillment of a number of objectives set out in the Harmel Report, have significantly improved the overall security of the Allies. The monolithic, massive and potentially immediate threat which was the principal concern of the Alliance in its first forty years has disappeared. On the other hand, a great deal of uncertainty about the future and risks to the security of the Alliance remain.

7. The new Strategic Concept looks forward to a security environment in which the positive changes referred to above have come to fruition. In particular, it assumes both the completion of the planned withdrawal of Soviet military forces from Central and Eastern Europe and the full implementation by all parties of the 1990 CFE Treaty. The implementation of the Strategic Concept will thus be kept under review in the light of the evolving security environment and in particular progress in fulfilling these assumptions. Further adaptation will be made to the extent necessary.

Security challenges and risks

8. The security challenges and risks which NATO faces are different in nature from what they were in the past. The threat of a simultaneous, full-scale attack on all of NATO's European fronts has effectively been removed and thus no longer provides the focus for Allied strategy. Particularly in Central Europe, the risk of a surprise attack has been substantially reduced, and minimum Allied warning time has increased accordingly.

9. In contrast with the predominant threat of the past, the risks to Allied security that remain are multi-faceted in nature and multi-directional, which makes them hard to predict and assess. NATO must be capable of responding to such risks if stability in Europe and the security of Alliance members are to be preserved. These risks can arise in various ways.

10. Risks to Allied security are less likely to result from calculated *aggression against the territory* of the Allies, but rather from the adverse consequences of instabilities that may arise from the serious economic, social and political difficulties, including ethnic rivalries and territorial disputes, which are faced by many countries in Central and Eastern Europe. The tensions which may result, as long as they remain limited, should not directly threaten the security and territorial integrity of members of the Alliance. They could, however, lead to crises inimical to European stability and even to armed conflicts, which could involve outside powers or spill over into NATO countries, having a direct effect on the security of the Alliance.

11. In the particular case of the Soviet Union, the risks and uncertainties that accompany the process of change cannot be seen in isolation from the fact that its conventional forces are significantly larger than those of any other European State and its large nuclear arsenal comparable only with that of the United States. These capabilities have to be taken into account if stability and security in Europe are to be preserved.

12. The Allies also wish to maintain peaceful and non-adversarial relations with the countries in the Southern Mediterranean and Middle East. The stability and peace of the countries on the southern periphery of Europe are important for the security of the Alliance, as the 1991 Gulf war has shown. This is all the more so because of the build-up of military power and the proliferation of weapons technologies in the area, including weapons of mass destruction and ballistic missiles capable of reaching the territory of some member states of the Alliance.

13. Any armed attack on the territory of the Allies, from whatever direction, would be covered by Articles 5 and 6 of the Washington Treaty. However, Alliance security must also take account of the global context. Alliance security interests can be affected by other risks of a wider nature, including proliferation of weapons of mass destruction, disruption of the flow of vital resources and actions of terrorism and sabotage. Arrangements exist within the Alliance for consultation among the Allies under Article 4 of the Washington Treaty and, where appropriate, co-ordination of their efforts including their responses to such risks.

14. From the point of view of Alliance strategy, these different risks have to be seen in different ways. Even in a non-adversarial and co-operative relationship, Soviet military capability and build-up potential, including its nuclear dimension, still constitute the most significant factor of which the Alliance has to take account in maintaining the strategic balance in Europe. The end of East-West confrontation has, however, greatly reduced the risk of major conflict in Europe. On the other hand, there is a greater risk of different crises arising, which could develop quickly and would require a rapid response, but they are likely to be of a lesser magnitude.

15. Two conclusions can be drawn from this analysis of the strategic context. The first is that the new environment does not change the purpose or the security functions of the Alliance, but rather underlines their enduring validity. The second, on the other hand, is that the changed environment offers new opportunities for the Alliance to frame its strategy within a broad approach to security.

CHRONOLOGY

1945   U.N. Charter is signed in San Francisco on 26 June.

1947   On 12 March President Harry S. Truman urges Congress "to
            support free peoples who are resisting attempted subjugation
            by armed minorities or by outside pressure" (Truman
            Doctrine) and requests financial aid to Greece and Turkey.
            In his Harvard University commencement speech on 5 June,
            Secretary of State George C. Marshall announces a plan for
            the economic rehabilitation of Europe (the Marshall Plan).

1948   Britain's secretary of state for foreign affairs, Ernest Blevin,
            proposes to Parliament on 22 January a form of the Western
            Union. The Brussels Pact is signed on 17 March by Belgium,
            Britain, France, Luxembourg, and the Netherlands. The
            U.S. Senate adopts Resolution 239 (the Vandenberg
            Resolution) on 11 June. The Soviet Union's Berlin blockade
            begins 24 June. Representatives of the United States,
            Canada, and the Brussels Pact powers meet in Washington,
            D.C., on 6 July and again on 10 December to negotiate the
            drafting of a North Atlantic Treaty.

1949   On 15 March the North Atlantic Treaty negotiating powers
            invite Denmark, Iceland, Italy, Norway, and Portugal to join. On
            4 April the treaty is signed in Washington, D.C., by Belgium,
            Canada, Denmark, France, Iceland, Italy, Luxembourg, the

---

Adapted from *The North Atlantic Treaty Organisation* (Brussels: NATO Information Service, 1984), 327–56, and *NATO Handbook* (Brussels: NATO Information Service, 1986), 98–101.

Netherlands, Norway, Portugal, Britain, and the United States. The Council of Europe is set up in London on 5 May. The Berlin blockade is lifted on 9 May. The North Atlantic Treaty goes into effect on 24 August. The Mutual Defense Assistance Act is signed by President Truman on 6 October.

1950   On 27 January President Truman approves plan for integrated defense of the North Atlantic area, releasing $900 million in military aid. On 9 May France proposes the creation of a single authority to control the production of steel and coal in France and Germany (Schuman Plan). North Korea attacks South Korea on 25 June. On 24 October France's prime minister, René Pleven, outlines his plan for a unified European army, to include Germans, within the framework of the North Atlantic Council plan. The council appoints General Dwight D. Eisenhower as Supreme Allied Commander Europe (SACEUR) on 16 December. The Consultative Council of the Brussels Pact powers decide to merge the military organization of the Western Union into the North Atlantic Treaty Organization (NATO) on 20 December.

1951   On 2 April Supreme Allied Command Europe becomes operational with Supreme Headquarters Allied Powers Europe (SHAPE) in Rocquencourt, near Paris. On 18 April Belgium, France, Italy, Luxembourg, the Netherlands, and West Germany set up the European Coal and Steel Community.

1952   Greece and Turkey accede to the North Atlantic Treaty on 18 February. At a meeting in Lisbon (20–25 February) the North Atlantic Council reorganizes the alliance: NATO becomes a permanent organization with its headquarters in Paris, and the Channel Command is established, with Admiral Sir Arthur John Power appointed its commander-in-chief. On 12 March Lord Ismay of Britain is appointed vice chairman of the North Atlantic Council and secretary-general of NATO. Supreme Allied Command Atlantic becomes operational on 10 April, with headquarters in Norfolk, Virginia. On 27 May the European Defense Community (EDC) is established with a treaty signed by

Belgium, France, Italy, Luxembourg, the Netherlands, and West Germany.

1954   Abortive conference on German reunification between the ministers of France, Britain, the United States, and the Soviet Union is held in Berlin, 25 January–18 February. On 29 August the French National Assembly declines to ratify the EDC treaty. Representatives of Belgium, Britain, Canada, France, Italy, Luxembourg, the Netherlands, the United States, and West Germany meet in London, 28 September–3 October, seeking an alternative to the EDC. Britain, France, the United States, and West Germany meet in Paris, 20–22 October, and adopt a protocol terminating the occupying regime of West Germany. The Paris Agreements are signed on 23 October: West Germany is invited to join NATO, and West Germany and Italy accede to the Western European Union (WEU).

1955   West Germany becomes a member of NATO on 5 May. On 14 May the Soviet Union concludes the Warsaw Pact with Albania, Bulgaria, Czechoslovakia, East Germany, Hungary, Poland, and Romania. Abortive meeting on German reunification between the ministers of France, Britain, the United States, and the Soviet Union is held in Geneva, 27 October–11 November.

1956   On 13 December the North Atlantic Council adopts resolutions on the peaceful settlement of disputes between member countries and on nonmilitary cooperation in NATO.

1957   The Saar is politically integrated with West Germany on 1 January. The Rome Treaties are signed 25 March: they set up Euratom and the European Economic Community (European Community). Paul-Henri Spaak of Belgium becomes NATO's secretary-general. The first Soviet *Sputnik* is launched on 2 October.

1958   Soviet Premier Nikita Khrushchev announces that the Soviet Union wishes to terminate the four-power agreement on the status of Berlin.

1959   Cyprus's independence is decided on 19 February at a meeting between Britain, Greece, and Turkey. The ministers of France, Britain, the United States, and the Soviet Union again meet in Geneva, 11–19 June, to discuss German reunification. The European Free Trade Association is established at 20 November convention attended by Austria, Denmark, Norway, Portugal, Sweden, Switzerland, and Britain.

1960   An American U-2 aircraft is shot down over Soviet territory on 1 May. The ministers of France, Britain, the United States, and the Soviet Union hold an abortive meeting in Paris, 16 May, on the German situation. Cyprus becomes an independent republic on 16 August.

1961   On 21 April Dirk U. Sikker of the Netherlands becomes NATO's secretary-general. President John F. Kennedy meets with Khrushchev in Vienna, 2–3 June. The Berlin Wall goes up on 13 August. At 13–15 December meeting in Paris the North Atlantic Council strongly condemns the building of the Berlin Wall and approves renewed diplomatic contacts with the Soviet Union to try to resolve the Berlin situation.

1962   At 4–6 May meeting in Athens the North Atlantic Council reviews the circumstances in which NATO might use nuclear weapons. On 11 December U.S. Defense Secretary Robert S. McNamara announces in London the canceling of the Skybolt air-to-ground nuclear missile. At 13–15 December meeting in Paris the North Atlantic Council approves the United States' action in the Cuban Missile Crisis and affirms position on Berlin and disarmament. President Kennedy meets with British Prime Minister Harold Macmillan in Nassau, Bahamas, where they agree to contribute part of their respective strategic nuclear forces to NATO.

1963   On 14 January French President Charles de Gaulle objects to Britain's entry in to the European Community (EC). The Franco-German Treaty of Cooperation is signed 21–22 January. On 10 October the Nuclear Test Ban Treaty—initiated by the United States, Britain, and the Soviet Union in Moscow in July—goes into effect.

1964   At North Atlantic Council meeting in the Hague, 12–14 May, ministers reaffirm their full support for the United Nations in its actions to restore law and order in Cyprus. Manlio Brosio of Italy becomes NATO's secretary-general. Khrushchev is removed from office on 15 October and is replaced by Aleksey Kosygin as prime minister and Leonid Brezhnev as party leader.

1965   President de Gaulle announces that French military integration within NATO will end at the latest by 1969.

1966   On 7 March de Gaulle informs President Lyndon B. Johnson of France's intention to cease participation in NATO's integrated military commands—with the consequent need for the removal from France of allied military forces and military headquarters. On 10 March he makes this announcement publicly. On 29 March the French government announces that French force assignments in NATO will end on 1 July and that the transfer of allied facilities from France should be completed by 1 April 1967. On 21 June the Belgian Chamber of Representatives approves the transfer of SHAPE to Belgium, and on 13 September it is decided to transfer SHAPE to Casteau, near Mons, Belgium. On 26 October the North Atlantic Council decides to move NATO headquarters to Brussels. NATO's Defense Planning Committee (DPC) decides on 10 November to transfer the Military Committee from Washington to Brussels. The DPC establishes the Nuclear Defense Affairs Committee and the Nuclear Planning Group on 14 December.

1967   SHAPE officially opens at Casteau on 31 March. The Nuclear Planning Group meets for first time on 6–7 April in Washington, D.C. Military regime takes power in Greece on 21 April. NATO Headquarters officially opens in Brussels on 16 October. At 13–14 December meeting the North Atlantic Council approves the Harmel Report on the Future Tasks of the Alliance. The DPC approves establishment of a Standing Naval Force Atlantic.

1968   The United States and the Soviet Union agree on 19 January on a draft of the nuclear nonproliferation treaty but table this at the Geneva Disarmament Conference. At a 24–25 June North Atlantic Council meeting in Reykjavik, Iceland, ministers issue a declaration on Mutual and Balanced Force Reductions (MBFR). The council meets on 21 August to discuss the crisis created by the invasion of Czechoslovakia. Maritime Air Force Mediterranean is activated in Naples to improve NATO surveillance of the Mediterranean area.

1969 The North Atlantic Council approves the establishment of a Committee on the Challenges of Modern Society to study the problems of the human environment, on the basis of a proposal by President Richard M. Nixon.

1970 The Nonproliferation Treaty on Nuclear Weapons comes into force on 5 March. U.S.-Soviet Strategic Arms Limitations Talks (SALT) open in Vienna on 16 April.

1971 Joseph Luns of the Netherlands becomes NATO's secretary-general on 1 October.

1972 President Nixon visits Peking on 1 February, which leads to normalization of relations between the United States and China. At 30–31 May meeting in Bonn the North Atlantic Council ministers agree to start multinational preparatory talks for a Conference on Security and Cooperation in Europe (CSCE) and propose multilateral exploration of MBFR. SALT II opens in Geneva on 1 November. Multilateral preparatory talks on a CSCE open in Helsinki on 2 November. The "Basic Treaty" between West and East Germany is signed in East Berlin on 21 December.

1973 Denmark, Ireland, and Britain join the EC on 1 January. Multilateral exploratory talks on MBFR are held in Vienna from 31 January to 29 June. Conference on MBFR opens in Vienna on 30 October. On 23 December the Organization of Petroleum-Exporting Countries announces it will double the price of crude oil.

1974 Military stages coup in Cyprus on 15 July, followed by landing of Turkish troops. Military regime resigns in Athens on 23 July; Constantine Karamanlis, returning from exile, is named Greek prime minister, and restrictions on civil liberties are removed. Greek forces withdraw from NATO's integrated military structure on 14 August.

1975 Heads of state sign the final act of the CSCE in Helsinki on 1 August.

1978 SALT II agreement is signed in Vienna on 18 June by Presidents Jimmy Carter and Leonid Brezhnev. U.S. embassy in Iran is seized by Islamic revolutionaries on 4 November. Soviet military intervenes in Afghanistan on 21 December.

1980   Military assumes leadership of Turkey on 12 September. Greek forces are reintegrated into NATO's military structure on 20 October.

1981   Greece becomes the tenth EC member on 1 January. The United States and the Soviet Union open Intermediated-Range Nuclear Force (INF) negotiations in Geneva on 30 November. The North Atlantic Council signs the Protocol of Accession of Spain to the North Atlantic Treaty on 10–11 December.

1982   Falklands conflict, 2 April to 14 June. Spain becomes NATO's sixteenth member. Strategic Arms Reduction Talks (START) open in Geneva on 30 June. Brezhnev dies on 10 November and is succeeded by Yuri Andropov as the Communist Party's general secretary.

1983   On 30 March the United States announces its readiness to agree to an equal level of warheads substantially below the number planned for deployment in the December 1979 dual-track decision provided that the Soviets reduce their warheads on land-based LRTNF missiles on launchers to the same level. The Soviet Union decides on 23 November to discontinue the current round of INF negotiations in Geneva. Current round of U.S.-Soviet START negotiations in Geneva is concluded on 8 December without a date set by the Soviets for talk resumption. INF deployments begin in West Germany, Italy, and Britain in December.

1984   The Stockholm Conference on Confidence- and Security-Building Measures (CSBMs) and Disarmament in Europe opens on 17 January. Yuri Andropov dies on 9 February and is succeeded by Konstantin Chernenko as the Communist party's general secretary. On 25 June Lord Carrington is named NATO secretary-general. At 26–27 October WEU meeting in Rome ministers decide to increase cooperation within the WEU.

1985   Chernenko dies on 11 March and is succeeded by Mikhail Gorbachev as the Communist party's general secretary. On 12 March the United States and the Soviet Union begin new arms control negotiations in Geneva, encompassing defense and space systems, strategic nuclear forces, and INF. On 2 July Andrei Gromyko becomes president of the Soviet

Union; Eduard Shevardnadze succeeds Gromyko as foreign minister.

1986   Spanish voters support via a 12 March referendum the continued membership of Spain in the Atlantic alliance without participation in NATO's integrated military structure. Responding to terrorist attacks attributed to Libya, U.S. forces attack targets in Tripoli and Benghazi on 15 April. Nuclear accident occurs at the Chernobyl power station in the Soviet Union on 26 April. Stockholm Conference concludes 22 September, advocating mandatory measures for notification, observation, and on-site inspection of military maneuvers of participating countries. President Ronald Reagan meets with Gorbachev on 11–12 October at summit meeting in Reykjavik, Iceland.

1987   Talks begin on 17 February in Geneva between NATO and Warsaw Pact countries on a mandate for negotiations on Conventional Forces in Europe (CFE) from the Atlantic to the Urals. On 22 July Gorbachev announces Soviet readiness to eliminate all intermediate-range nuclear weapons, including those deployed in the Asian part of the Soviet Union in the context of a U.S.-Soviet INF treaty. At 20 August meeting in the Hague, the WEU considers joint action in the Persian Gulf to ensure freedom of navigation in the region's oil shipping lanes. On 28–30 August U.S. inspectors attend military maneuvers near Minsk. On 5–7 October Soviet inspectors attend NATO exercises in Turkey. On 8 December in Washington, D.C., Presidents Reagan and Gorbachev sign the INF treaty, agreeing to eliminate globally land-based intermediate-range nuclear missiles. On 9 December the United States and the Soviet Union agree on measures allowing the monitoring of each other's test sites.

1988   West Germany and France establish the Joint Security Council on 22 January and also agree to the formation of a Franco-German army corps. The Soviets begin troop withdrawals in Afghanistan on 15 May. At summit meeting in Moscow on 31 May, Presidents Gorbachev and Reagan exchange documents implementing the INF Treaty. Manfred Woerner of Germany becomes NATO's secretary-general on 1 July. Addressing the U.N. General Assembly on 7 December, Gorbachev announces unilateral conventional force reductions; a major earthquake in Armenia devastates several cities and kills thousands.

1989   Vienna CSCE meeting concludes on 19 January with the adoption of mandates for new CFE and CSBM negotiations. On 15 February the Soviet Union completes the withdrawal of military forces from Afghanistan. CSCE representatives meet in Vienna on 6 March to open negotiations on CFE among NATO and Warsaw Pact countries and on CSBMs among all CSCE member states. Agreements are signed in Warsaw on 5 April leading to free elections in Poland and the registration of the previously banned trade union movement, Solidarity. President George Bush proposes on 12 May the confidence-building "Open Skies" program, with reciprocal opening of airspace and acceptance of overflight by participating countries. On 29–30 May President Bush announces major new initiatives for conventional force reductions in Europe. Solidarity wins big in Poland's free elections on 4 and 18 June. START negotiations reopen in Geneva on 10 June. On 24 August, Tadeusz Mazowiecki becomes prime minister of the first non-Communist-led Poland in 40 years. On 10 September Hungary opens its western border, enabling large numbers of East Germans to leave the country. On 3 October some 20,000 East German emigrants congregate at West Germany's embassies in Prague and Warsaw. East Germany's Communist leader, Erich Honecker, is replaced by Egon Krenz on 18 October. The Republic of Hungary becomes a democratic state on 23 October. The East German cabinet resigns on 7 November and the Politburo the following day. The gates of the Berlin Wall are opened on 9–10 October and travel restrictions to the West are lifted. The east German Parliament elects reformist Hans Modrow as prime minister on 14 November. Czechoslovakia's Civic Forum, led by Vaclav Havel, emerges on 17 November. Presidents Bush and Gorbachev meet in Malta on 2–3 December. On 4 December the Warsaw Pact countries denounce their 1968 invasion of Czechoslovakia and repudiate the Brezhnev Doctrine. Czech President Gustav Husak resigns on 7 December and a coalition government is formed. Havel is elected president of Czechoslovakia on 13 December. Foreign Minister Shevardnadze visits NATO Headquarters for talks with Wöner and perma-nent representatives of NATO countries. The regime of Romanian leader Nicolai

Ceausescu falls on 22 December, and Ceausescu is executed three days later; the National Salvation Front, headed by Ion Iliescu, takes control and promises free elections. On 29 December Poland's Parliament abolishes the leading role of the Communist party and restores the country's name as the Republic of Poland.

1990   On 15 January, Bulgaria's government abolishes the Communist party's power monopoly. At a Central Committee session on 6 February, Gorbachev addresses major aspects of his reform program, including the abandonment of the Communist party's leading role and the introduction of political pluralism. At "Open Skies" conference in Ottawa, ministers agree on 13 February to discuss external aspects of German unification in a "Two-Plus-Four" framework. On 8 March the North Atlantic Council consults on the position of West Germany regarding developments in East Germany and related security matters. On 11 March the Lithuanian Parliament votes for independence from the Soviet Union. In East German elections on 18 March citizens vote overwhelming for the conservative Alliance for Germany, furthering the process of German unification. On 26 March the Czech government orders barricades along its borders with Austria and West Germany to be dismantled. Portugal and Spain formally enter the WEU on 27 March. Hungarian elections on 7 April result in victory for the center-right Democratic Forum. On 12 April East Germany's coalition government declares itself in favor of German unification. President Bush announces on 3 May the cancellation of modernization program for nuclear artillery shells deployed in Europe and for a "follow-on" to the Lance missile; he calls for negotiations on U.S. and Soviet short-range nuclear missiles to begin shortly after the CFE Treaty is signed. On 7 May the Latvian Parliament declares independence; the next day Estonia's Parliament modifies the republic's name and constitution and restores its prewar flag. On 20 May Iliescu is elected Romanian president, and the National Salvation Front obtains a majority in Parliament. On 22–23 May, Hungary announces it will withdraw from the Warsaw Pact. Boris Yeltsin is elected president of the Russian republic on 30 May. In Czech parliamentary elections Civic Forum and allied parties win a majority on 8 June. Bulgarian elections of 10 and 17 June result in the parliamentary majority for the Bulgarian

Socialist party. On 2 July monetary union is established between East and West Germany. On 6 July NATO publishes the London Declaration, proposing cooperation with countries of Central and Eastern Europe on a wide spectrum of political and military activity. West German Chancellor Helmut Kohl and President Gorbachev agree on 16 July on measures enabling Germany to regain full sovereignty and to exercise its right to remain a full member of the North Atlantic Alliance. The Two-Plus-Four conference on German unification concludes in Paris on 17 July. Iraqi troops invade Kuwait on 2 August following a dispute between the two countries on exploitation of oil rights in the Persian Gulf. The North Atlantic Council holds special meeting on 10 August to consult on developments in the Gulf. On 22 August the East German legislature votes in favor of German unification on 3 October. U.S. Secretary of State James Baker briefs a special meeting of the North Atlantic Council on 10 September regarding the U.S.-Soviet meeting on the Gulf crisis. On 14 September NATO calls on Iraq to free those seized in NATO embassies in Kuwait and to refrain from further aggressive acts. Germany is unified on 3 October. The CSCE adopts the Vienna Document on CSBMs on 17 November. NATO and Warsaw Pact countries sign the CFE Treaty in Paris on 19 November. The North Atlantic Assembly meets in London on 26–28 November and accords associate delegate status to the Soviet Union, Bulgaria, Czechoslovakia, Hungary, and Poland. The Defense Planning Committee and the Nuclear Planning Group meet in Brussels on 6–7 December and support U.S. Resolution 678 demanding that Iraq withdraw its forces from Kuwait by January 1991. Lech Walesa is elected president of Poland on 10 December. Albania's Communist party announces on 11 December the legalization of opposition parties after 45 years of one-party rule. EC leaders meet in Rome on 15 December and open conferences on economic, monetary, and political union. On 20 December Soviet Foreign Minister Shevardnadze resigns, warning of risks of renewed dictatorship in the Soviet Union.

1991   On 2 January NATO deploys aircraft of the ACE Mobile Force to southeast Turkey in an operational role. On 9 January Soviet troops are deployed around the Lithuanian capital to enforce mandatory conscription. At a 9 January meeting between U.S. and Iraqi foreign ministers in

Geneva, Iraq maintains its refusal to withdraw forces from Kuwait. NATO issues a statement on 11 January urging the Soviets to refrain from using force and intimidation in the Baltic republics. The Gulf War begins on 17 January as the coalition forces launch air attacks against Iraq after Iraq refuses to comply with U.N. resolutions on withdrawal. In 11 February plebiscite election in Lithuanina 85 percent of the voters favor independence. Soviet peace plan for ending the Gulf War fails on 19 February. Coalition forces begin ground offensive into Kuwait on 24 February. Warsaw Pact countries meet in Budapest on 25 February to announce the dissolution of the bloc's military structure. Coalition forces liberate Kuwait on 28 February; Iraq accepts unconditionally all 12 U.N. resolutions regarding its withdrawal of forces from Kuwait. In 3 March referendums held in Estonia and Latvia, votes favor independence by 77 percent and 73 percent, respectively. On 4 March the Soviet legislature ratifies the treaty permitting German unification. On 12 May the Soviet Union eliminates its remaining SS-20 missiles in accordance with the INF Treaty. On 21 May the U.S. House calls for U.S. troop reductions in Europe from 250,000 to 100,000 by 1995. Albania becomes participating CSCE state on 19 June. The CSCE Council meets in Berlin on 19–20 June and creates an emergency mechanism allowing for meetings of senior officials to be called at short notice subject to agreement by 13 CSCE states. On 20 June, German legislators vote to reinstate Berlin as the country's official capital. On 25 June the parliaments of Slovenia and Croatia, of the former Yugoslavia, proclaim independence. Comecon is dissolved on 28 June. The Warsaw Pact is officially disbanded on 1 July. On 30 July President Yeltsin signs a treaty with Lithuania recognizing its independence. Presidents Gorbachev and Bush meet on 30–31 July to sign the START Treaty. On 19 August President Gorbachev is removed from office in a coup and replaced by an "emergency committee"; Russian President Yeltsin calls for a general strike as tanks flying Russian flags position themselves near the Parliament building in Moscow. The North Atlantic Council condemns the unconstitutional removal of President Gorbachev and calls for the restoration of democratic reform. The Soviet coup collapses on 21 August and Gorbachev returns to Moscow. On 25 August the Soviet Union announces purge of the military high command; Gorbachev proposes that the Communist party be disbanded and resigns as its general secretary. On 26 August the EC agrees to establish diplomatic ties with the three Baltic republics. On 29 August Soviet legislators vote to suspend all Communist party activities. The Soviet Congress of People's Deputies agrees to hand over key powers to the republics before disbanding on 5 September. Estonia, Latvia, and Lithuania are admitted to the United Nations on 17 September. President Bush announces on 27 September sweeping cuts in U.S. nuclear weapons and calls on the Soviet Union to do likewise. Gorbachev announces on 6 October the abolition of Soviet short-range nuclear weapons and the removal of all tactical nuclear weapons from ships, submarines, and land-based naval aircraft. At 17 October meeting in Taormina, Italy, NATO defense ministers announce reductions in the current stockpile of substrategic nuclear weapons in Europe by approximately 80 percent. On 8 December the republics of Russia, Belorussia, and Ukraine set up the Commonwealth of Independent States (CIS) to replace the Soviet Union. At 9–10 December meeting in Maastricht, the Netherlands, the EC adopts treaties (subject to ratification) on economic, monetary, and political union. Representatives from NATO and Central and Eastern European countries meet on 20 December to inaugurate the North Atlantic Cooperation Council (NACC). On 21 December 11 former Soviet republics sign agreements creating the CIS. Gorbachev announces his resignation as Soviet president on 25 December.

1992 The United States sponsors international coordinating conference on assistance to the former Soviet Union on 22–23 January in Washington, D.C. The CSCE Council meets in Prague on 30–31 January; it recognizes the Russian Federation and admits 10 former republics as CSCE participating states. On 26 February the Canadian government informs the alliance that it will cancel plans to maintain 1,100 Canadian forces in Europe after 1994. In a 26 February statement on Yugoslavia, the North Atlantic Council appeals to all parties to respect cease-fire arrangements to follow the deployment of U.N. peacekeeping troops. On 24 March, Croatia, Georgia, and Slovenia become CSCE participating states; "Open Skies" agreement is signed. U.S. General John M. Shalikashvili is appointed as SACEUR on 29 April. NATO's Naval On-Call Force for the Mediterranean is replaced by the Standing Naval Force Mediterranean on 30

April. CIS leaders meet in Tashkent on 15 May and agree to appoint member rights and obligations with respect to the CFE Treaty. In a 2 June national referendum Danish votes reject the Maastricht treaties on political and monetary union (50.7 to 49.3 percent). The Extraordinary Conference is held in Oslo on 4–5 June: NATO ministers there announce their readiness to support conditionally peacekeeping activities under the responsibility of the CSCE; the NACC welcomes Georgia and Albania as NACC members (Finland attends as observer); a final document formally establishes the obligations under the CFE Treaty of the eight CIS republics with territory to which the treaty applies. On 16 June Presidents Bush and Yeltsin sign an agreement to cut nuclear warheads on strategic missiles significantly beyond the limits of the START Treaty. On 2 July the United States notifies the allies of the completion of withdrawal from Europe of land-based nuclear artillery shells, Lance missile warheads, and nuclear depth bombs, as well as the removal of tactical nuclear weapons from U.S. surface ships and attack submarines. On 10 July the North Atlantic Council agrees on a NATO maritime operation in the Adriatic in coordination and cooperation with the operation decided by the WEU to monitor compliance with U.N. Security Council sanctions imposed on Serbia and Montenegro by Resolutions 713 and 757. The NATO-Spanish coordination agreement on air defense is signed in Naples on 28 July. The North Atlantic Council agrees on 2 September to make available alliance resources in support of U.N., CSCE, and EC efforts to bring about peace in the former Yugoslavia, including the provision of resources for the protection of humanitarian relief and support for U.N. monitoring of heavy weapons. In a 20 September national referendum French voters approve the Maastricht treaties on political and monetary union (50.82 to 49.18 percent). On 22 September the CSCE Forum for Security Cooperation is inaugurated in Vienna; the U.N. General Assembly votes to exclude Serbia and Montenegro and rules that Belgrade must make an application to be admitted to the United Nations. On 1 October the United States ratifies the START Treaty, which cuts U.S. and Russian nuclear forces by one-third. NATO's Allied Command Europe Rapid Reaction Corps is inaugurated in 2 October in Lielefeld, Germany, by SACEUR Shalikashvili. On 14 October the North Atlantic Council authorizes the use of NATO airborne early-warning forces to monitor the U.N.-mandated "no-fly" zone in effect over Bosnia-Herzegovina. The CFE Treaty officially enters force by ratification of all 29 signatory states on 9 November.

NOTES AND REFERENCES

CHAPTER 1

1. Armin Rappaport, "The American Revolution of 1949," *NATO LETTER* 12 (February 1964):3–8.

2. Raymond Aron, *The Century of Total War* (Boston: Beacon Press, 1955), 3.

3. *Encyclopedia Britannica*, 15th ed. (Chicago: Encyclopedia Britannica, 1987), 21:799.

4. Alan Milward, *The Reconstruction of Western Europe 1945–1951* (Berkeley: University of California Press, 1984), 465.

5. Walter Lipgens, *A History of European Integration, 1945–1947*, trans. P. S. Falla and A. J. Ryder, vol. 1 (Oxford: Clarendon Press, 1982), 2.

6. Richard Coudenhove-Kalergi, *Pan Europe* (New York: Knopf, 1926), xv.

7. Felix Gilbert, *To the Farewell Address: Ideas of Early American Foreign Policy* (Princeton: Princeton University Press, 1961), 73.

8. James H. Hutson, *John Adams and the Diplomacy of the American Revolution* (Lexington: University Press of Kentucky, 1980), 144, 146.

9. See Leonard Silk and Mark Silk, *The American Establishment* (New York: Basic Books, 1980), and Robert D. Schulzinger, *The Wise Men of Foreign Affairs: The History of the Council on Foreign Relations* (New York: Columbia University Press, 1984).

CHAPTER 2

1. James F. Byrnes, *Speaking Frankly* (New York: Harper & Row, 1947), 239.

2. George F. Kennan, "The Sources of Soviet Conduct," *Foreign Affairs* 25 (July 1947):566–82.

3. Truman Message to Congress, 12 March 1947, in *Public Papers of the Presidents, 1948* (Washington, D.C.: U.S. Government Printing Office, 1963), 178–79.

4. Ibid., 180.

5. Joseph M. Jones, *The Fifteen Weeks (February 21–June 5, 1947)* (New York: Harcourt, Brace & World, 1955), 259.

6. Marshall commencement address at Harvard University, 5 June 1947, *Department of State Bulletin* 16 (15 June 1947):1160.

7. Ibid.

8. Great Britain, *Parliamentary Debates* (Commons) 5th ser., 446 (1948): cpl. 383ff.

9. See Lipgens, *A History of European Integration,* 468–70.

10. Carl Van Doren, *The Great Rehearsal: The Story of the Making and Ratifying of the Constitution of the United States* (New York: Viking, 1948), ix–x.

11. Oral History Interview, Theodore C. Achilles, Harry S. Truman Library, Independence, Missouri.

12. Secretary of state to the British ambassador, 20 January 1948, *Foreign Relations of the United States, 1948,* 3:8. Hereafter cited as *FRUS.*

13. Memorandum, Hickerson to secretary of state, 19 January 1948, *FRUS, 1948,* 3:6–7; Memorandum, Kennan to secretary of state, 20 January 1948, ibid., 7–8; Memorandum of conversation by Hickerson, 21 January 1948, ibid., 9–12.

14. Oral History Interview, John D. Hickerson, Harry S. Truman Library, quoted in Thomas G. Paterson, *On Every Front: The Making of the Cold War* (New York: W. W. Norton & Co., 1979), 63.

15. NSC-1/3, report to the NSC by the executive-secretary on "The Position of the U.S. with Respect to Italy," 8 March 1949, Record Group 59, National Archives and Record Service.

16. Memorandum by the director of the Office of European Affairs to the secretary of state, 8 March 1948, *FRUS, 1948,* 3:40–42.

17. Truman message to Congress, 17 March 1948, *Public Papers of the Presidents, 1948,* 184.

18. See Lawrence S. Kaplan, *The United States and NATO: The Formative Years* (Lexington: University Press of Kentucky, 1984), 115–20.

19. NSC-7, *FRUS, 1948,* 1:545–50.

20. NSC-9, ibid., 3:85–88.

21. Theodore C. Achilles, "U.S. Role in Negotiations That Led to Atlantic Alliance," *NATO Review* 27 (August 1979):13.

22. *Congressional Record,* 80 Cong., 2nd sess., 11 June 1948, 4:7791.

23. NSC-14/1, *FRUS, 1949,* 4:585–88.

24. Minutes of the Fifth Meeting of the Washington Exploratory Talks on Security, 9 July 1948, *FRUS, 1948,* 3:171.

25. *North Atlantic Treaty Hearings,* Senate Committee on Foreign Relations, 81 Cong., 1st sess. (Washington, D.C.: U.S. Government Printing Office, 1949), 2:368–69.

26. Minutes of the Twelfth Meeting, Exploratory Talks, 8 February 1949, *FRUS, 1949,* 4:73–75.

27. Kenneth W. Condit, *The History of the Joint Chiefs of Staff: The JCS and National Policy, 1947–1949* (Wilmington, Del.: Michael Glazier, 1979), 291, 296.

28. Claude Delmas, "France and the Creation of the Atlantic Alliance," *NATO Review* 28, no. 3 (August 1980):24.

29. Minutes of the Twelfth Meeting, Exploratory Talks, 8 February 1949, *FRUS, 1949*, 4:85.

30. Kaplan, *The United States and NATO*, 115–20.

31. Dean Acheson, *Present at the Creation: My Years in the State Department* (New York: W. W. Norton & Co., 1969), 284.

32. Oral History Interview, Theodore C. Achilles, Harry S. Truman Library.

CHAPTER 3

1. Requests from the Brussels Treaty Powers to the U.S. Government for Military Assistance, 5 April 1949, *FRUS, 1949*, 4:285–87.

2. Memorandum, Kennan to acting secretary of state, 1 June 1949, *FRUS, 1949*, 4:301.

3. Memorandum of conversation, 24 June 1949, Acheson Papers, Harry S. Truman Library.

4. Record of discussions at meeting of Senate Committee on Foreign Relations, 21 April 1949, *FRUS, 1949*, 1:288–89.

5. Senate Committee on Foreign Relations, *The North Atlantic Treaty Hearings*, on Executive L, 81 Cong., 1st sess., 27 April–18 May 1949, 3 pts.

6. *North Atlantic Treaty Hearings*, 3:1121.

7. Ibid., 1:30.

8. Ibid., 1:146.

9. Speech to Jewish War Veterans, New York, 5 April 1949, in *New York Times*, 6 April 1949.

10. *North Atlantic Treaty Hearings*, 1:117.

11. *New York Times*, 29 September 1949.

12. Kaplan, *The United States and NATO*, 118, 139.

13. Acheson, *Present at the Creation*, 329.

14. The text of the strategic plan is in *FRUS, 1949*, 4:353–56.

15. Kaplan, *The United States and NATO*, 142–43.

16. See Lawrence S. Kaplan, *A Community of Interests: NATO and the Military Assistance Program, 1948–1951* (Washington, D.C.: U.S. Government Printing Office, 1980), 85–90.

17. "United States Interests, Positions, and Tactics at Paris," 5 November 1949, *FRUS, 1949*, 3:295.

18. The text of NSC-68 is in *FRUS, 1950*, 1:234–92.

19. Marshall Shulman, *Stalin's Foreign Policy Reappraised* (Cambridge, Mass.: Harvard University Press, 1963), 80–103. This chapter deals with the peace movement as an instrument of Soviet diplomacy.

20. *Le Monde*, 4 April 1950.

21. 15–18 May 1950, London, North Atlantic Council, in *Texts of Final Communiqués, 1949–1974* (Brussels: NATO Information Service, n.d.), 54.

22. Konrad Adenauer, *Memoirs, 1945–1964* (Chicago: Henry Regnery Co., 1965), 273.

23. Schuman's qualified statement on German units in a European army before the North Atlantic Council is recorded in *Verbatim Record 3*, C-5-VR/3, 16 September

1950, M-88, Box 152 (2206), Foreign Affairs Documents and Reference Center, Department of State, Washington, D.C.

24. Secretary of state to president, SECT 13, tel., 15 September 1950, White House Central Files, Harry S. Truman Library.

25. Gruenther to Eisenhower, 12 September 1950, Presidential File, Dwight D. Eisenhower Library, Abilene, Kansas.

26. Acheson, *Present at the Creation*, 437.

27. Kaplan, *The United States and NATO*, 167.

28. 20–25 February 1952, Lisbon, North Atlantic Council, *Final Communiqués*, 68.

29. Ibid., 70.

30. Hastings, Lord Ismay, *NATO: The First Five Years, 1949–1954* (Paris: NATO, 1955), 28.

31. Ismay to Churchill, 12 February 1954, Ismay Papers, III/12/23a, Liddell Hart Centre for Military Archives, King's College, London.

CHAPTER 4

1. Acheson, *Present at the Creation*, 626.

2. Protocol to the North Atlantic Treaty, 27 May 1952, in Clarence W. Baier and Richard P. Stebbins, eds., *Documents on American Foreign Relations, 1952* (New York: Harper & Bros., 1953), 245.

3. Excerpt from Kirk H. Porter and Donald Bruce Johnson, eds., *National Party Platforms, 1840–1956* (Urbana: University of Illinois Press, 1956), 497.

4. O. William Perlmutter, "The 'Neo-Realism' of Dean Acheson," *Review of Politics* 26 (January 1964):107.

5. U.S. Congress, Senate Foreign Relations Committee, *Supplemental Hearings on Agreement Regarding Status of Forces of Parties of the North Atlantic Treaty*, 83 Cong., 1st sess., 24 June 1953, 3.

6. Ibid.

7. Ismay, *NATO: The First Five Years*, 47.

8. Quoted in Robert E. Osgood, *NATO: The Entangling Alliance* (Chicago: University of Chicago Press, 1963), 103.

9. John Foster Dulles, "Policy for Security and Peace," *Foreign Affairs* 32 (April 1954):359.

10. Morris Honick and Ed M. Carter, "SHAPE Histories: the New Approach, July 1953–November 1956," unpublished preface, Historical Section, Office of the Secretary of the Staff, SHAPE, viii.

11. 14–16 December 1953, North Atlantic Council, Paris, *Final Communiqués*, 80–82; 17–18 December 1954, North Atlantic Council, Paris, ibid., 88; 11–14 December 1956, North Atlantic Council, Paris, ibid., 102; 16–19 December 1957, North Atlantic Council, Paris, ibid., 113.

12. 4–5 May 1956, North Atlantic Council, Paris, ibid., 98.

13. John Foster Dulles, "A Survey of Foreign Policy Problems," *Department of State Bulletin* 28 (9 February 1953):214.

14. Legislative Leadership Meeting, Supplementary Notes, 18 December 1953, Legislative Meeting Series, Box 3, Dwight D. Eisenhower Library.

15. Edward Fursdon, *The European Defence Community: A History* (New York: St. Martin's Press, 1979), 297.

16. Dulles to Eisenhower, 27 October 1954, Dulles/Herter Series, Anne Whitman files, Box 3, Dwight D. Eisenhower Library.

17. 27 December 1954, Papers of John Foster Dulles, Dwight D. Eisenhower Library.

18. *New York Times*, 21 November 1954.

19. Konrad Adenauer, "Germany: the New Partner," *Foreign Affairs* 33 (January 1955):82.

20. Report of the Committee of Three on Nonmilitary Cooperation in NATO (December 1956), in Robert S. Jordan, *Political Leadership in NATO* (Boulder, Colo.: Westview Press, 1979), 281–93.

21. Ibid., 289–90.

22. Dulles's statement on 15 December 1956 after a meeting of the North Atlantic Council, *Department of State Bulletin* 35 (31 December 1956):981.

23. Andrej Korbonski, "The Warsaw Pact," *International Conciliation*, no. 573 (May 1969):13.

24. "An Historic Week," report of the secretary of state to the president, 17 May 1955, *Department of State Bulletin* 32 (30 May 1955):871; president's news conference, 18 May 1955, *Public Papers of the Presidents: Dwight D. Eisenhower, 1955*, 505–18.

25. *New York Times*, 21 November 1954.

26. Anthony Eden, *Full Circle: The Memoirs of Anthony Eden* (Boston: Houghton Mifflin, 1960), 324; Harold Macmillan, *Tides of Fortune* (New York: Harper & Row, 1969), 607.

27. *Public Papers of the Presidents: Dwight D. Eisenhower, 1955*, 484; Dwight D. Eisenhower, *The White House Years: Mandate for Change* (Garden City, N.Y.: Doubleday & Co., 1963), 506.

28. *New York Times*, 17 July 1955; Livingston Merchant, in John Foster Dulles Oral Histories, Dulles Papers, Princeton University.

29. Eisenhower, *The White House Years*, 523.

30. George F. Kennan, *Russia, the Atom, and the West* (New York: Harper & Bros., 1958), 62.

31. Adam Rapacki to U.S. Ambassador Jacob Beam, *Department of State Bulletin* 38 (19 May 1958):822–23.

32. Dean Acheson, "The Illusion of Disengagement," *Foreign Affairs* 36 (April 1958):373–81.

33. George F. Kennan, *Memoirs, 1950–1963* (Boston: Little, Brown & Co., 1972), 249.

CHAPTER 5

1. *New York Times*, 19 September 1959.

2. Quoted in Walter LaFeber, *America, Russia, and the Cold War, 1945–1980*, 4th ed. (New York: John Wiley & Sons, 1980), 200.

3. Quoted in David Schwartz, *NATO's Nuclear Dilemmas* (Washington, D.C.: Brookings Institution Press, 1983), 58.

4. John Foster Dulles, "Challenge and Response in United States Policy," *Foreign Affairs* 36 (October 1957):30–33.

5. Quoted in Stephen E. Ambrose, *Eisenhower: The President* (New York: Simon & Shuster, 1984), 2:579.

6. *Public Papers of the Presidents, 1955*, 713–16.

7. "Declaration on Berlin," Paris, 16–18 December 1958, *NATO Final Communiqués*, 123.

8. Robert Divine, *Eisenhower and the Cold War* (New York: Oxford University Press, 1981), 134–35.

9. Harold Macmillan, *Riding the Storm* (London: Macmillan, 1971), 652–56.

10. Quoted in Ambrose, *Eisenhower*, 579.

11. 16–18 December 1960, North Atlantic Council, Paris, *NATO Final Communiqués*, 133.

12. Inaugural Address, 20 January 1961, *Public Papers of the Presidents, 1961*, 1.

13. Joseph Kraft, *The Grand Design: From Common Market to Atlantic Partnership* (New York: Harper, 1962).

14. Address at the Paulskirche, Frankfurt, 25 June 1963, *Public Papers of the Presidents, 1963*, 517.

15. Denise Artaud, "Le Grand dessein de J. F. Kennedy: Proposition mythique ou occasion manquée?" *Revue d'histoire moderne et contemporaine* 29 (Spring 1982):266.

16. Frank Costigliola, "The Failed Design: Kennedy, de Gaulle, and the Struggle for Europe," *Diplomatic History* 8 (Summer 1984):228.

17. News conference, Kremlin, 12 July 1960, recorded in *New York Times*, 13 July 1960.

18. Arthur Schlesinger, Jr., *A Thousand Days: John F. Kennedy in the White House* (Boston: Houghton Mifflin, 1965), 397.

19. The full text of President Johnson's letter of 5 June 1964 was published in the Turkish newspaper *Hurriyet*, 14 January 1966.

20. J. William Fulbright, "Old Myths and New Realities," *Congressional Record*, U.S. Senate, 88 Cong., 2nd sess., 62227–29.

21. Ronald Steel, *The End of the Alliance: America and the Future of Europe* (New York: Viking Press, 1964), 9–11.

22. David Horowitz, *The Free World Colossus* (New York: Hill & Wang, 1971), 264.

23. Quoted in David N. Schwartz, *NATO's Nuclear Dilemmas* (Washington, D.C.: Brookings Institution Press, 1983), 38.

24. Interview with Jacques Tournoux, 30 November 1956, in Jacques Tournoux, *La Tragédie de général* (Paris: Librairie Plon, 1967), 215 (translated for General Lemnitzer), Box 62, de Gaulle file, Lyman L. Lemnitzer Papers, National War College (NWC), Washington, D.C.

25. Colin Gordon, "NATO and the Larger European States," in Lawrence S. Kaplan and Robert W. Clawson, eds., *NATO after Thirty Years* (Wilmington, Del.: Scholarly Resources, 1981), 68.

26. Quoted in Alistair Buchan, "Mothers and Daughters (or Greeks and Romans)," in William P. Bundy, ed., *Two Hundred Years of American Foreign Policy* (New York: New York University Press, 1977) 56.

27. Ibid., 56–57.

28. Schlesinger, *A Thousand Days*, 871.

29. Quoted in Jordan, *Political Leadership in NATO*, 83.

30. 16–18 December 1960, North Atlantic Council, Paris, *NATO Final Communiqués*, 134.

31. George W. Ball, *The Past Has Another Pattern: Memoirs* (New York: W. W. Norton, 1982), 267.

32. Quoted in Keith W. Baum, "Treating the Allies Properly: The Eisenhower Administration, NATO, and the Multilateral Force," *Presidential Studies Quarterly* 13 (Winter 1983):35.

33. 31 May-1 June, Meeting of Defense Ministers, Paris, *NATO Final Communiqués*, 165.

34. Harlan Cleveland, *NATO: The Transatlantic Bargain* (New York: Harper & Row, 1970), 102; Ball, *The Past Has Another Pattern*, 334.

CHAPTER 6

1. 15–16 December 1966, Paris, North Atlantic Council, *Texts of Final Communiqués, 1949–1975* (Brussels: NATO Information Service, n.d.) 179–80.

2. Memorandum, 29 March 1966, in *NATO Letter* 14 (May 1966):24.

3. *New York Times*, 15 March 1966.

4. Cleveland, *NATO*, 106; Oral Interview, John M. Leddy, 12 March 1969, Oral History Collection, Lyndon B. Johnson Library, Austin, Texas; Oral Interview with Andrew J. Goodpaster, 21 June 1971, ibid.

5. Cleveland, *NATO*, 105–6.

6. Charles E. Bohlen, *Witness to History* (New York: W. W. Norton, 1973), 507–8.

7. Lemnitzer to Margaret and Ernest Lemnitzer, 1 July 1966, Box 66 (Family), Lyman L. Lemnitzer Papers, NWC.

8. Lemnitzer to Major H. E. Simpson, Jr., 26 September 1966, ibid.

9. Report No. 85 of Special Subcommittee visiting American military installations and NATO bases in France, Committee on Armed Services, H.R., 89 Cong., 2nd sess., 12 September 1966, 10387.

10. News Release No. 67–22, SHAPE, Belgium, 20 November 1967, Remarks by General Lemnitzer at the Thirteenth Annual Session of the North Atlantic Assembly, Brussels, Box 109, L-1000-71, Lyman L. Lemnitzer Papers, NWC; *New York Times*, 21 November 1967; see "Collective Defense–the Basis of Military Security," *NATO Letter* 26 (January 1968):6.

11. C. L. Sulzberger, *New York Times*, 31 July 1966.

12. 13–14 December, 1967, Brussels, North Atlantic Council, *Final Communiqués*, 197.

13. "The Atlantic Alliance," hearings before the Subcommittee on National Security and International Operations of the Committee on Governmental Operations, U.S. Senate, 89 Cong., 2nd sess., pt. 6, 21 June 1966, 187.

14. Cyrus L. Sulzberger, *New York Times*, 8 June 1966.

15. "The Future Tasks of the Alliance," in 13–14 December 1967, Brussels, North Atlantic Council, *Final Communiqués*, 199.

16. Lemnitzer, "Collective Defense," 4.

17. Remarks by General Lemnitzer at Conference on "Leadership in NATO–Past and Present," 14–15 October 1982, Dwight D. Eisenhower Library.

18. 15–16 November 1968, Brussels, North Atlantic Council, *Final Communiqués*, 214–15.

19. 24–25 June 1968, Reykjavik, North Atlantic Council, *NATO Final Communiqués*, 208.

20. 22 November 1972, *Atlantic Community Quarterly 11*, no. 1 (Spring 1973):55.

21. Jordan, *Political Leadership in NATO*, 171.

22. William T. R. Fox and Annette B. Fox, *NATO and the Range of American Choice* (New York: Columbia University Press, 1967), 252.

23. "The Future Tasks of the Alliance," *Final Communiqués*, 206.

24. Ibid., 206.

25. *New York Times*, 10 March 1967.

26. Denis Brogan, "The Illusion of American Omnipotence," *Harper's Magazine* 205 (December 1952): 21–28.

27. Henry A. Kissinger, "The Viet Nam Negotiations," *Foreign Affairs* 47 (January 1969):211–34; Informal Remarks on Guam with Newsmen, 25 July 1969, *Public Papers of the President, Richard Nixon, 1969* (Washington, D.C.: U.S. Government Printing Office, 1971), 544ff.

28. Radio Address, 13 October 1968, "The Time to Save NATO," *Atlantic Community Quarterly* 6 (Winter 1968–69):481–82.

29. Remarks to the North Atlantic Council in Brussels, 24 February 1969, *Public Papers of the President, 1969*, 106.

30. U.S. Senate, *Congressional Record*, 91 Cong., 1st sess., 1969, 115:36147–49.

31. *New York Times*, 13, 16 May 1971.

32. Raymond Aron, "Richard Nixon and the Future of American Foreign Policy," *Daedalus 101* (Fall 1972):18.

33. James Chace and Earl C. Ravenel, *Atlantis Lost: U.S.-European Relations after the Cold War* (New York: New York University Press, 1976), 52.

34. Quoted in Richard J. Barnet, *The Alliance: America, Europe, Japan—Makers of the Post-war World* (New York: Simon & Schuster, 1983), 313.

35. Ibid., 314.

36. News Conference, 31 January 1973, *Public Papers of the Presidents, 1973*, 57; Kissinger, "A New Atlantic Charter," address delivered to Associated Press Editors' Annual Meeting, New York, 23 April 1973, *Department of State Bulletin* 68 (14 May 1973):593–98.

37. Barnet, *Alliance*, 319.

38. Wilfred Kohl, "The Nixon-Kissinger Foreign Policy System and U.S. European Relations: Patterns of Policy Making," *World Politics 28* (October 1975):18.

39. Fourth annual report to the Congress on U.S. foreign policy, *Public Papers of the Presidents, 1973*, 402–4.

40. 14–15 June 1973, Copenhagen, North Atlantic Council, *NATO Final Communiqués*, 294.

41. *New York Times*, 21 October 1973.

42. *The Memoirs of Richard Nixon* (New York: Warner Books, 1978), 2:476.

43. Henry Kissinger, *Years of Upheaval* (Boston: Little, Brown & Co., 1982), 708.

44. *Wall Street Journal*, 16 November 1973.

45. *U.S. Statutes at Large* 87, sec. 812, (1973):6199620.

46. Question and answer session at the Executives' Club of Chicago, 15 March 1974, *Public Papers of the Presidents, 1974*, 267.

47. "Twenty-Five Years of Ups and Downs," *NATO Review* 22 (April 1974):3.

CHAPTER 7

1. North Atlantic Council, *Final Communiqués*, 13–14 December 1979, *NATO Review* 28 (February 1980):28.

2. Kissinger, *Years of Upheaval*, 980–81.

3. Declaration on Mutual and Balanced Force Reductions, 24–25 June 1968, Reykjavik, North Atlantic Council, *Final Communiqués*, 210.

4. Quoted in Christopher S. Raj, *American Military on Europe: Controversy over NATO Burden Sharing* (New Delhi: ABC Publishing House, 1983), 316.

5. "Declaration on MBFR," 26–27 May 1970, Rome, *NATO Final Communiqués*, 238.

6. Alistair Buchan, "The United States and the Security of Europe," in David Landes, ed., *Western Europe: Trials of Partnership* (Lexington, Mass.: D. C. Heath, 1977), 300.

7. U.S. Congress, Senate, Committee on Armed Services, *NATO and the New Soviet Threat: Report of Senator Sam Nunn and Senator Dewey Bartlett*, 95 Cong., 1st sess., 24 January 1977.

8. S. Victor Papacosma, "Greece and NATO," in Lawrence S. Kaplan et al., *NATO and the Mediterranean* (Wilmington, Del.: Scholarly Resources, 1985), 197.

9. Quoted in Albano Nogueira, "Portugal's Special Relationship: The Azores, the British Connection, and NATO," ibid., 93.

10. Gerald R. Ford, *A Time to Heal: The Autobiography of Gerald R. Ford* (New York: Harper & Row, 1979), 285.

11. U.S. Congress, *Nunn and Bartlett Report*, 1.

12. George W. Ball, "Capitulation at Helsinki," *Newsweek* 86 (4 August 1975):13.

13. *New York Times*, 2 March 1976.

14. Leslie H. Gelb, "The Kissinger Legacy," *New York Times Magazine*, 31 October 1976, 13ff; Oriana Fallaci, *Interviews with History* (New York: Liveright, 1976), 41.

15. Address at Commencement Exercises at University of Notre Dame, 22 May 1977, *Public Papers of the Presidents, 1977*, book 1, 961–62.

16. Barnet, *The Alliance*, 364.

17. *NATO and the Warsaw Pact: Force Comparisons* (Brussels: NATO Information Service, 1984), 45.

18. *NATO and the New Soviet Threat*, 1.

19. Cyrus R. Vance, *Hard Choices: Critical Years in American Foreign Policy* (New York: Simon & Schuster, 1983), 66.

20. *New York Times*, 12 June 1970, 5 December 1975, and 25 December 1977; Chinese journalists' delegation to Denmark, Great Britain, Italy, and Switzerland in

November and December 1977 repeatedly endorsed Western Europe's defense against potential Soviet aggression, *Peking Review* 21 (17 February 1978):22–26.

21. Robert W. Komer, "Treating NATO's Self-Inflicted Wound," *Foreign Policy* 13 (Winter 1973–74):36–37.

22. Department of Defense Appropriation Authorization Act of 1976, *U.S. Statutes at Large* 90, sec. 902: 930–31.

23. Scott L. Bills, "Congress and Western European Policy," in *Congress and Foreign Policy—1978*, committee print for U.S. House of Representatives (Washington, D.C.: U.S. Government Printing Office, 1978), 209.

24. Quoted in Robert Kennedy, "Precision ATGMs and NATO Defense," *Orbis* 22 (Winter 1979):897.

25. Quoted in Schwartz, *NATO's Nuclear Dilemmas*, 203.

26. Official text and protocol of SALT II, signed in Vienna, 18 June 1979, *Facts on File 1979*, 450–56.

27. Helmut Schmidt, "The 1977 Alastair Buchan Memorial Lecture," *Survival* 20 (January-February 1978):4.

28. Cited in Barnet, *The Alliance*, 373.

29. Defense Planning Committee, 6–7 December 1977, Final Communiqué, *NATO Review* 26 (February 1978):25.

30. Quoted in Barnet, *The Alliance*, 376.

31. *New York Times*, 8 July 1977.

32. Ibid., 29 April 1978.

33. Z. Brzezinski, *Power and Principle: Memoirs of a National Security Adviser* (New York: Farrar, Straus & Giroux, 1983), 302, 304–5.

34. Jimmy Carter, *Keeping Faith: Memoirs of a President* (New York: Bantam Books, 1982), 229.

35. Drew Middleton, *New York Times*, 5 January 1979.

36. Special meeting of the foreign and defense ministers, 12 December 1979, Final Communiqué, *NATO Review* 28 (February 1980): 25.

37. *New York Times*, 25 September 1983.

38. Brzezinski, *Power and Principle*, 463.

39. The president's news conference, 29 January 1981, interview with Walter Cronkite, 3 March 1981, ibid., 193, Public Papers of the Presidents, Ronald Reagan, 1981, 57.

40. Strobe Talbott, *Deadly Gambits: The Reagan Administration and the Stalemate in Nuclear Arms Control* (New York: Alfred A. Knopf, 1984), 3.

41. Quoted in Walter LaFeber, *America, Russia, and the Cold War, 1945–1984*, 5th ed. (New York: Alfred A. Knopf, 1985), 304.

42. Richard Burt, "The Evolution of the US START Approach," *NATO Review* 30 (September 1982):2.

CHAPTER 8

1. McGeorge Bundy, George F. Kennan, Robert S. McNamara, Charles Schulze, and Gerard Smith, "Nuclear Weapons and the Atlantic Alliance," *Foreign Affairs* 60 (Spring 1982): 753–68.

2. Bernard W. Rogers, "Follow-on Forces Attack (FOFA): Myths and Realities," *NATO Review* 32 (December 1984): 1–9.

3. Ted Galen Carpenter, "Standing Guard over Europe," *Reason* (August 1984): 47.

4. *New York Times*, 29 October 1983.

5. Final Communiqué, North Atlantic Council, 17–18 May 1982, *NATO Review* 30 (August 1982):29.

6. *New York Times*, 7 July 1985.

7. EUROGROUP Communiqué, 29 November 1982, *NATO Review* 30 (February 1983): 28; "Western Defense: The European Role in NATO" (Brussels: EUROGROUP 1985), 6. The percentages are higher when France's forces are included.

8. Quoted in *NATO Review* 33 (February 1985): 10.

9. *NATO Review* 34 (October 1986): 15.

10. "Developments in Europe, October 1986," hearings before the Subcommittee on Europe and the Middle East of the Committee on Foreign Affairs, H.R., 99 Cong. 2nd sess., 7 October 1986, 2.

11. George P. Schultz, *Turmoil and Triumph: My Years as Secretary of State* (New York: Charles Scribner's Sons, 1993), 777–80.

12. Quoted from *Facts on File Yearbook, 1986*, October 1986, 803.

13. *NATO Review* 5 (October 1986): 10.

14. "The INF Treaty," hearings before the Senate Committee on Foreign Relations, 100 Cong., 2nd sess., pt. 1, 25 January 1988, 15.

15. "NATO Defense and the INF Treaty," hearings before the Senate Committee on Armed Services, 100 Cong., 2nd sess., pt. 1, 1 February 1988, 103.

16. Statement issued by the North Atlantic Council, meeting in Ministerial Session, Brussels, 8–9 December 1988, *NATO Review* 6 (December 1988): 25–26.

17. Lord Carrington, "East-West Relations: A Time of Far-Reaching Change," *NATO Review* 3 (June 1988): 13.

18. Quoted in *NATO Review* 2 (April 1988): 3.

19. Statement by EUROGROUP minister, *NATO Review* 3 (June 1989): 33.

20. Special report of the North Atlantic Assembly, "NATO in the 1990s," 26.

21. *New York Times*, 17 April 1989.

22. "The Nuclear Weapons Requirements Study, 1991–1998," summarized in Nuclear Planning Group communiqué, Brussels, 19–20 April 1989, *Texts of NATO Final Communiqués, 1986–1990*, 111.

23. "A Comprehensive Concept of Arms Control and Disarmament," adopted by the heads of state and government at meeting of North Atlantic Council, Brussels, 29–30 May 1989, *NATO Review* (June 1989): 23.

24. Richard Burt, "START Talks—President Bush Proposes Verification Measures," *NATO Review* 4 (August 1989):10.

25. Defense Planning Committee communiqué, *NATO Review* 6 (December 1989):29.

26. The president's news conference, 3 May 1990, *Public Papers of the Presidents, George Bush, 1990*, 608.

CHAPTER 9

1. Francis Fukuyama, "The End of History?" *National Interest* (Summer 1990): 4.

2. Ivo Daalder, "The CFE Treaty: An Overview and an Assessment" (Washington, D.C.: Johns Hopkins Foreign Policy Institute, 1991), 29.

3. "The CFE Treaty," hearings before the Subcommittee on European Affairs of the Senate Committee on Foreign Relations, 102 Cong., 1st sess., 31 July 1991, 318.

4. Ibid., 25 July 1991, 164–65.

5. Special report of the North Atlantic Assembly, "NATO in the 1990s," 13.

6. *NATO Review* 4 (August 1991): 6.

7. North Atlantic Cooperation Council Statement on Dialogue, Partnership, and Companion, *NATO Review* 1 (February 1991):29–30.

8. "London Declaration of a Transformed North Atlantic Alliance," North Atlantic Council meeting, London, 5–6 July 1990, *NATO Review* 4 (August 1990): 32–33.

9. "Charter of Paris for a New Europe," 19–21 November 1990, *NATO Review* 6 (December 1990): 26ff.

10. Charles A. Kupchan, "NATO and the Persian Gulf: Examining Intra-Alliance Behavior," *International Organization* 42 (Spring 1988): 322.

11. Secretary-General Woerner's press statement at special ministerial meeting of the North Atlantic Council on the Gulf crisis, 10 September 1990, *NATO Review* 5 (1990): 33.

12. Statement on the Gulf, North Atlantic Council meeting, Brussels, 17–18 December 1990, *NATO Review* 6 (December 1990): 5.

13. Defense Planning Committee and Nuclear Planning Group communiqué, North Atlantic Council meeting, Brussels, 28–29 May 1991, *NATO Review* 3 (June 1991): 33.

14. Ibid, 34–35.

15. "The Alliance's New Strategic Concept," agreed by heads of state and government in meetings of the North Atlantic Council, Rome, 7–8 November 1991, *NATO Review* 6 (December 1991): 26.

16. Ibid., 31–32.

17. CRS Report for Congress, 28 September 1992, Edward F. Bruner, "U.S. Forces in Europe: Military Implications of Alternative Levels," 1–2.

18. Jeff Sallot, "Allies Let Fly at Canada over Pullout," *Toronto Globe and Mail,* 9 April 1992.

19. Dick Cheney, "Defense Strategy for the 1990s: The Regional Defense Strategy," January 1993, 19.

20. Report, 38th Ordinary Session (First Part, "WEU after Maastricht"), Document 1308, 13 May 1992; *New York Times,* 8 March 1992.

21. *London Financial Times,* 5 June 1991.

22. *Jane's Defence Weekly,* 6 June 1992.

23. *Washington Times,* 21 May 1992.

24. *New York Times,* 23 May 1992.

25. *Armed Forces Journal International,* December 1991.

26. Rudolph Chimelli in *Süddentschland Zeitung* (Munich), 21 May 1992.

27. "The Alliance's New Strategic Concept," *NATO Review* 6 (December 1991): 30.

28. Defense Planning Committee communiqué, Brussels, 26–27 May 1992, *NATO Review* 3 (June 1992): 35.

29. Ibid., 30.

30. *European Stars and Stripes,* 2 May 1992.

31. *Independent*, 16 August 1992.

32. Statement on 15 July 1992 by the secretary-general on monitoring by NATO forces of compliance with U.N. embargo on Serbia and Montenegro, *NATO Review* 4 (August 1992): 8.

33. Statement on former Yugoslavia issued by ministerial meeting of North Atlantic Council, 17 December 1992, *NATO Review* 6 (December 1992) 31–32.

34. "Coping with Violence and Disorder in Post-Cold War Europe: The Role of America, the Role of Europe," paper presented for the ECPR workshop, The Response of Western European Institutions to the Changes in the Former Soviet Union and Central and Eastern Europe, Leiden, April 1993.

35. Interview with Robin Knight, *U.S. News & World Report*, 29 March 1993.

36. Christopher Coker, "Limited Options, Unlimited Choices?" *Policy/Strategy* (February 1993), 4.

37. Conor Cruise O'Brien, "The Future of 'the West,'" *National Interest* (Winter 1992–93): 3.

38. *Die Zeit*, 24 May 1991, quoted in Frank Costigliola, *France and the United States: The Cold Alliance Since World War II* (New York: Twayne Publishers, 1992), 221.

39. *European Stars and Stripes*, 23 April 1993.

40. *Washington Post*, 29 March 1993.

41. Ronald Steel, *The End of the Alliance: America and the Future of Europe* (New York: Viking Press, 1964); Irving Kristol, "Does NATO Still Exist?" in Kenneth A. Myers, *NATO: The Next Thirty Years* (Boulder, Colo.: Westview Press, 1980), 361–81; Melvin Krauss, *How NATO Weakens the West* (New York: Simon & Schuster, 1986).

42. Ted Galen Carpenter, *A Search for Enemies: America's Alliances after the Cold War* (Washington, D.C.: Cato Institute, 1992), 45. See also James Chace, "Exit, NATO," *New York Times*, 14 June 1993.

43. Ronald D. Asmus, Richard L. Kugler, and F. Stephen Larrabee, "Building a New NATO," *Foreign Affairs* 72 (October 1993): 28–40; excerpts from remarks by Senator Richard Lugar to reporters on 7 September 1993 after a visit to Europe, *Indianapolis Star*, 8 September 1993.

GLOSSARY

AFCENT	Allied Forces, Central Europe
AFSOUTH	Allied Forces, Southern Europe
ANF	Atlantic Nuclear Force
ATGMs	antitank guided missiles
CENTO	Central Treaty Organization
CFE	Conventional Forces in Europe (Treaty)
CSCE	Conference on Security and Cooperation in Europe
DPC	Defense Planning Committee
EC	European Community
ECA	European Cooperation Administration
EDC	European Defense Community
ERP	European Recovery Program
ERWs	enhanced radiation weapons
ET	emerging technologies
EUCOM	U.S. European Command
EUROCOM	European Communications System
EUROGROUP	European Group
EUROLOG	European Logistics System
EURONAD	European Defense Equipment Group
GLCMs	ground-launched cruise missiles
IEPG	Independent European Programme Group
INF	Intermediate-Range Nuclear Force (Treaty)
ICBMs	intercontinental ballistic missiles
IRBMs	intermediate-range ballistic missiles
JCS	Joint Chiefs of Staff (U.S.)
LRTNF	Long-Range Theater Nuclear Force
MBFR	Mutual and Balanced Force Reductions
MLF	Multilateral Force

MPSB	Military Production and Supply Board
MTDP	Medium-Term Defense Plan
NACC	North Atlantic Cooperation Council
NADGE	NATO Air Defense Ground Environment
NATO	North Atlantic Treaty Organization
NDAC	Nuclear Defense Affairs Committee
NCS	National Security Council (U.S.)
NPG	Nuclear Planning Group
PGMs	precision guided missiles
RDF	Rapid Deployment Force
SACEUR	Supreme Allied Commander Europe
SACLANT	Supreme Allied Commander Atlantic
SALT	Strategic Arms Limitation Talks
SDI	Strategic Defense Initiative
SEATO	Southeast Asia Treaty Organization
SHAPE	Supreme Headquarters Allied Powers Europe
START	Strategic Arms Reduction Talks
TNF	Theater Nuclear Force
WEU	Western European Union

BIBLIOGRAPHIC ESSAY

From 1949 onward there has been a steady outpouring of publications on NATO in its many dimensions. Most of them inevitably were ephemeral, the products of problems of a particular crisis, military or political. Only a trickle of books has concentrated on the history of the United States and NATO, as opposed to a flood of books on worldwide American foreign policy since World War II. Those few that have given more than a carefully measured portion of attention to the Atlantic alliance include Richard W. Barnet, *The Alliance: America, Europe, Japan—Makers of the Postwar World* (New York: Simon & Schuster, 1983); A. W. DePorte, *Europe between the Superpowers: The Enduring Balance* (New Haven: Yale University Press, 1979); David P. Calleo, *The Atlantic Fantasy: The United States, NATO, and Europe* (Baltimore: Johns Hopkins University Press, 1970); and William T. R. Fox and Annette Baker Fox, *NATO and the Range of American Choice* (New York: Columbia University Press, 1967). Additionally, with *L'Alliance atlantique* (Paris: Editions Gallimard/Juillard, 1979) Pierre Mélandri has written a useful French survey of NATO's first 30 years. Lawrence S. Kaplan et al., *NATO after Forty Years* (Wilmington, Del.: Scholarly Resources, 1990), is a collection of essays covering most of NATO's concerns in its first generation.

Two useful bibliographies are Colin Gordon, *The Atlantic Alliance: A Bibliography* (New York: Nichols Publishing Co., 1978), and A. Norton et al., *NATO: A Bibliographical and Research Guide* (New York: Garland Press, 1985). A thorough review of the literature of the early years of NATO can be found in Lawrence S. Kaplan, "NATO and Its Commentators: The First Five Years," *International Organization* 8 (November 1954): 447–67. An updating of this bibliographical essay was made 30 years later in "NATO and Its Commentators: The First Five Years Revisited," in Lawrence S. Kaplan, *The United States and NATO: The Formative Years* (Lexington: University

241

Press of Kentucky, 1984), 204–21. The most recent major contribution is Bert Zeeman, "The Origins of NATO: An International Bibliography," *Bulletin of Bibliography* 47, no. 4 (December 1990).

The major monographs on the establishment of NATO are Escott Reid, *Time of Fear and Hope: The Making of the North Atlantic Treaty, 1947–1949* (Toronto: McClelland & Stewart, 1977), and Nicholas Henderson, *The Birth of NATO* (Boulder, Colo.: Westview Press, 1983), the commentaries of a Canadian and British diplomat, respectively. Other noteworthy studies of the formative years include Alan K. Henrikson, "The Creation of the North Atlantic Alliance, 1948–1952," *Naval War College Review* 32 (May–June 1980): 4–39, and Timothy P. Ireland, *Creating the Entangling Alliance: The Origins of the North Atlantic Treaty Organization* (Westport, Conn.: Greenwood Press, 1981). Lawrence S. Kaplan, *A Community of Interests: NATO and the Military Assistance Program, 1948–1951* (Washington, D.C.: U.S. Government Printing Office, 1980), and Chester J. Pach, Jr., *Arming the Free World: The Origins of the United States Military Assistance Program, 1945–1950* (Chapel Hill: University of North Carolina Press, 1991), deal with one of the most significant aspects of the alliance. With *Forging the Alliance: NATO, 1945–1950* (London: Secker & Warburg, 1991) Don Cook has written a readable journalistic acount of the formation of the alliance.

With the reorganization of NATO after the Korean War came the institution of official publications, of which the *NATO Letter* (1951–69) and the *NATO Review* (1969–) are the most significant. Additionally, the NATO Information Service produces the annual *NATO Handbook* and *The North Atlantic Treaty Organization: Facts and Figures* and has published such important records as *Texts of Final Communiqués* from the ministerial sessions of the North Atlantic Council, the Defense Planning Committee, and the Nuclear Planning Group. The Department of State publishes addresses and important official commentaries on NATO in its *Bulletin*. Even more revealing are the frequent hearings on NATO problems published by the Senate Foreign Relations Committee and the House Foreign Affairs Committee.

The decade of the 1950s has attracted considerable interest as the records of the National Archives in Washington, D.C., the Eisenhower Library in Abilene, Kansas, and the Dulles papers in Princeton, New Jersey, have become available to scholars. Where documents or correspondence are not available, memoirs of leading participants help to provide the raw materials.

On the issue of German rearmament and membership in NATO, Robert McGeehan, *The German Rearmament Question: American Diplomacy and European Defense after World War II* (Urbana: University of Illinois Press, 1971), and James L. Richardson, *Germany and the Atlantic Alliance: The Interaction of Strategy and Politics* (Cambridge, Mass.: Harvard University Press, 1966), have made major contributions. The most preceptive examination of German-American relations in the period is Thomas A. Schwartz, *America's Germany: John J. McCloy and the Federal Republic of Germany*

(Cambridge: Harvard University Press, 1991). The most recent studies of the French portion of the triangle are Irwin M. Wall, *The United States and the Making of Postwar France, 1945–1954* (New York: Cambridge University Press, 1991), and Frank Costigliola, *France and the United States: The Cold Alliance since World War II* (New York: Twayne Publishers, 1992). For a French view of the German question in the early 1950s, see Jules Moch, *Histoire de réarmament allemand depuis 1950* (Paris: R. Laffont, 1965). The "Great Debate" and the assignment of troops to Europe have been treated in David R. Kepley, "The Senate and the Great Debate of 1951," *Prologue* 14 (Winter 1982): 213–26, and Phil Williams, *The Senate and US Troops in Europe* (New York: St. Martin's Press, 1985). The experience of American troops in Europe is described in Christopher S. Raj, *The American Military in Europe: Controversy over NATO Burden Sharing* (New Delhi: ABC Press, 1983). Samuel R. Williamson, Jr., and Stephen L. Rearden, *The Origins of U.S. Nuclear Strategy, 1945–1953* (New York: St. Martin's Press, 1993), provides an authoritative account of U.S. nuclear strategy in this period.

The question of European integration has been of consistent interest to scholars, with speculations and predictions appearing periodically. Two of the more interesting, reflecting thoughts of two generations, are Mary Margaret Ball, *NATO and the European Union Movement* (New York: Praeger, 1959), and Pierre Mélandri, *Les Etats-Unis face al'unification de l'Europe* (Paris: A. Pedone, 1980). A recent addition to the literature is Francis H. Heller and John R. Gillingham, *NATO: The Founding of the Atlantic Alliance and the Integration of Europe* (New York: St. Martin's Press, 1992).

Just as the Truman and Eisenhower libraries have facilitated studies of NATO in the 1940s and 1950s, the Kennedy and Johnson libraries have stimulated inquiries into the 1960s. Charles de Gaulle and the appearance of *Sputnik* have inspired considerable literature on the direction NATO would take to meet these challenges. The most notable responses to the early Soviet nuclear challenge are Henry Kissinger, *Nuclear Weapons and Foreign Policy* (New York: Harper, 1957), and Robert E. Osgood, *NATO: The Entangling Alliance* (Chicago: University of Chicago Press, 1963). Kissinger's volume is a seminal study of the potential of limited nuclear weapons for the defense of NATO, while Osgood's was the first major scholarly work to place the European-American conflict over nuclear weapons into a historical context. De Gaulle's conception of American-European relations is reflected favorably in Robert Kleiman, *Atlantic Crisis: American Diplomacy Confronts a Resurgent Europe* (New York: Norton, 1964), and Henry Kissinger, *The Troubled Partnership: A Reappraisal of the Atlantic Alliance* (New York: McGraw-Hill, 1965). Another reaction was pessimism over the future of the alliance in the 1960s. This is best expressed in Ronald Steel, *End of the Alliance: America and the Future of Europe* (New York: Viking, 1964), and Richard W. Barnet and Marcus Raskin, *After Twenty Years: The Decline of NATO and the Search for a New Policy in Europe* (New York: Random House,

1965). On the other hand, Joseph Kraft, in *The Grand Design: From Common Market to Atlantic Partnership* (New York: Harper, 1962), looks ahead with the optimism of the Kennedy administration to a two-pillared NATO, with Europe and America sharing authority and responsibility equally. Harlan Cleveland, writing in the wake of France's removal from the organization, reflected a continuing faith in *NATO: The Transatlantic Bargain* (New York: Harper & Row, 1970).

The literature of the 1970s and the 1980s reflects both the hopes for stability to be produced by détente and the disillusionment over its failings. Sherri Wasserman, *The Neutron Bomb Controversy: A Study in Alliance Politics* (New York: Praeger, 1983), examines a divisive issue in the Carter administration. Robert S. Jordan has written two authoritative studies on the office of the secretary-general as a stabilizing force: *The NATO International Staff/Secretariat, 1952–1957* (Oxford: Oxford University Press, 1967), and *Political Leadership in NATO: A Study in Multinational Diplomacy* (Boulder, Colo.: Westview Press, 1979). Jordan has also edited *Generals in International Politics: NATO's Supreme Allied Commander, Europe* (Lexington: University Press of Kentucky, 1987).

On the importance of nuclear weaponry, Catherine McA. Kelleher, with *Germany and the Politics of Nuclear Weapons* (New York: Columbia University Press, 1975), has made a major contribution to the subject. The domination of nuclear politics can be found in such significant works as Lawrence Freedman, *The Evolution of Nuclear Strategy* (New York: St. Martin's Press, 1981); David N. Schwartz, *NATO's Nuclear Dilemmas* (Washington, D.C.: Brookings Institution Press, 1983); Richard W. Stevenson, *The Rise and Fall of Détente: Relaxation of Tension in U.S.-Soviet Relations, 1953–1954* (Urbana: University of Illinois Press, 1985); Jeffrey D. Boutwell et al., *The Nuclear Confrontation in Europe* (Dover, Mass.: Auburn House, 1986); and Robert B. Killibrew, *Conventional Defense and Total Deterrence: Assessing NATO's Strategic Options* (Wilmington, Del.: Scholarly Resources, 1986). Among the contributions of the last five years are Jane Stromseth, *The Origins of Flexible Response* (New York: St. Martin's Press, 1988), and Ivo Daalder, *NATO Strategy and Theater Response since 1967* (New York: Columbia University Press, 1991).

Projections of the future can be found in Kenneth A. Myers, ed., *NATO: The Next Thirty Years* (Boulder, Colo.: Westview Press, 1980), and Stanley W. Sloan, *NATO's Future: Toward a New Transatlantic Bargain* (Washington, D.C.: National Defense University Press, 1985). Melvin Krauss, *How NATO Weakens the West* (New York: Simon & Schuster, 1986), offers a gloomier projection of NATO's future. Reflecting the view that NATO's future is at best limited are David Calleo, *Beyond American Hegemony: The Future of the Western Alliance* (New York: Twentieth Century Fund/Basic Books, 1987), and Ted Galen Carpenter, *A Search for Enemies: American Alliances after the Cold War* (Washington, D.C.: Cato Institute, 1992). Joseph Nye, *Bound to Lead: The Changing Nature of American Power* (New York: Basic Books, 1990), offers a more positive projection of NATO after the cold war.

INDEX

THE AUTHOR

Lawrence S. Kaplan is university professor emeritus of history and director emeritus of the Lyman L. Lemnitzer Center for NATO and European Community Studies at Kent State University. He is currently adjunct professor of history at Georgetown University. Prior to coming to Kent State in 1954 he was with the Historical Office, Office of the Secretary of Defense. He has written numerous articles, monographs, and books on U.S. diplomatic history and NATO affairs, including *A Community of Interests: NATO and the Military Assistance Program, 1948–1951* (1980), *The United States and NATO: The Formative Years* (1984), and (ed.) *American Historians and the Atlantic Alliance* (1991).